Fidelis Morgan is an actress and playwright whose published work includes *The Female Wits* (1981), *A Woman of No Character* (1986), *The Well-Known Troublemaker: A Life of Charlotte Charke* (1988) and *A Misogynist's Sourcebook* (1989). She is co-editor with Paddy Lyons, of *Female Playwrights of the Restoration: Five Comedies*, published in Everyman in 1991. She lives in London.

To Rosalind Knight who frequented my drawing room while I worked on this book.

The Female Tatler

Edited and introduced by
Fidelis Morgan

J. M. Dent & Sons Ltd
London
Charles E. Tuttle Co., Inc
Rutland, Vermont
EVERYMAN'S LIBRARY

First published in Everyman's Library in 1992

Typeset at The Spartan Press Ltd,
Lymington, Hants.
Printed and bound in Great Britain by
The Guernsey Press Co. Ltd, Guernsey, C.I.
for J. M. Dent & Sons Ltd
91 Clapham High St
London SW4 7TA
and
Charles E. Tuttle Co., Inc.
28 South Main Street
Rutland, Vermont
05701, USA

ISBN 0 460 87074 2

Everyman's Library
REG US PATENT OFFICE

CONTENTS

INTRODUCTION

On 8 July 1709 the first issue of *The Female Tatler* hit the streets of London. A double-sided sheet attributed to the satiric pen of 'Phoebe Crackenthorpe, a lady that knows everything', it was printed by B. Bragge and issued three times a week, on days alternating with Addison and Steele's *Tatler*, which had been in business for only three months. The printers obviously decided on this tactic so that it would become a complementary rather than a rival paper, thereby increasing sales.

'Mrs Crackenthorpe' split from her printer five weeks later, and took her paper to the printing house of Mrs A. Baldwin. But B. Bragge had obviously enjoyed success with the paper for, despite the loss of his authoress, he continued to print a spurious paper, still ostensibly by 'Mrs Crackenthorpe' but infinitely inferior in style and content. This fake *Female Tatler* managed to survive for twenty-five issues, selling alongside and passing itself off as the real thing. Thus for a few weeks London had two 'genuine' *Female Tatlers*, spitting venom at each other and each accusing the other of being the fake paper.

Following a cryptic signing off at the end of Mrs Baldwin's paper 51, 'Mrs Crackenthorpe' left the paper to the joint authorship of 'a Society of Ladies', writing under the names Lucinda, Artesia, Emilia, Rosella, Arabella and Sophronia. The last extant issue by the Society was printed on 31 March 1710. It is possible the paper folded then, or it may have continued and no copies have survived. Whichever, on 26 September 1710, Addison's and Steele's *Tatler* 229 declared *The Female Tatler* dead.

The identity of the contributors who languished behind these wonderful soubriquets is still the subject of scholarly speculation. The most convincing arguments identify 'Mrs Crackenthorpe' as Delarivier Manley, playwright and novelist. The prologue to Mrs Susanna Centlivre's play *The Man's Bewitched* [which is discussed in FT 69, p. 139] makes allusion to Steele's *Tatler* (referring to him by his *nom de plume* Isaac Bickerstaff), closely followed by mention of Delarivier Manley:

Tho Bickerstaff's vast genius may engage,
And lash the vice and follies of the age;
Why should tender Delia tax the nation;
Stickle and make a noise for reformation
Who always gave a loose herself to inclination?

Mrs Manley's scandalous *romans à clefs*, *Secret Memoirs from the New Atalantis* and *Memoirs of Europe*, became two of the best sellers of the time, and her political pamphlets and editorship of *The Examiner* (after Swift) helped bring down John Churchill, 1st Duke of Marlborough. *The General Postscript*, a journal printed on 27 September 1709, when describing the newspapers of London says that *The Female Tatler* was written by 'Scandalosissima Scoundrelia and her two natural brothers'. As London's queen of scandal, Mrs Manley is obviously intended.

The British Library catalogue ascribes *The Female Tatler* to a lawyer, Thomas Baker, and according to verses in a rival paper, *The British Apollo*, when issue 24 of *The Female Tatler* (31 August 1709) poked fun at a City Deputy and his daughters, Baker was beaten up for it. The most likely attribution of authorship is to Manley and Baker working in tandem. (According to *The General Review* they may even have had a third contributor.) *The British Apollo*, which was frequently at loggerheads with *The Female Tatler*, describes its authors thus:

You'll say she is some Mother Mab [Mrs Manley] in disguise,
Trained up from her birth in abuses and lies;
Or else you may think by her scurrilous tongue,
From Billingsgate, Bridewell or Newgate she sprung;
Admitting all this (as it seems pretty plain)
Regard to her sex might have warded the cane.
But others will swear that this wise undertaker
By trade's an at——ney, by name is a B——r,
Who rambles about with a female disguise on,
And lives upon scandal, as toads do on poison.

It has been suggested that the fake *Female Tatler* was written by mathematician Thomas Lydal. His books are consistently advertised in it, and in her paper Mrs Crackenthorpe makes sarcastic reference to her rival's 'Calculated Tables'. Lydal published *A New Interest Pocket-Book . . . Also tables of Compound Interest* in 1710. Another theory is that Baker in fact wrote the fake *Female Tatler*, Manley the real one, and that Lydal was Baker's assistant.

The Ladies are even harder to identify. Dr Bernard Mandeville, translator of La Fontaine's *Fables*, certainly contributed something to the paper, particularly the Lucinda and Artesia papers, and a poem of his appears in one of the Crackenthorpe *Female Tatlers*. Susanna Centlivre may also have written as one or more of the Society of Ladies. After some inside information concerning the behaviour of the actors at a rehearsal of one of her plays was published in *The Female Tatler*, she wrote an impassioned denial of her own supposed contribution, declaring 'who they are that write that paper, or how distinguished, I am perfectly ignorant, and declare I never was concerned either in writing or publishing any of the Tatlers.' (Note that she says, delicately, Tatlers, not Female Tatlers.) So she denies having written the offending paper but, given the difficult situation she must have been in at the Playhouse, with the actors who were appearing in her play up in arms at having their behaviour exposed in print, her best option would have been denial, whether she was responsible or not. The fact is, *someone* who was at that rehearsal must have given the information to 'The Society of Ladies', in the hope of showing how badly the actors had treated Mrs Centlivre, and it is unlikely to have been the actors themselves. So even if she was not actually writing for the paper, it seems that she was contributing information. Much later in her career, when *The Female Tatler* was long gone, she used a plot taken from a *Female Tatler* story for her play *The Artifice*. Maybe she wrote the original story, maybe she just stole it.

The writing style and subject matter of some of the later papers make me suspect that Mrs Manley, having resigned the paper to the Society of Ladies on her arrest in October 1709, later became one of the Ladies herself. She had been briefly held in custody, after complaints about her book *New Atalantis*, but after her release there is no reason why she should not have gone back to the paper. It is also possible that some of her old material was left at the printer's office and used at a later date.

Undoubtedly Mrs Manley and Mrs Centlivre have been identified as possible Female Tatlers because of their very high profile in the London literary scene at this time. There were, however, other less well-known female writers who may also have contributed, but arguments on behalf of anybody else, male or female, famous or not, can only be based on the flimsiest of evidence: the text of the paper itself.

*

In 1709 a number of papers and broadsides were on sale in London. *The Female Tatler* refers to some of them: *The Observator*, *The Flying Post*, *The English Post*, *The British Apollo* and *The Review*. Apart from the flourishing social scene of London's private drawing rooms, the men who attended public coffee houses and gaming clubs, and the women who frequented India Houses – tea shops with a large female clientele – obviously provided a good market for this kind of scandal-based paper. Both *The Tatler* and *The Female Tatler* declared themselves to be interested in the 'improvement of ladies', but the content of the papers themselves shows this declaration to be at best ironic and, at worst, a cover for a more prurient attitude.

The Female Tatler frequently announces its desire to improve – in the same way that much of the tabloid press does today – by exposing folly and vice in malicious detail. Parallels with the modern press do not end there. *The Female Tatler*, along with Defoe's *Review*, was brought before the Grand Jury of Middlesex on 15 October 1709 and declared 'a great nuisance'. Real people were satirised and their private lives were exposed in all their folly. According to a hand-written note in the margin of the Bodleian Library's copy of the paper, 'Deputy Bustle' was one Deputy Skinner. Many actors and theatrical associates including Colley Cibber, Anne Oldfield and Robert Wilks are easy to identify, and there is no doubt that to the regular readers, gathered round their cups of coffee, tea and chocolate, Ladies 'Meanwell', 'Fadler', 'Bumfiddle' and 'Lantern-Jaws' together with 'Cynthio' and 'Parthenissa' were personalities utterly recognisable and, possibly, seated at the next table. In 1709 London was a very small place.

The Female Tatler took a firm stance on class and race and this reflected the attitudes of the time. The uncouth behaviour of servants and upstarts from the country is frequently mocked, along with the pretentions of the nouveaux riches and of city merchants. There are also many strongly expressed sentiments against the French and Irish. *Plus ça change* . . .

The philosophy of *The Female Tatler* is also very much of its own time. It is not a feminist paper, although it believes implicitly in the equal intelligence and ability of women. In the early eighteenth century arguments for female equality were not thought of as radical but logical. In 1697 Defoe had pleaded for female education in his *Essay on Projects*, and by 1709 many women already worked for a living, in the theatre, education, brewing, bar-keeping, writing, publishing,[1] farming, shopkeeping, dressmaking and many other areas, some in very important posts, and many owning their own businesses.

These powerful and busy women, along with their more leisured sisters, would no doubt have relished a relaxing half-hour, three times a

[1] It is worth noting that England's first daily newspaper, the shortlived *Daily Courant*, had been edited by a woman, and that Mrs Crackenthorpe's second publisher was Mrs A. Baldwin.

week, with a dish of tea and a few tasty morsels from the pen of Mrs Crackenthorpe and her successors, Lucinda, Artesia, Emilia, Rosella, Arabella and Sophronia, the Female Tatlers.

FIDELIS MORGAN

NOTE ON THE TEXT

The original text of *The Female Tatler* has been modernised and repunctuated to make it accessible to modern readers.

PART ONE

The Female Tatler

By Mrs Crackenthorpe

A LADY THAT KNOWS EVERYTHING

Sum Canna Vocalis[1]

FRIDAY JULY 8, 1709 *Number 1*

 hope Isaac Bickerstaff, Esq.[2] will not think I invade his property, by undertaking a paper of this kind, since tatling was ever adjudg'd peculiar to our sex; my design is not to rival his performance, or in the least prejudice the reputation he has deservedly gain'd: but as more ridiculous things are done every day than ten such papers can relate, I desire leave to prate a little to the town, and try what diversion my intelligence can give 'em. My acquaintance, which is a very great part of the town (for I am intimate with everybody at first sight) have encourag'd me to this attempt, by saying I have the character of knowing everybody's actions, and have sometimes pretended to declare people's intentions. 'Tis true I have twice a week a very great assembly of both sexes, from his Grace my Lord Duke to Mr Sagathie the spruce Mercer[3] in the City; and from her Grace my Lady Duchess, to Mrs Top Sail, the sea captain's wife at Wapping. Not that my drawing room ever had the least ill character, tho' a foolish baronet once call'd it the scandal office. But as I am courteous to all persons, and strangers have the same respect paid 'em as my former acquaintance, half the nation visits me, where I have a true

1 I am the singing reed.
2 The pseudonym of the author of *The Tatler*, Richard Steele.
3 textile dealer

history of the world; and to oblige those who are absent from me, by turns, shall endeavour to give it 'em again. I shall date all my advices from my own apartment, which comprehends, White's, Will's, the Grecian, Garraway's,[4] in Exchange-Alley, and all the India houses[5] within the Bills of Mortality.[6] Since grave statesmen, airy beaus,[7] lawyers, cits,[8] poets and parsons, and ladies of all degrees assemble there, each person delivers himself according to his talent, which gives me a superficial smattering for all of 'em.

The variety of our conversation affords general satisfaction; books are canvas'd, removals at court suggested, law cases disputed, the price of stocks told, the beaus and ladies inform us of new fashions, and the first long pocket that was seen in town receiv'd its reputation from being approved of at Mrs Crackenthorpe's drawing room. But when we get into general tittle-tattle, 'tis every little story that happens to get air, those of quality are as liable to reflection as their inferiors, and seldom any person obliges the company with a new piece of scandal, but 'tis repaid him with above twenty more. And tho' to support my visiting days, I am forc'd to act the good Lady Praise-all myself, yet the moment any visitor retires to give place to a fresh comer-in, some one of the company breaks out into (if a gentleman), 'Really, Mrs Crackenthorpe, Sir Charles is mighty good company wou'd he not rail at people so behind their backs.' 'Pray what estate has he?' says another, 'I hear but small and they say damnably dipp'd.' (If a Lady) 'Cousin Crackenthorpe, D'you think that lady handsome? She's horrid silly however, and not a bit genteel; but what a load of jewels she had on!' 'Ay,' says another, 'they say she lies in 'em; I don't believe her earrings were right.'

As to particular stories, I shall begin my second paper with them; but in that, and every following piece, as I find encouragement to proceed, shall be very careful, unjustly or ungenteely not to reflect upon any person whatsoever, but gently to correct the vices and vanities which some of distinction, as well as others, wilfully commit. Shou'd we be so bless'd as to procure an honourable and lasting peace,[9] things of this kind will be a very good amusement for the public, when our news papers are laid aside; peace will produce plenty, plenty makes every body grow mercurial; and when a happiness so long wish'd for, and with such difficulty obtain'd shall, instead of promoting religion, virtue, and sobriety, so far intoxicate men's minds as to draw 'em into pride, luxury,

[4] smart clubs frequented by wits   [5] tea shops

[6] official returns of death rate in London   [7] men   [8] citizens

[9] In the eighth year of the War of Spanish succession, after a number of British and allied victories, hopes were high that a peace was soon to be arranged.

and all manner of ridiculous excursions, an ingenious tatler will conduce more to the reformation of mankind than an hypocritical society,[10] who have made a trade of it. Would people of rank proceed with honour, justice, and a nobleness of spirit, and let their actions, not their equipage, support the dignity of their station, we might hope for a true Golden Age; but when we daily hear of unaccountable whims and extravagant frolics committed by the better sort, we must expect those of inferior classes will imitate them in their habits of mind, as well as body, and the only way to correct great men's foibles, is handsomely to ridicule 'em; a seasonable banter has often had a reclaiming effect, when serious advice from a grave divine has been thought impudence.

I wou'd intreat those who are not particularly acquainted with me, that they wou'd not imagine I write this paper merely for the profit that may accrue to me by it; for all that I have the honour to be intimate with, know that I have an estate of £300 *per annum* and always kept two maids and a footman; but if I should happen to succeed beyond my expectation, it might so far advance my fortune that I may be able to keep a coach as well as my sister Micklethwaite. I shall follow Mr Bickerstaff's method to get a footing into the world, and deliver the first paper *gratis*, afterwards those that will receive them at the price of 1d[11] will in some measure repay the charge and trouble of such an undertaking; and to prevent mistakes, which may happen by peoples' enquiring for either of the tatlers, I shall publish mine the contrary days, *viz.* Mondays, Wednesdays and Fridays.

Phoebe Crackenthorpe

FRIDAY JULY 8 TO MONDAY JULY 11 *Number 2*

My good Lady Coupler, that is always doing one kind office or another, had no sooner read my name in print, but she came hurrying to me as fast as her old horses could draw her; said she had a little private business with me, and complaining of wind, desir'd a dram of cinnamon water;[12] she told me, she was in a rapture at my undertaking, since it was not an impertinent rotation of

[10] The Society For the Reformation of Manners, founded in 1699, now beginning to make an effect on the content of plays etc.

[11] One penny

[12] an alcoholic cordial

chit-chat, but a well-grounded design, divertingly to lead people into good moral instruction, whose intent in reading this paper might be only to find out some invidious reflection, or laugh at an idle story; that she was thoroughly persuaded no body cou'd object against so glorious a project, and that the ladies, more particularly, would encourage it, for, as Horace says, *Bidentem dicere verum quid vetat.*[13] She begg'd of me to be very severe upon those people that behave themselves indecently at church, that religion was not to be trifl'd with; and she had observ'd several ladies at Ormond-chapel squat when they should kneel, eat carraways[14] when they shou'd say after the minister, and that a creature who sat next to her last Sunday devour'd a quarter of a pound of orange chips, and had not the manners to offer her a bit.

But the affair she had to impart to me was this: 'You know Mrs Crackenthorpe,' said she, 'I have had a very great value for you ever since I was invited down for a whole summer to your father's at Nottingham.' The wind returning upon her Ladyship's stomach, she drank the other half-pint glass, and proceeded; that she was very intimate with Isaac Bickerstaff, Esq. and his whole family, the same Nurse suckling his sister, Mrs Jenny Distaff, and her Ladyship's daughter Prudence, that she could not propose any match half so suitable as Mr Bickerstaff and myself; 'What wondrous things,' continues she, 'might two such headpieces in conjunction produce, and for our progeny, the sons would be all bishops, judges and recorders, and the daughters Behns, Philips' and Daciers.'[15]

I was so much confounded at her ladyship's proposal, having never suffer'd my mind to entertain the least idea of man's private conversation, that I was just upon swooning, but her Ladyship clapping her hartshorn[16] to my nose, and assuring me she had not mention'd the matter to Mr Bickerstaff. I recover'd, told her I should think my self infinitely happy in Mrs Jenny Distaff's acquaintance, and if her brother would honour my drawing room with his company any public day, he should be extremely welcome.

Immediately stopped seven or eight coaches, as many more came rattling after, and chairs to an infinite number. I was supris'd to have so much company in summertime, but my first paper had so alarm'd my acquaintance that they all assembled, and several from Hampstead, Epsom and seats within twenty miles of London came up on purpose,

[13] Tell the forbidden truth at your peril [14] sweet biscuits

[15] Aphra Behn (1640–89), playwright and poet, Katherine Philips (1631–64), poet and Anne Dacier (1654–1720), translator, editor and critic

[16] smelling salts

every body having something to say to me about it; Mrs Judy Skrew disapprov'd of the paper, and said, 'Truly there was scandal enough in the other Tatler, and as for the story of Mrs Goddy and Mrs Slim, positively the fellow meant her and her sister.' But the multitude were mightily for it. My Lord Plausible said, 'Let it be never so scurrilous, nobody can be offended at what a Lady writes, and shou'd you, Madam, stamp me the greatest rake and libertine in the kingdom, so far from being disturb'd at it, I should think my self highly honoured that you are pleas'd to take Notice of me at all.'

MONDAY JULY 11 TO WEDNESDAY JULY 13 — *Number 3*

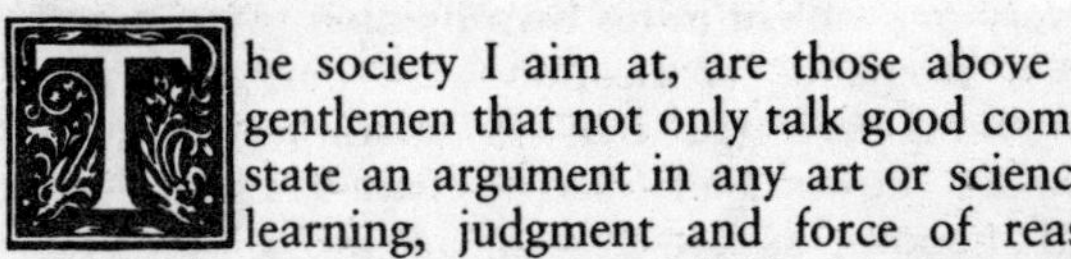

The society I aim at, are those above the common level, gentlemen that not only talk good common sense, but can state an argument in any art or science and dispute with learning, judgment and force of reason. Wit is entertaining, but people are not oblig'd always to be upon the grin. I would have the ladies to relish somewhat above mere tittle-tattle, and tho' they want the benefit of profound learning, yet conversing with ingenious persons would so far improve their natural parts, as to give 'em a more noble idea of things, and create in 'em at least a value for matters serious and instructive, which would stifle a world of scandal and detraction.

The French nation have so complaisant a regard for the fair sex, that they always mix with 'em in conversation, entertain 'em with discourses on every topic, which gives them a short knowledge of the world, what other nations are agitating as well as their own; and if a lady has the misfortune to lose a husband, or brother in the field of battle, it must in very great measure abate her grief to know he died honourably in the service of his country. But English ladies, the moment they rise from dinner are pack'd off to their tea tables, where they spend half their live's time in talking of fans and tea-cups, sugar-tongs, salt shovels and gloves made up in walnut-shells.

Therefore as I would avoid reprimanding any body in my own apartment, I take this opportunity to entreat the absence of all effeminate fops, that drink milk and water, wear cherry colour'd stockings and stitch'd waistcoats and, in a counter-tenor voice, complain of vapours and the spleen; impudent beau-Jews, that talk obscenely in modest womens' company, then stare 'em in the face and burst out a-laughing, who, so far from being admitted into civil society, ought to be expell'd the nation; all comic gentlemen that act in tragedies for the diversion; designing persons, that make assignations at public drawing-rooms, and foreign beaus, that assume the title of counts, who just make an outside show to engage some great fortune, and when they have received her money, fly away with it into their own country . . . .

English gentlemen are strangely ridicul'd by foreigners, for misapplying their education. Men of estates should imbibe a general knowledge, since learning is to them an ornament and not a business. History shows 'em the world; mathematics makes them talk properly, music relieves 'em from more anxious studies, and dancing gives them an agreeable address; poetry and painting discover a bright genius, but are not absolutely necessary. Foreigners of rank attain a mighty character in mixing their studies, talk genteely to every art and science, without being particularly fond of any; but our nation, as it is divided into parties, and every one violent in his own opinion, so in point of breeding, we give a strenuous application to a particular study, regardless of every thing else. He that affects music, forgets the gentleman, and becomes a downright fiddler, his chambers are fill'd with semiquavers instead of books, his conversation is to prove there's more mathematics in one of Corelli's sonatas than in all Euclid, old B—n—ster[17] is his bosom friend, and if he gets acquainted with your B—n—ster, Nine's the Main[18] – four to nine and 'tis ten to five if he's not bubbled[19] out of his estate. He that is fond of books is a mere pedant, will tell you every corner in Rome, and yet lose himself in his own country village; and he that's bewitch'd to poetry, players dine with him, players sup with him, he gives them precedence in all places, and carries 'em into all societies, where he's very coldly received for the sake of his companions; 'tis a strange reflection to make that men of fortune should dwindle from their characters, having at the same time sense enough to know they act like fools.

*

The Lady Well-bred, at Eltham, in Kent, is willing to dispose of a romping daughter, aged fifteen years. Her Ladyship passing thro' the hall last week to order some whipped syllabubs when a great deal of company was there, saw Miss sit very quietly in the footman's lap to be

17 John Banister (1630–79), violinist and composer

18 a gambling term, i.e. a stake, the odds

19 cheated

kiss'd. She took no notice of the matter, but when the girl came into the dining room: 'See me no more this month,' says my Lady, 'you confident thing, to let a nasty fellow that stinks of the stables flop you at that rate. I perceiv'd you, but said nothing, being resolved to shame you before all this company.' Miss star'd her in the face and cry'd – 'Well, what if he did? I like it.' My lady instead of dashing her daughter, was so out of countenance herself, she knew not which way to look; which, the girl perceiving, made mouths at her, and hoyden'd out of the room. Whoever can like her person with two thousand pounds, may have a full view of her at Eltham-Church, where by her manner of behaviour, she distinguishes herself from the whole congregation.

*

A very agreeable young lady at Epsom, having made complaint that an impudent parrot, on Clay-hill, whenever she happens to pass by, is always bawling, 'When did you see Captain Thumper, Oh! the dear Captain, the pretty, pretty Captain', till she was forc'd to remove her lodgings, tho she knows not, nor ever heard of any such Captain. The gentleman believes the parrot meant her no affront, humbly begs her pardon and henceforward, Poll shall have less victuals than formerly, that he may not be so very pert, and be hung next the garden instead of the street.

WEDNESDAY JULY 13 TO FRIDAY JULY 15 — *Number* 4

Went into Holborn to see my grandmother, but met with a great misfortune by the way, for in Chancery Lane a drayman's horse splashed me all over, which I set down as a memorandum never to go through Chancery Lane again.

Mrs Crackenthorpe desires people not to trouble their heads so much with her footman, Francis. One teases him, and t'other teases him, and the fellow don't love to be teased. She is loathe to entertain her visitors with complaints against her servants, but t'other day several of my Lord Outside's swearing equipage, got him to The Bear and Ragged Staff, where they called him Mr Francis, pulled the papers off his hair,[20] and

[20] curling papers

tore his fine shirt that cost three guineas. Francis is as tractable a servant as ever came into a house, and can turn his hand to anything; when the cook-maid's sick, he'll dress a joint of meat or make a pudding, scour down the stairs and mend the kitchen towels. If he's sent to keep his mistress a place in the box,[21] the Ladies are very easy with Francis, and will sometimes do him the honour to talk to him. Or if his mistress goes to Tunbridge without a maid-servant, Francis pins up a gown beyond e'er a mantua-woman[22] in Christendom. 'Tis true he loves a little diversion, and 'tis fit he should have it, since his going abroad is not to game away his wages or spoil his livery at the Bear Garden,[23] but only to take a walk, see the wax-work[24] or drink tea with his Aunt Dobson. And tho' the wenches don't love him because he's sober and virtuous, yet while he is Mrs Crackenthorpe's servant and behaves himself modestly, she will not have him affronted by anybody.

*

Whereas the Society of Fiddlers have taken notice that several ladies, whose constitutions are impaired by the spleen, the hyppo,[25] the flatus[26] and the hurry of the spirits, want a musical support; that if they walk the length of a street they are ready to drop down dead, yet can hold out at country dances twenty-four hours together without being in the least fatigued. And whereas Hackney-coach-men[27] are very abusive, especially to women, and the water[28] is what not one lady in ten dares venture upon, the Society have appointed seven hundred able performers to ply at the corner of every noted street, that when any lady has a mind to dance about town, she may have a fellow to play before her at sixpence an hour; if she trips out of town at five shillings a day (the price of a coach being ten) or to any part of England at reasonable rates.

*

Whereas several gentlemen and ladies have accustomed themselves to a very indecent laugh (one hallows till people are deaf, another splutters in everybody's face, a third grins as if she fleered at the whole company, a fourth screams five notes above the pitch) Solomon Simper, laughing master, who was prentice to Mr Giggle, and has since improved himself

[21] servants were frequently sent ahead to save a good seat at the playhouse

[22] dress-maker

[23] A park which held rough public entertainments – bear-baiting, wrestling, sword-play etc.

[24] A wax work with mechanical parts was exhibited for some time in The Strand.

[25] hypochondria

[26] wind

[27] drivers of hired carriages

[28] travel by river was popular

under the famous Myn Heer Van Grin, is willing to instruct any gentleman or lady in the rules of laughing, according to notes, which he thinks ought to be as musical as singing; at the usual rates of other masters. Note: he is a very great beau.

FRIDAY JULY 15 TO MONDAY JULY 18 *Number 5*

Tho' most women are fond of ridiculing one another, it was always my temper to extenuate, rather than aggravate, the frailties of my own sex, when at the same time, I have blush'd for other womens infirmities, as much as if they had been my own. If a lady appears impertinently talkative, and will rather sermonise than converse, I impute it to her youth. Nature has given her a ready wit, which time and experience will ripen to a good judgment, for every woman that talks well must think before she speaks. If a lady appears rustic, awkward, and ill-bred – what can be expected from a country education? Plays, drawing-rooms, and observation in company, will insensibly bring her into an easy method; or if an agreeable young creature is always setting her hair, altering her Patches[29] and practising airs in a looking glass, then every body allows her to be a fine woman; men have flatter'd her into a deity, but matrimony will soon convince her she must have charms of mind as well as body to secure a heart her beauty drew into that fatal snare – but as this paper is impartially to laugh at the foibles of both sexes, I think my self oblig'd to publish the following letter.

To Mrs Crackenthorpe

Madam,
Above a hundred gentlemen having been intolerably affronted by two ridiculous affected bar-keepers (*viz*, Rebecca Rhenish near Lincoln's Inn great gate, and Winifred Whitewine by the May-pole in the Strand), desire the favour of you to impart their characters to the town. These creatures are wondrous great cronies, and always together when business will permit; they send a drawer[30] every

[29] A small piece of black silk applied to the face to cover a blemish or add adornment.

[30] boy who works the pumps in a tavern

Monday to know how one another does and most evenings to keep 'em places in the box, where they elbow women of the first quality in tawdry painted calicoes, wash'd gloves, and steel crosses,[31] – 'Lord,' says Rhenish, 'here's horrid company tonight. I don't see one woman tolerably well dress'd. 'Ay,' says Whitewine, 'and as ill-bred as if they came out of the city; I have curtsy'd to five or six ladies, and because they don't know me, they had not the manners to return it again; their husbands might pay what they owe at our houses before the proud things take so much state upon 'em.' 'My dear,' says Rhenish, 'don't you see Col. Sturdy yonder? Well he's a sweet man! What legs he has!'. And are so fond of officers, that if they see but a red coat[32] they'll run the length of a street to look after him.

At every review in Hyde Park these trollops are certainly in a hackney, will stop the coach to drink pint glasses with 'em at Phillips's, yet wonder at the liberties some women take, and tho' they are ready to eat every fellow they see, can't believe any of their own sex virtuous but themselves. At home, they are so very scornful, they take antipathies to people – 'this set of company are the ugliest fellows they ever saw – show 'em into a dark dirty low room, and give 'em the prick'd wine we send to funerals'. Another set are rude puppies, that pass'd by the bar without paying her any respect, a third are idiots, for having a supper dress'd and not inviting her to table. And when a society shall spend ten guineas in the house, instead of 'gentlemen you're welcome,' they will make mouths after them, and cry, 'Such wretches! Bar up the doors, and draw me a pint of canary,[33] for my stomach kecks[34] at the very idea of them.' Your opinion, Madam, how two such impertinent things ought to be us'd will infinitely oblige your humble servant.

Andrew Allnight

As I never was conversant in taverns, I know not how gentlemen ought to be treated there. 'Tis certain everybody ought to be courteously us'd where they spend their money, and have respect paid 'em suitable to their quality. I have met with several morose tradesmen that have affronted people of rank for undervaluing their goods, which they bring upon themselves; for sometimes they ask so extravagantly out of the way, customers know not what to bid 'em. But that grievance is easily redress'd by avoiding such shops another time. As to these bar-keepers, I am inform'd they are little more ridiculous than the rest of their tribe;

[31] washable gloves (rather than leather), and steel rather than silver crosses.

[32] soldier

[33] light sweet wine

[34] retches

their rattling, ringing, noisy profession gives an assurance unbecoming the character of their sex; and, by seeing such a variety of company, they pretend to a general knowledge, and if gentlemen are affronted, mimick'd and ridicul'd by such pert amazons (amongst whom, rarely, very rarely you find a modest woman), the reflection I make is upon themselves; for if men of estates would not treat them at the bar, and call 'em 'dear' and 'jewel' – 'Thou blossom of a cauliflower', or worship 'em with 'angel', 'goddess', 'cherubim', and such stuff; and sometimes lend them their chariots, to stare the whole park out of countenance, but pass by 'em with a cold common civility, Mrs Rhenish, and Mrs Whitewine would know their proper distance, and give companies the obliging attendance they require.

I was carrying on this day's paper with some particular advices I receiv'd yesterday, but must defer 'em to oblige my Lady Betty Modish, who rattled five times at the door before Francis could possibly let her in. 'Mrs Crackenthorpe,' says she, 'if you would pleasure all the maiden ladies in the kingdom that they may know how to chose husbands, nay, the whole sex, for we are all upon the violentest titter, you must immediately clap this story into print.' Lady Scandal pops in with the same story, but vary'd a little in the relation. But however, as I have gather'd it from 'em both, 'tis in part as follows.

Five baronets who have been observed to be very intimate for some years past, and a select company to themselves; (for tho' they use the Smirna, and other coffee houses, their conversation extends but to one another) have been discover'd by some prying ladies to understand needle-work and are very curious in cross-stitch, Irish stitch, etc., that they have a very great genius to cut-work, patch-work and filigrees, and have each of 'em a closet at private lodgings fill'd with wonderful curiosities of that kind, which their intimates obtain the favour of seeing, but, like the beauties at Hampton Court, are not visible to every body. These baronets it seems, have a sweet meat club at a confectioners in York Buildings, where they meet three times a week to work a fine waistcoat for a brother beau's wedding – Sir Formal did the border, Sir Tawdry a sun-flower, Sir Finical a tulip, Sir Plump an artichoke, and Sir Dapper a primrose. The gentleman who was to wear the waistcoat for their sakes, walk'd about the room with a white wand, and when any one of 'em was idle, he gave him a rap on the fingers, which for want of witty conversation created a world of laughter, and when they had finish'd their several tasks, they refresh'd themselves with a collation of wet sweetmeats, and every one had a pint of sack and an orange. They hugg'd themselves two months with this mighty secret, and thought themselves very happy in making business a pleasure; but an odious thing, as ugly as the devil, bolting unawares into the room, the matter was blown up, and the ill-bred creature instead of begging pardon for her rudeness, tir'd six pair of horses to carry the jest about town.

My answer to Lady Betty was that tho' the meeting was ridiculous enough, and might give diversion to those who have nothing better to talk of, yet these gentlemen are not so blameable as their parents. Master Neddy, being heir to a great estate, and my Lady's darling, she can't bear him out of her sight for fear an earthquake should swallow him up, or a house tumble down upon his head. He must not go to school for the bare thoughts of a rod or ferula[35] put her Ladyship upon the rack. If he knows his letters by sixteen 'tis scholarship enough for one of his estate. He's not suffer'd to have any acquaintance for fear of ill courses which would break her Ladyship's heart, but goes a visiting with my Lady, where he imbibes all effeminacies, lies with my Lady's woman till she begins to make complaints, and then a wife provided him.

Miss Jenny is her father's dotage, my Lady abominates her, she is so horrid rude; but being a girl of quick parts, her father won't have her spirit broke. One moment she's a straddle upon a five bar gate, her father is ready to die with laughing; the next, fighting amongst the boys, he commends her courage. If she calls the servants to naught, 'tis wit and repartee. As she grows up, she rides a hunting with her father, goes to the bowling-green with her father and, if he'd encourage her, she'd take to smoking and drinking. And the product of her education is this: that when she marries, she'll certainly beat her husband. If people had a right management of their children, Miss would mind her embroidery, and Sir Finical his books and manly diversions.

MONDAY JULY 18 TO WEDNESDAY JULY 20 — *Number 6*

An advertisement lately given about town concerning the poor actors (who complain what small allowances they have had this last winter from the patentees of the Drury Lane Play-House,[36] as if they had receiv'd no more than so many poor Palatines,[37] coming to my hands) I thought it highly necessary to make some reflections thereon.

[35] cane

[36] Drury Lane was going through a managerial crisis. The patentee, Christopher Rich, was ordered to close down by the Lord Chamberlain for disobeying an order forbidding deductions of more than £40 from actors' benefits.

[37] Protestant refugees from Bavaria were settling in England, but lived in extreme poverty.

The patentees are undoubtedly to blame for not doubling the salary of the head actors, since it is not to be suppos'd but Dorimant and Sir Fopling[38] enter so far into the fop and the fine gentleman, and are so far intoxicated with the applause given 'em, as that they'll do their utmost off the stage to appear the persons they represent on it, and sometimes out-do 'em in dress and extravagant living. Could any one be so barbarous to desire Statira,[39] after all her attendance at the theatre, to pin up her petticoats, trudge home in pattens,[40] without anybody to guard her honour, then tell over her week's pay and make a solitary supper upon cold beans, supported only with the melancholy refreshment of – 'Where is the best brandy?' – 'No, a chair, a link[41] here' – 'let Daniel run before and see if supper's ready' – 'Wax candles light up, a dish of ortelans,[42] a bottle of tocai, and the baronets to sing to her.' Or would any one desire Sergeant Kite[43] to sit at Pervil's and drink beer and beer, when men of quality are ravish'd with his company, tho' he mimics them to their faces. There's a vast difference between what the world in general thinks of players, and the opinion they have of themselves. If the town would not tantalise 'em further than to give 'em loud claps on every just performance, and despise 'em when the play's over, they'd value themselves upon good action only: but when people of note shall caress 'em, and embrace 'em ('do me the honour, dear Hamlet, to let me have you this evening,' 'I was charm'd with you in such an act,'), they forget they are but parrots of other men's elaborate studies, and begin to value themselves upon realities. Antony wears his buskins at the alehouse, and Cleopatra has her tail spread in Clare market.[44]

Players nowadays rise to a mighty pitch, the suppos'd Lord associates with the real one, and they are every day seen publicly together at picquet.[45] Nay, a certain gentleman is so fond of 'em, he has turn'd his chapel into a theatre, invites 'em into the country every autumn for two months, where they are receiv'd like people of quality: Moll Kent lies in the best damask bed, and Jubilee Dicky[46] has a footman to attend him in his chamber. They are seated at his own table, entertain'd with thirty dishes every day, and if a nobleman comes up after they have begun to scramble, his Lordship dines at a side table, since the gentleman's bosom

38 Robert Wilks and Colley Cibber

39 Jane Rogers and Mrs Bradshaw had both played the role of Statira in Lee's *The Rival Queens* in the previous season.

40 wooden over-shoes worn to raise the wearer above the mud on the streets.

41 a pitch torch

42 delicate edible birds

43 Richard Estcourt had played the role of Kite this season.

44 a low-life area of sleazy tenements

45 card game

46 Henry Norris, actor

friends must not be displac'd. Last year one of 'em fancy'd a fine horse – 'twas presented him. And were players not people of wondrous modesty, another would have fancy'd the furniture of a room, a third a set of gold dressing plate, and a fourth the coach and six horses 'till they had fancy'd away all the gentleman's moveables. When they took their leaves, Sir Comedy could not make THEM presents in *specie*;[47] and as rings and snuff- boxes were scarce in the country, each of 'em had twenty guineas slip'd into their coat pockets, to please themselves in town – 'twas mighty handsome, and genteel – marry it was.

These are your people of spirit and address, who are really kings, emperors, princesses, and sultanas, because they will be so. 'Tis true, they sometimes condescend to be valets and waiting-women, but 'tis as their brother monarchs divert themselves from affairs of government that lie heavy upon their shoulders.

Now can it be thought, four or five hundred pounds a year can maintain people of such public dispositions? Therefore the patentees, let the winter prove never so bad, should give them a larger supply, since they are a sort of quality few people care to trust.

*

Several ladies of quality in Piccadilly who play cards o' Sundays have been reflected on by a Puritanical sort of people, which they think a very great piece of impudence, and desire they'd exercise as much religion as they please and not trouble their heads with those that have none.

47 in cash

WEDNESDAY JULY 20 TO FRIDAY JULY 22 *Number 7*

esterday being my visiting-day, I had the most agreeable select set of company that ever yet grac'd my drawing-room. Our discourse ran chiefly upon the different manner of people's behaviour in public; their birth, their education, their dispositions. What is nature and what affectation are easily discover'd by their way of address. Just as the most rustical habit cannot hide the fine gentleman, nor the gayest embroidery give an air to the clown, so true wit and breeding, notwithstanding all modest endeavours to conceal 'em, will, to people of observation, discover themselves from the vain pretences of impertinence and fluttering assurance. A sophister[48] may pass upon the generality for a man of learning, a prating quack for a great physician, and a conceited punster[49] for a youth of quick repartee. But persons, who have truly study'd mankind, dart thro' such false appearances, and to make a right judgment of things in so deceitful an age is a happiness inexpressible, both for admiration and ridicule . . .

Since I undertook this paper, I have discover'd the impertinence of the world to be infinitely greater than I could have imagin'd it. I receiv'd yesterday above thirty letters, in all of which I could not find one tolerable observation. They consist of silly amours, petty reflections, frivolous tales and scandalous aspersions. Young people and fools think the TATLERS give 'em a mighty opportunity to expose their superiors, and when a mother shall justly correct her daughter, a lady her servants, or a tradesman his prentices, they make no reply, but letters are immediately dispatch'd to ridicule them in print. Should such people be encourag'd, a paper of this kind would be not only useless, but pernicious, since most families harbour a detractor, and masters must be afraid to direct those they feed, lest they should draw their characters. But if gentlemen or ladies please to write any thing that may be serviceable to the public, it will be kindly receiv'd.

*

Mrs Crackenthorpe gives her service to the authors of *The British Apollo*, *Review*, *Observator*, *Flying Post*, *English Post* and *Supplement*[50] and does hereby discharge 'em from troubling the town any longer, the coffee houses making heavy complaints against 'em;

48 a second or third year student
49 a person who makes puns
50 rival papers all in print at this time

neither does she think it reputable that her paper should be seen upon the table in such intolerable company.

FRIDAY JULY 22 TO MONDAY JULY 25 *Number 8*

'm obliged to the gentleman, who wrote the following letter, for the compliments he makes me. But if he saw my face he'd think no more of adoration. Beauty was ever the least of my aim, I would rather chose to recommend myself by a tolerable understanding. 'Tis true, it heightens a lady's character, and when a fine woman shall deliver herself in an elegant manner, her beauty, like sweetening a note in music, is a grace to her expression, and the men are ravish'd with her, when they'd be but barely pleas'd with one less agreeable. But, if gentlemen would not value a woman chiefly for her person, and think the silliest things wit, that come from youth and beauty, our sex would employ some time in cultivating their minds, and take more pains to place their words, than their patches . . .

An express from Peckham gives an account that Mrs Margaret and Mrs Millicent Trott are grown so very ridiculous not a neighbour will receive a visit from them. They affect every thing that's masculine, their shifts are called shirts, their headclothes are their perriwigs, their wrapper is their double-button'd coat, and their furbelow-scarves[51] their roquelaures.[52] They are very intimate with Obadiah Subpoena, an impudent attorney, and Frank Fore-castle, a ranting sea-captain, are frequently dress'd in man's clothes, and gallop with 'em to the Palatines, where, tho' they have not taught 'em English, 'tis suspected they have given some of 'em to understand that conversation may be held between people of different nationals without knowing one another's language. But the worth of the matter is, they have seduc'd Miss Lack-it from the boarding-school, who steals out when her mistress is a-bed, to ramble with 'em. They'll sit down tightly to a bowl of punch, and then scour the streets, break windows, and have so little regard to their own sex as to abuse every woman they meet. They are women of condition as well as fortune, and their relations, having in vain us'd all arguments to reclaim 'em, were forc'd to entreat a public reprimand.

[51] flounced scarves [52] knee-length cloak

The two ladies I have little to say to. A wound taken early may be easily cur'd, and one foolish frolic the town may have good nature enough to forget; but a reputation once lost, like a mortification, is almost irrecoverable. As to the girl, her mistress is more to blame for not keeping a stricter eye over her. Her actions confirm me in the dislike I ever had to boarding-schools. People of fashion nowadays educate their children at home, and whereas, formerly, Miss was a romp at twenty, she is now, by the management of her parents, a discreet young lady at fifteen.

*

A ship laden with monkeys is lately come into the river; the young ones are fit for ladies' pages, the middle ag'd ones, ladies' impertinents, and the old ones will make admirable C——n C——l[53] men. They are to be seen any hour of the day, at the St George near the Tower.

MONDAY JULY 25 TO WEDNESDAY JULY 27 *Number 9*

This afternoon, some ladies, having an opinion of my fancy in clothes, desir'd me to accompany 'em to Ludgate-Hill, which I take to be as agreeable an amusement as a lady can pass away three or four hours in; the shops are perfect gilded theatres. The variety of wrought silks, so many changes of fine scenes; and the mercers are the performers in the opera, and instead of 'Viviture Ingenio',[54] you have in gold capitals 'No Trust by Retail'. They are the sweetest, fairest, nicest dish'd out creatures, and by their elegant address and soft speeches, you would guess 'em to be Italians. As people glance within their doors, they salute 'em with: 'garden silks, ladies, Italian silks, brocades, tissues, cloth of silver, or cloth of gold, very fine Mantua silks, any right Geneva velvet, English velvet, velvets emboss'd' – and to the meaner sort – 'fine thread satins, both strip'd and plain, fine mohairs, silk satinets, burdets, perfianets, Norwich crepes, auterines, silks for hoods and scarves – any camlets, drudgets, or sagathies; gentlemen, nightgowns ready made, shalloons, durances and right Scotch plaids'.

53 Common Council

54 'Long Live Genius' (refers to the inscription over the door)

We went into a shop which had three partners, two of 'em were to flourish out their silks and, after an obliging smile and a pretty mouth made, Cicero-like, to expatiate on their goodness; and the other's sole business was to be gentleman-usher of the shop, to stand completely dress'd at the door, bow to all the coaches that pass by, and hand ladies out and in.

We saw abundance of gay fancies fit for sea captains wives, sheriffs feasts, and Taunton-Dean Ladies – 'This madam, is wonderful charming' – 'This madam is so diverting a silk' – 'This madam – my stars! how cool it looks'. 'But this, madam, ye gods, would I had ten thousand yards of it' (then gathers up a sleeve and places it to our shoulders), 'It suits your ladyship's face wonderfully well.' When we had pleas'd ourselves, and bid him ten shillings a yard for what he ask'd fifteen. 'Fan me, ye winds, your ladyship rallies me! Shou'd I part with it at such a price, the weavers wou'd rise upon the very shop – Was you at the park last night, madam? – Your ladyship shall abate me sixpence – Have you read *The Tatler* today, pretty lady? A smart fellow I'll assure you.'

But being tir'd with his impertinence, as very ridiculous things soon cloy people, we agreed the point. He whipp'd us off twenty-eight yards with as much dexterity as Young G——y shall dash you out glasses of wine, and Mr Fantast at the door reconvey'd us into the coach.

These fellows are positively the greatest fops in the kingdom; they have their toilets,[55] and their fine night-gowns, their chocolate in a morning, and their green-tea two hours after, turkey polts for their dinner, and then perfumes, washes and clean linen equip 'em for the parade. 'Tis fit those whose professions invite the ladies shou'd appear decent before 'em. But if some women of note wou'd not countenance their foppery, and cry, 'Really Mr Farendine, you are too well bred, and have too good an air for a tradesman, but a mercer is a genteel calling. Suppose you had been bred a soap-boiler' . . . 'Fogh!', says he. 'Oh filthy!', says she, nor invite 'em to collations,[56] and be seen in a hackney coach with 'em, they'd leave off their conceited niceties and keep within the sphere of industry, for sure, no composition can be more ridiculous, than a creature made up of beau and business. Our sex indeed have a mighty ascendant, and those poor animals may be a little excus'd, when some women shall have power to coin fops and fools out of the greatest statesmen and politicians.

*

Mrs Y——g at Chiswick, who has sixteen lap-dogs that lie in beds, blankets and fine quilts, and have every day roast pullets,[57] and a

55 dressing tables 56 meals 57 young chickens

footman to attend 'em, would have Madamoiselle Javillot to teach them to dance. She has tried several English masters that have begun 'em in minuets and rigadoons,[58] they have given 'em no air. As she pays for their learning, tho' they are dogs, she expects to have 'em civilly treated, since they are dear creatures to her; for several that have lately affronted 'em she has had before their betters.

*

In a few days will be published:
The Art of Tautology, written by Valentine Verbose of the Inner Temple, Esq. who is a wonderful proficient in the fluency of words; he can, by needless recitals, extend a bill in chancery to six hundred sheets, and has made considerable and approved additions to the introduction of an answer, as, 'This defendent saying to himself' etc. and to the conclusion 'Without that that' etc.—— To which will be added a small tract, entitled *The Art of Saying Something Upon Nothing*, very useful to those who draw preambles to noblemen's patents. —— A Poem in praise of Sine Cures; by Timothy Tunbelly, vicar of Cellarton in Derbyshire.

WEDNESDAY JULY 27 TO FRIDAY JULY 29 *Number 10*

Last night the Honourable Charles Empty, Esq. brought a gentleman to my drawing-room whom I had never seen before. The whole company seem'd very uneasy at his appearance, and some ladies went away the moment he sat down. He gave a loose to[59] talk, and us'd a sort of familiarity I had never heard of. 'Mrs Phoebe,' says he, 'I long'd mightily to see you; for by your papers, I fancy'd you must be a comical slut.' I was a little struck at his oddness of address, as everybody was, and burst out laughing. He mimick'd and ridicul'd all the quality in the kingdom; this lady was a trapes,[60] t'other a puss, a third was in love with a trooper, and a fourth, he knew enough of her! Then rak'd into people's families. One's father was a foot soldier, and t'other's grandmother an old match-maker; gave 'em the nick-names of Sue Stately, Jenny Jigg-it, Bess Bob-tail, and Kate

58 lively jigs 59 started to 60 a slut

Wriggle, and practis'd over all their airs. This sort of behaviour was perfectly new to me, and I couldn't forbear telling him such treatment was not fit for people of rank, that as he had had the honour to be admitted into most great families he might have observ'd they never took those liberties with one another, and I thought it very indecent for an inferior to mention 'em with so little respect. His answer was, 'Pray, my Lady Scribble, hold you your clack, I have a fine story about you! And so, Madam, your Servant. I believe I shall dine with you one day this week.'

When he was gone, Col. Aiery gave me the following account of him. That he was formerly in a genteel post that brought him into the best of company, but lost it by the grossness of his ridicule; that he was a man of parts, but had suffer'd his wit to dwindle into mere buffoonery, which had often cost him a good bearing. Some families who can bear his jokes (as great men formerly kept jesters) are very fond of him still. But the generality have thrown him off, since the nobleman he sups with tonight is certainly diverted with a ridiculous character of those that entertain'd him yesterday. So that gentlemen who are above scandal, and pleas'd to hear one another abus'd, admire him as a living lampoon. He is the soonest acquainted with you of any man; give him but a pinch of snuff in the side-box, he's at your *levée*[61] next morning, dines with you, sups with you, commends your wines and desires you to present him with a chest of it, and then – you are an odious creature. He's so far from pride, that he wants a decent decorum for 'tis equal to him whether he drinks burgundy at Lockets[62] with my Lord, or stout and ale with his footman in a cellar; and is never difficult of access but to counter-officers. Withal, so very good natur'd, that whatever tradesman arrests him he's the first that runs in his debt again. He has lately got a footing into city entertainments, and would dine with those custard-eating wretches oftener, cou'd he contain his laughter. But the punch bowl cap of maintenance, the ridiculous songs of 'Tis my Lady's birth day,' and 'O raree show, pretty show,' and those frightful harridans their wives are what he is no more able to bear than to see the judges dance round the coal fire on All Saints Day. Those that know him perfectly, fancy him to be a little craz'd, for in winter you shall meet him in silk camlet,[63] and in dog-days with a blue cloak on. And he's observed either to be very clean in a coach with a coronet, or very dirty a foot, with a crab in one hand and a handkerchief full of salad in the other.

61 a morning social reception
62 fashionable eating place
63 light garment of silk and mohair

These hangers upon families I never lik'd and have order'd Francis henceforward to deny me both to him, and the Honourable Mr Empty that introduc'd him. The number of buffoons, parasites and court beggars that follow people of quality is infinite, it shows a levity of mind, and that those who encourage 'em are very easily pleas'd. Some great men are very unaccountable in giving access to people. A gentleman, who has been serviceable to his country, has sustain'd misfortunes and really merits the interest he is endeavouring to make, shall be refus'd admittance, when an actress shall immediately be usher'd up with her benefit tickets. The first indeed is but doing a dull piece of christianity, which shou'd they perform once, they'd never be free from troublesome attendants; but the latter is a diverting charity, and obliges a Lady – a'nt please you. I think those whom we call leading men ought a little to refine their tastes. Their actions shou'd be great, like themselves, their diversions solid and substantial and their tables fill'd with learning and true friendship instead of contemptible mimics and designing sycophants.

The City of London has of late been very unfortunately in insurrections; the weavers rose, and frightened all the French people into morbleu, tettebleu, ventrebleu, etc. which the valiant trainbands[64] soon dispers'd; chiefly owing to the glittering appearance and magnanimous looks of Mr Noisy, the pewterer, who calls himself Prince Huge-One, at the head of 'em. But their sieges, skirmishes and the rest of their heroic imaginations so alarm'd the tranquillity of Moorfields and the adjacent parts, that the inhabitants fancy'd themselves at Tournai.[65] However the suppos'd town being taken, the venison pasties eat, and a peace concluded between the aldermen, colonels, and the republic of Old Street they were hastily dismiss'd by a shower of rain and, saluting their wives with an over charg'd volley which does no other mischief than to fright old women into enthusiasm.

*

The lady that lost her self lately in St James's Park, at two o'clock in the morning, may hear of her self again at Mrs Crackenthorpe's drawing-room, she paying the charge of this advertisement.

*

Last Monday Mrs Crackenthorpe's man Francis ask'd leave to go to Ratcliffe to see his Aunt Dobson, and had as handsome a suit of clothes

64 citizens in arms

65 site of a recent battle in Marlborough's Low Country campaign

on of his own, as any young fellow need to wear. Some slovenly tars[66] met him at Shadwell, press'd him,[67] and would have carry'd him on board had he not screamed out and two strong women rescu'd him. The poor fellow has been always subject to fits, and the family have been scarce able to keep life in him ever since. Whoever shall discover any of the rude rabble that assaulted him will receive a guinea reward of his Aunt Dobson, and Mrs Crackenthorpe will give another. For nobody that sees him can suppose he was ever bred to climb ropes, disorder his hair with boisterous winds, and lie in dirty hammocks; for, shou'd a peace[68] happen, and Mrs Crackenthorpe take a trip to France, the very crossing from Dover to Calais wou'd almost fright him out of his wits.

FRIDAY JULY 29 TO MONDAY AUGUST 1 — *Number 11*

Yesterday I gave a release to Stud[69] and repaid some visits, which our sex have made book-debts. One lady was not at home, another wou'd not be at home, and a third saw no company, having lately buried her squirrel. At last I fixed myself with Mrs Townly, and the company I met there were all monsters. Nothing is so amazing to me as the choice of some women's conversation who dream away their time in incoherent stuff which makes 'em useless to the world. But fools have this happiness – to be easy with themselves, and let other people blush for 'em. Mrs Save-all is reckon'd a good housewife and gives you a history of her management: she had twenty maids last year, and all of 'em prov'd sluts, her dining-room is in nice order, for she carries her visitors into the kitchen, and the best fashion that ever came up is not to treat people.

They have two prentices, who, tho' provisions be dear, have as monstrous stomachs as ever, and her sister had the conscience to bring a footman that's enough to breed a famine in the nation. By a prudent care to lock up everything, the beggars never molest her doors. She grudges

66 sailors

67 Press-gangs were groups of men employed to force men to join the Army or the Navy.

68 See M. 9, p. 2

69 presumably Stud was the name of Mrs Crackenthorpe's horse

her husband necessaries. Her children are dispers'd among her relations, and her poor kindred, for she hates idleness, work out her benevolence, and then her charity is well bestow'd. She's observed, however, to be very kind to herself, has many a private collation, and cherry-colour'd damask, tho' she's turned of fifty, is hardly gay enough for her. Ask her about news, she'll tell you the barber's wife is brought to bed, and her brother-in-law's cat has kitten'd. Books she never converses with, yet is so well read in the history of her neighbours that she sets the whole parish together by the ears.

Lady Wou'd-be is a learned piece, and has puzzled most divines. She's a great admirer of Suckling. Milton she has by heart and Cowley is her bed-fellow. Plays are infinitely below her, Alexander[70] she can bear, but a comedy's fit only for her woman. She understands architecture, and talks of the Corinthian, the Doric, Ionic and Tuscan Orders; her language is seraphic and supernatural; and for those who use familiar phrases, their discourse is uncouth and *jejune*,[71] and bears no symmetry or concatination.

Ask her, if she can make a tansy?[72] – She's never hear'd of it.

Mrs Prim is wonderfully dizen'd out, makes a visit of an hour long, and then stalks off without having spoke a word all the while, till the town has reported her to be dumb.

But Mrs All-talk gives you a rotation of the French king and the parson of Huntington, Dr Trotter in Moorfields, and the black woman under St Dunstan's Church, till she deafens the whole room.

Another set came in, which if it be possible, are more ridiculous than these: Mrs Dandler, Mrs Mince-it, Mrs Fore-fight, Mrs Hoyden-Tail. Dandler entertain'd us with discourses of her children; that Master Bobby was the cunningest little Boy, and Miss Dolly the sweetest girl that a woman cou'd bring into the world, she had wit at will tho' but five years old, and said such smart things she put her pious grand-mother into the violentest tee-hee, that had not laugh'd before these thirty years! Fore-sight talk'd of news and as loud as if she had bawl'd it about the streets. She said Louis XIV[73] was necessitated to sign the preliminaries, his country being in a deplorable condition, and that we shou'd certainly have a peace by Lord-mayor's day, for letters from Turin advise that the army under the Count de Thaun, decamp'd from Suza the 10th Instant, the 11th they began to pass Mount Cenis, and the greatest part of the troops are since arriv'd at Termignon near Laneburgh; that the body commanded by General Schuylenburgh in the Valley of Aosta, has been

70 *The Rival Queens; or, The Death of Alexander the Great* by Nathaniel Lee (1677)

71 empty 72 pudding

73 of France, who had offered peace

reinforc'd to 5 or 6,000 men, with which he is to enter the Tarantaise in order to join General Thaun, and penetrate into Marienne.

Mince-it labours under a mighty uneasiness to inform you of her equipage and all her fine trinkets, but at length hauls 'em in by head and shoulders. That last Christmas, going to bed, she was frighted to that degree, her woman was putting on her nightclothes, her chamber-maid airing the bed, her middle-maid blowing up the fire, and her cook-maid preparing somewhat for her to take, when somebody in the next street cried out, 'Thieves! Thieves!' Her coach-man and all the six footmen ran out, the butler's hair stood on end about the plate, and where to hide her jewels, that were worth six thousand pounds, her watch, tweezer-case, gold snuff-box and the five hundred broad pieces Sir John lately gave her, put her into the greatest confusion imaginable. And tho' her fright was mere invention, she tells it all over the town till she believes it herself. And for Mrs Hoyden-tail, she cou'd not sit two minutes in a place, but was for hotcockles, blind-man's-buff, and a king-I-am,[74] that she might be commanded into the kitchen to kiss the fellows.

This sort of society is mighty edifying truly, and I told Mrs Townly, tho' no lady can be refus'd bringing a foil with her, yet she ought to take all opportunities of dropping such acquaintance, as some men of letters once a year clear their libraries of silly and impertinent books. As virtue or vice, so wit and folly are adjudg'd people according to the company they keep, and as every man's sobriety is suspected that associates with a libertine, I shou'd question his understanding that is seen often with a coxcomb. Vanity does indeed sometimes touch men of parts, and much company they think gains them a popular esteem, but 'tis a mistaken notion the man of sense gives a lustre to the peer at the expense of his own judgment. And I had rather be seen a-foot with honest thread-bare Timon,[75] than flying to Hyde Park in a coach and six with my Lord Feather-fool.

*

Lady Whimsey and Lady Sqeamish, that are ever altering and contriving, fidgeting about town, and buying all the year round, make complaints that seamstresses shops have such loads of fellows in 'em saunt'ring, sneering and treating the creatures with fruit. They are not offended with a pretty gentleman at any hour or place, but in one shop sat a filthy fat fellow, in another a frightful fiery-face fellow, in a third, a washy hatchet-face fellow and one bold trollop had a dozen rakish

74 parlour games

75 a Timon is a misanthrope and hermit.

officers about her. Ladies have occasion for several gimcracks,[76] not proper to ask for before men, and, if these enormities are not rectify'd, they must be forc'd to buy of women that sell in chambers, and sure the fellows won't have the impudence to come there.

*

Whereas several ill-bred critics have reported about town that a woman is not the author of this paper, which I take to be a splenetic and irrational aspersion upon our whole sex, women were always allow'd to have a finer thread of understanding than the men, which made them have recourse to learning, that they might equal our natural parts, and by an arbitrary sway have kept us from many advantages to prevent our out-vying them; but those ladies who have imbib'd authors, and div'd into arts and sciences have ever discover'd a quicker genius, and more sublime notions. These detractors must be a rough-hewn sort of animals that cou'd never gain admittance to the fair sex, and all such I forbid my drawing-room.

MONDAY AUGUST 1 TO WEDNESDAY AUGUST 3 — *Number 12*

Last week an extraordinary piece of mortality came to the printer of this paper. Her attire, which was painted calico, lemon colour'd knots, patches beyond arithmetic, and her scarf a mere cobweb furbelow'd with butterflies, suppos'd her to be fifteen; but her face discover'd seventy. Her equipage was suitable to her appearance, for she had a hundred boys after her, and the loudness of our talk alarmed the gaping neighbourhood. She had a story which Mrs Crackenthorpe must needs insert or she'd take it very ill, *viz*: that a young lady of her acquaintance took too much notice of the men, which made the men take a great deal of notice of her, and what might be the issue of the matter she could not tell; that tho' her relations and friends had advised her not to be civil to any man, yet she paid more respect to a handsome young fellow than to her mother who bore her into the world; that she had a great deal more to say of her, and desir'd the printer to write it down, who told her the story ought to be a little

[76] knick-knacks

digested; that no body was so capable of penning it as herself, and Mrs Crackenthorpe was too well bred to disoblige one of her figure. Her ladyship return'd three times before this important affair could be settled. At last she resolv'd to put pen to paper, and said the young lady's name she must by all means conceal, and therefore he must ask her no questions about it, for it must not be known for the world. However, that the lady herself might know who was meant by the story, she was resolved to put the first and last letters of her name with a dash; but because she was no mistress of spelling, desired him to tell her the beginning and ending letters of the name 'Crisp'. For which, being laugh'd at by her rude attendants, Mrs Crackenthorpe has lost the story; for madam told him in a very great huff that there was a third Tatler coming out, and truly she'd carry her intelligence to them; so tucked up her tail, and march'd off.

People little think that an impertinent satire upon others is a severe libel upon themselves.

*

Last week a gentleman-beggar came to Mrs Crackenthorpe's pretending he was related to her, his mothers name being Crackenthorpe, and desir'd her charity, but she not thinking him a proper object, gave him a civil denial. Upon which, the fellow presents a pistol at her, and Francis, interposing, had like to have been shot; but the cookmaid running in, who had been in love with Francis three years, they got the pistol from him, and Elsabeth and he thrash'd him severely. Mrs Crackenthorpe has since been informed that he has visited most families in town, and desires to speak with people privately, pretending his mother was of every lady's name, and when he's refus'd money, out comes the pistol. She therefore desires those who have as yet escaped his impudent visits to be cautious in trusting themselves alone with such strangers.

*

Complaints are made that the linen drapers of Cheapside and Cornhill daily set up for wits, damn plays before they are acted, cry down books before they are published and take towns before they are besieged. They'd be very much surpriz'd to hear a gentleman at will's talk of Bag-Hollands and Sheer-Muslins.[77] Books and Bengals[78] are very inconsistent; and whatever linen draper would get an alderman's estate must publicly declare he has no wit. Mrs Crackenthorpe likewise thinks it as

[77] fabrics [78] silk fabrics

ridiculous for tradesmen, who don't pretend to swords, to walk with their hats under their arms as 'tis for attorneys clerks to buy a sword betwixt two of 'em.

*

The States of Holland having desired the favour of Mrs Crackenthorpe's picture, she designs to sit speedily, and desires Mr Richardson[79] to let her know when he's left at leisure. The posture she is to be in has been the subject of very learned debates. This lady says that being a studious person, she should lie on a couch, with one leg dangling off. Another lady would have her walking in a solitary grove. A third, as rising from her chair to receive company; and a West Country lady advis'd her to be smoking a pipe of tobacco. As she was in fifty minds who should draw it, she is now in fifty more how it shall be drawn; and when 'tis finished perhaps it must be as many times alter'd before it pleases her.

*

Mrs Crackenthorpe thinks it very ridiculous for my Lady Fullmoon, who is so extreme fat, to dance minuets in public.

WEDNESDAY AUGUST 3 TO FRIDAY AUGUST 5 — *Number 13*

Of all the fools this nation shares among 'em, to me an old fool is the most preposterous, and happening yesterday to meet some of these extraordinary personages, I shall just touch upon four of 'em. The imperious, dogmatical old fool, the peevish, fretful fool, the snarling, quarrelsome Oliverian[80] and the comical old fiddle-faddle.

An imperious, dogmatical old fellow is ever positive, and ever in the wrong. He stalks about the room like a citizen just knighted, lords it o'er his family with an arbitrary sway, his will's his reason, and he thunders out his commands to provoke fear and trembling. He is the worst companion breathing, his seat distinguishes him from the rest of the company, as if he paid the reckoning. Prescribes rules and methods without suffering other people's opinions, and whoever contradicts him is coxcomb. Young fellows are pert coxcombs, pragmatical coxcombs

79 Jonathan Richardson, celebrated portrait painter
80 Cromwellian

and a man must live to thirty years of age before he has wit enough to know he's a fool. If he's elected to any public office he's as fond of pageantry as children are of playthings, has hardly strength of reason to support so much grandeur, and with intoxicating pride, runs distracted at fourscore.

A peevish, fretful old fellow is always phthisicky,[81] pining and just going out of the world, and yet you'll find him in it twenty years hence. 'Tis the business of a whole family to nurse him, and yet he thinks everybody neglects him. His restlessness of mind, inequality of humour and inconstancy of heart show him to several men in one, and he multiplies himself as often as he changes his taste and manners. His youthful relations, in hopes of good legacies, give him a long series of attendance, and then all die before him.

The snarling Oliverian thinks himself heart-whole, true as steel and metal to the last. Smile at him and he breaks your head, mention but the Calves Head Club[82] he lugs out upon you, tells you what an army surrounded him in the civil wars, and how magnanimously he behaved himself. And let the stoutest hero of the present age speak a syllable against old Noll,[83] Bilboa's the word.[84] His garb, indeed, shows him to be of the rebel rout, but though his perriwig is as red as a fox, his neckcloth a piece of an old black hatband, his coat of the ancient long pockets, and a basket hilt sword with but half a scabbard to it, yet he values himself upon his scars, and is as obstinate in mischief as if the terror of his looks could frighten people into an insurrection.

But the old fiddle-faddle would make one die. He wears a patch and two favourites,[85] has a fan in his pocket and forty trinkets to his watch. He uses his coat of arms, but a letter to a fair lady is sealed with a bleeding heart, then cries 'hee, hee, hee' and gives you a pat on the cheek. He shakes the footman by the hand, asks the cook-maid how long she has lived there, what wages she has, and whether this mistress gives her the kitchen stuff, then takes the child out of the nurse's arms, will feed it himself, dandle it and talk foolish gibberish to it. Wherever he dines, he's sure they have some alteration lately, for he doesn't remember those window curtains; enquires for the whole family, is sorry to hear the coachman has the spleen, and has a sovereign remedy for it. He tells you yesterday he took a vomit, that there are a world of Palatines[86] come

[81] consumptive

[82] A club initiated to ridicule Charles I; the last toast of the night was always 'To those worthy patriots who killed the tyrant'.

[83] Oliver Cromwell

[84] a bully's sword; 'Bilboa's the word, and slaughter will ensue', Congreve in *The Old Bachelor* (1693).

[85] fashionable style of curl

[86] see n. 37, p. 12

over, and begins a relation of last night's dream, which, if you have the patience to hear, you'll never get rid of him.

People's dispositions are strangely different and persevering, and when they suffer themselves to be tainted with pride, ill-nature, vain-glory and impertinence, they are not to be rooted out, even in old age.

Letters from Highgate give an account of a very fine summer house there near the road, which a very fine lady gives herself abundance of airs in. She can't bear anything should pass by without seeing it, rises from table at a stage-coach, flies to a chariot-and-six, and a gentleman in scarlet with a footman after him, she'll come down in her shift too. Gaping at travellers is to her meat, drink, business, diversion and what-not, but the main design of it is to be seen herself. She curtsies to every stranger, and when a young fellow shall accost her with, 'Pretty lady, how far is it to Whetstone?' she tells him, not like her cousin ill-bred, that he must follow his nose, but that her name's Pepper, Deputy Pepper's daughter, that their town house is in Budge Row, and her father can give her five thousand pounds. She was bred in the city, is at all city entertainments, and tho' her fortune must come from the city, nobody makes so great a jest of it as herself. Tradesmen have great estates, but how those poor souls do purr about and get money is to her the greatest mystery in the world.

If a gentleman takes her out to a dance she presently tells him that Monsieur Seris is her dancing master, Nicholeni is her singing master, Barret her spinet master, Champelon her French master, and that her name's Pepper. Whoever dances a minuet she follows with the union; if they sing 'Celia my heart', she has 'fair Dorinda'; if they play Mr Purcell's Airs she knows a thorough bass, for nobody shall outdo her. If her father weren't a tradesman she could be civil to him, but all her family are the greatest fools and how she came by so much wit is another great mystery. Her garniture is fantastic beyond description, for, should she dress like other people, she'd look like other people, and whoever tells her of new fashion, she hates to imitate anybody. She says the court is distracted for her, and so would the city, if they had any brains to lose her. The whole town do so gaze at her (as they may very well do) and one person can't satisfy everybody, that she's forced to retire to Highgate, where she shines from the summer house, entices with her freedom, charms with her beauty, mortifies with her indifference that the despairing traveller passes mournfully along.

She fancies herself to have an influence in the skies, if she's obliged to stay at home it certainly rains, but when she puts on her whimsical suit, her crimped head and has taken a world of pains about her face, the sun shines brighter than she has lately observed it. Being sent for to a relation that lay a-dying, the family's in an uproar to equip her, but meeting four gentlemen in the street, she coquets with 'em an hour, hearing music at the boarding school she ran in there, stayed till the ball was done and then wondered people could sit so many hours to see the same thing over and over. Her relation died without seeing her, and when her parents reprimanded her ill conduct, she told 'em it was wit and humour.

A lady so extremely full of herself must be a most unhappy creature. Her jealousy of others and an invidious emulation must give her great disorders. Gaiety may be owing to nature, but gadding and affected airs are to gain admirers. And when she can endure a filthy fellow, perhaps she may dwindle into a wife,[87] but she'll sooner endure a husband than she'll get one. Men are prying creatures and in general have but a trifling opinion of our sex; they compliment us, then laugh at us, see through our little disguises, and think our discourse mere whipped syllabub, a mouthful of nothing.

*

Several ladies having made complaint that the title Madam is grown so common 'tis used to every seamstress and mantua-maker[88] if you go into an eating house it must be 'Madam' to the bar-keeper, and on Sundays, when chambermaids have got their best clothes on, the town is full of Madams. Mrs Crackenthorpe does hereby order the words Goody, Gammer, Mistress and Forsooth be used henceforward, as well in town as country; and that no person do henceforward assume the title of Madam that can't prove herself a gentlewoman, nor any citizen's wife suffer her servants to banter her at that rate, whose husband can't swear himself worth ten thousand pounds, on pain of Mrs Crackenthorpe's displeasure, and being prosecuted with the utmost severity of her paper.

*

Mrs Crackenthorpe having received some venison out of the country, designs to make an entertainment on Monday next, and having been bantered by some people about her long chin, she invites the whole family of long chins, spiritual and temporal, that they may consult how to bring 'em more in fashion, and spoil the grin of these ridiculous fellows who make a jest of so ornamental a proportion; and if her tittle-tattle can set all their chins a wagging, she shall think herself extremely happy.

*

Whereas several ladies about town keep coaches that can't afford to pay servant's wages, and several others, that haven't coaches, hate to make

87 lines from Congreve *The Way of the World* (1700)
88 dress-maker

visits in hackneys, 'tis agreed by all the decaying gentry, to save extravagant charges and unreasonable borrowing, that their equipage shall appear anywhere with any sort of people, and then pride, without foundation may flutter along, like French tailors to the Tuileries.[89]

*

Several people have complained of the brevity of this paper, which Mrs Crackenthorpe takes to be a very great compliment. A dull paper is too long by every line; and when this appears short 'tis for want of useful intelligence.

FRIDAY AUGUST 5 TO MONDAY AUGUST 8 — *Number 14*

The preference of so many persons of quality that yesterday crowded my drawing-room, made me lay aside a visit I intended to Madam Slender-sense, who is lately fallen ill of a swelling she receiv'd by a slip the last ball night. Some are so rude as to say that Beau Garsoon, the French dancing master, was the occasion of it; and Mrs Manlove, who generally searches into the bottom of such an affair, solemnly protests she saw them go up one pair of stairs together. What they did there she can't tell, but the lady has been ailing ever since. Be it as it will, I am satisfy'd she won't want attendance, which gives me the less uneasiness for laying aside such a piece of formality, especially since it is credibly reported that she does not intend to make a dying on't, as my niece Phoebe is like to do for the loss of her parrot.

Most part of the evening was spent in a rehearsal[90] of the misfortunes of the adorable Clarissa, who, tho' of a complexion really brunette, has something so agreeably charming and attractive in her features, shape and mien, that the most courageous mortal never had the temerity to stand a glance, without offering up his heart a sacrifice to the divinity of her perfections.

'Twas the beginning of Clarissa's misfortune to be born of, and brought up by, parents who were either ignorant or regardless of the singular beauty of her mind which, in her younger years, us'd to shoot

[89] a Parisian palace [90] a narration

forth such splendid rays of wit, as charm'd the auditors into surprise and admiration. She was scarce arriv'd to years wherein young virgins are generally reckon'd marriageable, when, by her too rigorous parents, she was privately contracted to Senioro, an old weather-beaten mortal, who by the motion of his body, and sometimes of his tongue, the acts of respiration, and such like evidences, gave most people occasion to think he was alive; whilst the shortness of his breath, and the rattling of his throat, made every one conclude that he was ready to make his exit from this wicked world. Tho' he was turn'd of seventy, and look'd as old as some do at four-score and ten, yet, his coffers being well-lined, his estate unmortgag'd and he always in a way of making additions to it, so tickled the covetous fancies of Clarissa's parents that they were resolv'd to sacrifice the irrefutable charms of their lovely daughter to one whose forbidding years made him altogether incapable using a jewel of that inestimable value as she really deserv'd, and no doubt would expect and desire.

'Twas reckon'd most advisable to prolong the completion of their marriage till the young lady was turn'd of fifteen, and then all on a sudden she was let into the destructive secret. Fear, horror, and amazement fill'd her tender soul and made her stifle some words she would have made use of to entreat her parents to avert that terrible doom. The conflict betwixt duty and the former, at last ended in a flood of tears, which they dry'd up. She found her self unable to resist, and so was forc'd to comply, notwithstanding she had some time before made a solemn promise of marriage to the lovely Cynthio, a neighbouring youth, whose inimitable perfections and excellent endowments entitled him with the greatest justice to Clarissa's esteem. But fate it seems had otherwise determin'd and the day came when with the utmost reluctancy she suffer'd Senioro to possess himself of all her charms.

Married they were and he led her home in triumph to her apartment, where she was for many years immur'd, to her unspeakable discontent. For a few months indeed, he suffer'd her to visit the church, accompanied by himself or an old maid who was her guardian, or rather mistress, till at last jealousy began to prey upon him, and then he resolv'd never to admit her that innocent privilege, upon a supposition that she might one day meet with a deliverer in a place where so much company resorted. Thus she was more strictly confin'd for four or five years, rather as his prisoner than his wife; till fame began to speak as loud of the injuries he did her, as of her virtuous and uncommon merits, which inspir'd the generous Cynthio, who had often in vain attempted to see her, with a stratagem of making love in disguise to her antiquated guardian, by which means he found an opportunity to divert her in those tedious hours, which before were wholly devoted to solitude and confinement.

As she knew him to be a man of too much honour to attempt her resolute virtue, she gave him greater freedoms than otherwise she would have done, and permitted him to snatch some small favours, which she thought he might rather attribute to chance than compliance. And as he did not reproach her with breach of promise, she was in hopes time would make him forget it. Cynthio was so transported, so amazed, and carry'd so far beyond himself with the fruition of these lesser endearments, that he neglected nothing on his part that might make her condition as easy as possible, tho' in the mean time he added to his own disquiet, by cherishing a flame it had been happy for him to have extinguish'd.

But this lasted not long. Fortune, who sometimes takes a delight to sport with the gay and beautiful, as well as with the mean and homely, unkindly separated these happy lovers by nipping their joys in the bud and laid open all their private intrigues to the wretched old man, and, nobody knows how, let him into a secret which dwelt in their breasts alone.

He no sooner heard or imagin'd such a thing to be, but his conscience suggested that he actually was what he knew well enough he deserv'd. Anger, jealousy and despair, made him resolve on the destruction of his chaste and lovely wife, which he had certain effected, had not a sudden sickness prevent him, which in a few days carry'd him off, and left the yet unfortunate Clarissa mistress of her own affairs. But tho' she had been so intolerably us'd and abus'd, yet such was her discretion, and she so tender of her reputation, that she was seen all in tears at his funeral, and accompany'd the corpse to the grave with as much solemnity as if he had been the most loving creature in the world.

On the other hand, Cynthio could not but entertain some secret joy at the prospect of his approaching happiness, notwithstanding he saw his dear Clarissa in tears. He gave her, as he thought, time sufficient to condole the misfortune of so small a loss and then made her a visit with such an awful modesty and becoming reverence, that one would have thought might have melted a harder heart than that of Clarissa's. But she receiv'd him so coldly and with such a negligent air that Cynthio could not forbear letting fall some expressions that seem'd to intimate his thoughts of deserving a better reception. She interrupted him just when he was going to reproach her with the breach of her former engagements, and told him, in short, that his presumption was a great uneasiness to her, that experience of a marriage state had given her such an aversion to it that she protested utterly against a second trial, and therefore desir'd him not give himself and her the trouble of seeing him any more.

'Is this the effect of all my tenderness, my long expectations, my tedious disquietudes and constant resolutions always to love you? Are these the returns you make me,' reply'd Cynthio, 'for the dangers I have run thro' to please you? May you meet with a man that loves you more, nay, that adores you as I do, and never have occasion to remember the unfortunate Cynthio.' At these words he darted out of the room without taking his leave, and has never been seen since. She repented immediately of her rashness, sent after him and, when it was too late, exclaim'd against herself for using him as she did. But all was now in vain. He was irrecoverably gone. The next morning an unknown hand brought her a letter, which prov'd to be Cynthio's last farewell. The tenor of it, said Polydamus, who gave us the relation, and who had a copy of the letter, was as follows.

> The unfortunate Cynthio to the adorable Clarissa: I give you the last proof of my love, Madam, by the exactness of my obedience. I go, my dear Clarissa, I go to seek death in a more fortunate clime, since you have banish'd me from your presence in this. 'Twas my good fortune to be once esteem'd, which gives a sharper edge to my present torment. Despair and continual grief reign sovereigns of my soul; and, as I shall never know any rest, since I have been deny'd it by you, I shall at least have this happiness, to die your slave. May Heaven continually crown you with prosperity, put an end to your sorrows, and make you unalterably happy. I wish you may never have occasion to repent of your cruelty to him, who so vehemently ador'd you, as did the miserable, Cynthio.

Hard-hearted as Clarissa was, she could not forbear expressing the anguish of her soul at the thoughts of her barbarity. She wish'd she could recall the fleeting time, that she might once more behold her lovely swain. But the Heavens were deaf to her prayers, and fate it seems had not yet put a period to her misfortunes. She calm'd her self at length with the thoughts that he had not quite abandon'd her; that 'twas possible this letter was only sent to terrify her in return to the ill-usage she had given him. But alas, some days and weeks being pass'd away, and no Cynthio appearing, she gave him over for lost.

In a revolution of some months, time, that defacer of all things, blotted him almost out of her thoughts, till a succeeding variety of troubles forc'd her to call him to mind again, and still to bewail his loss and her barbarity with a grief inexpressible.

The time of her widowhood was expir'd, and she appear'd public to the world at her own disposal, with a beauty if possible more dangerous than ever. Her killing eyes were now in the meridian of their lustre, and she quickly had adorers without number.

Among the rest who profess'd themselves her votaries and might boast of some place in her favour was Mr Rant, a young debauchée, who by a series of prodigalities had consum'd a fair estate at the Groom Porters,[91] the play-house and the tavern. His fortune was sunk to the lowest ebb when he first made his approaches to the divine Clarissa. As he was master of address, a proficient in the oratory of love, and one whom the gay part of mankind counted a wit, he was not long before he so insinuated himself into her favour, as to obtain the surrendry of that heart which Cynthio had so long sigh'd for in vain. The rakish youth was so transported with the conquest, that he scarce knew how to contain himself. But resolv'd to push on his good fortune whilst it was in his power, and being afraid that delays might prove dangerous in an affair of such consequence, he urged her to a speedy marriage. 'Twas not in her power to deny giving her hand where she had before resign'd her heart. The ladies blush'd for her; her relations endeavour'd to dissuade her from rushing into that certain ruin that must necessarily attend her present resolution; and in short all that knew her pity'd her extravagant humour. But all in vain. It was her destiny to be unfortunate, and therefore impossible to be prevented.

The marriage was celebrated with all the pomp and magnificence that cou'd be imagined; and Mr Rant with no small glory possess'd himself of the charming nymph, to her great delight and satisfaction. He deceitfully concealed his extravagancy for some time, and seemingly made it his whole delight to please her, till at length, having got what she had into his hands, and his humours and inclinations being only violently restrain'd, not really reform'd, broke out more impetuously than ever. He neglected his wife whole days and nights, nay sometimes whole weeks together, under pretence of riding into the country to see his relations. But in the meanwhile consuming her substance upon his harlots, till he left her as bare as himself was when he first made his addresses to her. He sold first her jewels, then her plate, and last of all what valuable furniture she had, and has for some time wholly forsaken her.

The poor lady, thus reduc'd, too late laments her rashness in banishing the generous Cynthio from her bosom. She is yet alive, bemoaning her condition in a retir'd country life, at a small seat of her own, which is her last refuge, and which her extravagant husband could never get from her. Her parents are long since dead. Her friends and relations have solemnly vow'd never to look on her more, since she despis'd their admonitions at a time when it was in her power to have made herself as happy as she is now miserable.

Polydamus having finish'd this mournful history, the company

91 a gaming club

entertain'd themselves with various reflections on that inevitable destiny that always attends us, and which it is impossible for us to avoid. Sophonisba, a lady of excellent perspicuity, was entering into a discourse on the variety of incidents that attend human life, when she was interrupted by the coming in of Monsieur Gusto, one of those fanatical fops, who, not content with the distinguishing character heaven has been pleased to bestow on mankind, take a peculiar pride in assuming such ridiculous habits and customs that make them look more like monkeys than men. We all perceived he was fluster'd, and as the ladies were in expectation of intolerable rudeness from one whom every body knew to have but little sense when sober and none at all when in drink, they all rose up to be gone. At which I was so nettled, 'twas next to a miracle I hadn't fallen into the vapours. I desired Polydamus to whisper Gusto, and let him know that the respect he ow'd the company required a decency in his behaviour, which had so good effect that, after adjusting his wig at the great glass, humming over an opera tune, and taking a pinch or two of musty,[92] he threw himself into an elbow-chair[93] that stood next him. But 'twas impossible to detain the company, who were all risen, and immediately withdrew. Monsieur fell fast asleep in the chair, where I left him, having some business upon my hands that required my attendance, and before I came back my gentleman was gone, to my no small satisfaction.

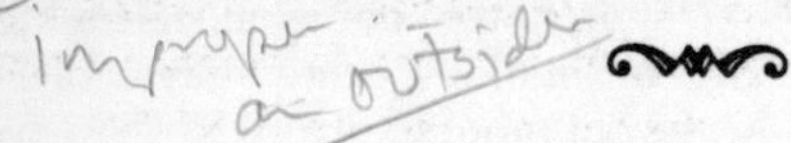

MONDAY AUGUST 8 TO WEDNESDAY AUGUST 10 — *Number 15*

The ingenious oxonian, who sent the following lines, complains that the pro-proctors[94] are such rigid disciplinarians they'd not allow their pupils wine, nor the society of women, two necessary things for love and poetry. 'Tis natural for our sex to side with youth, and, when I have observ'd parents to treat the children with unreasonable severity, I can't suppose tutors in general to have milder dispositions. But as young people are commonly too violent in their pleasures, 'tis fit such things as governors shou'd be, not tyrannically to curb their gaities, but judiciously to restrain their

[92] snuff [93] armchair [94] university officials

exorbitance. Hard students, fatig'd with crabbed Lycophron, or commenting upon Epictetus require a Bacchanalian refreshment (few know the labour of the mind) and when they associate, as I pronounce five to be the best company, I allow that the first bottle does no more than inform 'em of its goodness, the second exhilarates 'em, wit sparkles o'er the third, and the fourth makes 'em truly brilliant; Parthenissa is the toast, and the ravishing idea of a fine woman gives 'em an elevation above common soarers. Cou'd they part here, wit and beauty wou'd inspire sublime notions, and produce wonders in poetry; but when they shall want judgment to check the reins of their passions, and the heat of youth and wine makes 'em grow so immortal that no mortal can get 'em home, Bacchus laughs at Apollo, the muses are affronted, and the next morning, their pillow is their Parnassus and small beer their Helicon.

As to young students, who are gay, amorous, and irresistible, I can't approve of their conversing too frequently with women, except they be women of maturity, whose strict virtue may safely admit 'em, their experience improve 'em, and their wise conduct not only discourage every inordinate attempt, but discountenance every loose expression and *double entendre* in discourse, which, I have taken the liberty to tell several gentlemen, is very ill manners. Arguments from agreeable young fellows are very persuasive, and our sex, with all their seeming reservedness, are too apt to listen to 'em; admiration is repaid with complaisance, complaisance produces familiarity, familiarity breeds whispers, letters and assignations; and when Celadon has, by treats and importunities, insinuated himself into Florimel's good graces, time and place are the Devil – the Nymph surrenders, modesty takes its flight, religion and all moral virtues immediately follow after, and the person who has seduc'd the unhappy yielding maid, shall be the first to upbraid her weakness, and expose her to the world.

*

Arabella Tickle-pulse, wife to Tho. Tickle-pulse, doctor in physic, has elop'd from her husband. She's a little blackish woman, has a languishing eye, a delicious soft hand and two pretty jiggetting feet. She's suppos'd to be gone her husband knows not where, nor has she sent him word when she will return; therefore, all templars,[95] and other general lovers, are desir'd not to harbour her for the doctor will not pay for her board. She'd no occasion to run away, having a sufficiency of everything for a reasonable woman. However, tho' this be her third

95 law students

elopement, if she submits herself by the end of the Dog-days,[96] the doctor has good nature enough to receive her again.

*

The family of the Has-beens, are in very great wrath that the town has neglected toasting them lately. They think they might be kindly remember'd for former condescensions, but, when a girl of fifteen shall outvie them, whose elaborate compositions have been wonder'd at these thirty years, 'tis what flesh and blood can't bear. Should these ladies be bless'd with returning youth and beauty, which a very fine astrologer has taken but fourteen years to determine, they're resolved to use the men like snakes, vipers, toads, adders, and not suffer 'em to touch the hem of their garments, tho' they die o' the pip.[97] And my old Lady Has-been swears by all the great gods, and the little ones too, when that day happens, whatever fellow dares approach her, tho' it be a knight o' the shire, upon his bended marrow-bones, she'll call him ungrateful monster, perjur'd villain, pitiful scoundrel, and spit in his face.

*

Several gentlemen of finesse and ladies of delicatesse complaining of intolerable hot days, have agreed that the fields are wonderfully charming about twelve at night; but let them beware there be no snakes in the grass.

WEDNESDAY AUGUST 10 TO FRIDAY AUGUST 12 *Number 16*

I had the misfortune yesterday to disappoint my vintners by being hurry'd out early that morning to Mrs Qualm-sick the curate's wife, that annual disturber, who, by her own calculation, shou'd not have alarm'd us yet this fortnight. She was so extremely bad all day, I thought we must have sent for Sir David. But by the assistance of so many notable women, for the whole parish were assembl'd, she brought her husband the chopping'st boy, almost big enough to run alone, which made her number a complete

96 the hottest days of summer, usually August

97 a trivial irritation

dozen, and all of 'em alive. This business, which is but a ne pretence for half the gossips that come thither, being happily ove was retiring in great haste, for the cackling part of such an affair is to me intolerable, but was repuls'd by a regiment of furbelow'd nightrails[98] and aprons with Mrs Cherry-Mantle the midwife at the head of 'em.

'Good Madam – do us the honour, Madam – not taste the doctor's punch before you go – that wou'd be such a paradox – Dr Qualm-sick's chief study has been nicely to prepare a bowl of punch and Nurse Tape-lace, the sexton's wife, beseech'd my Ladyship to stay, and have a little fun with the company.' I was forc'd to yield my self to the mercy of their tongues, as great lawyers are oblig'd to bear the impertinence of some litigious women that know nothing, and more litigious persons who, tho' they have six counsel, are ever pleading their own causes; and being carry'd into another room, we sat down to a ham and chickens, which I thought were the best company there.

Their discourse was an incongruous medley of sights, clothes, husbands and hypochondriacs. One gave us a long account of the Palatines, which every body had been tir'd with; another talk'd of her new head that was dress'd at the Old Exchange; a third's Jonathon was a very honest sober man, but she had never a child by him; and a fourth's mother-in-law us'd to be mightily subject to vapours, but she had been dead a great while; but an apothecary's lady, whose tongue seldom lies still, happen'd to be very obliging for being in a violent flounce that the surgeon's wife sat above her, she would not speak one word. Some petty disputes we had at table, as, ''Tis well, madam, when servants have the luck to marry their masters'; ''Twou'd be better, Madam, if people that value themselves upon their family, wou'd pay their debts'; 'They say, Madam, tradesmen's wives are the junketing'st creatures, and have such loads of provision, it suffices a moderate stomach to look at it'; 'Ladies, Madam, often flock'd at an entertainment, because they are not invited to't'; 'Pray, Madam, when did you see Captain Smart, I must own him a pretty gentlemen; but they say, 'tisn't reputable to appear with him'; 'that disrepresentation, Madam, may arise from his being seen with some ladies'.

When one ask'd a country lady how her sow did, she said, 'Mightily upon the grunt till her belly was full'. But at the mediation of good Dr Qualm-sick matters were kept pretty quiet. However, when we rose, the whole company whisper'd me by turns that every woman there, except myself and her, was the most gadding, prating, busy, backbiting thing alive and by what she had heard, no better than she shou'd be.

98 loose wraps

When the doctor's punch arriv'd, they were wondrous friendly again, and after two or three healths, their clacks did run at that incessant rate, that one lady spoke in the cup, and grew so very noisy that, tho' I affected all the good humour imaginable, having a secret pleasure in their characters, I was forc'd to take an opportunity of slipping away.

*

Whereas several sprightly young fellows that keep horses and ride out every day to Hampstead Heath, Epping Forest, etc. are, thro' their idleness and extravagance, suspected by some malicious people to salute coaches in the dusk o' the evening. Mrs Mary Fanciful, having heard a world of stories about highwaymen, has a curiosity to see one. She sets out for the bath, on Monday next, with ten guineas (not hid in the privat'st part of her coach) therefore, if any of these gentlemen please to clap an uncharg'd pistol to her breast, only that she may know how it is to be robb'd, they shall receive the ten guineas with a sincere promise never to be prosecuted for the same. Her sister, Mrs Sarah Fanciful, wants mightily to see a ghost.

*

'The Catern-Wheel' at Henley-upon-Thames is the best inn for accommodating ladies that travel that road. The master of the house is so complaisant a creature that he says Sir and Madam to ladies' lap-dogs. He has very fine gardens, where ladies may stick themselves all over with flowers, and, as women o' quality in France keep valet-de-chambers, he is very handy about ladies, and will most obsequiously attend 'em in his laboratory with a dram of his *Aqua- anti-Splenetica*, or whatever else their pretty stomachs shall have a mind to.

FRIDAY AUGUST 12 TO MONDAY AUGUST 15 — *Number 17*

he discourse last night ran upon peoples' circumstances and their different way of living; the sordid frugality of some great men, the unaccountable extravagance of others, the prodigality of inferior classes, the falsity of reports, and in general, the deceitfulness of most men's appearance. But as distinction of rank is highly necessary for the economy of the

world, we ought to touch upon great peoples characters with the same consideration and awful respect as we approach their persons. Avarice in a nobleman, who has a vast estate and great employments, lessens him to his equals; and a gentleman that lives up to a small fortune, has more regard shown him. A penurious disposition makes people suspect his other qualities, whereas a truly great man regards his fortune only as 'tis subservient to his grandeur. His wonderful genius for politics and a head capable of forming noble designs distinguish him in the ministry; his delicate understanding, acute wit, and affable temper gain him friends among those of his own rank, and his regular hospitality, admirers among his inferiors.

On the other hand, extravagance in men of distinction, to outvie in dress, equipage, and luxurious entertainments, discover an empty pride and a groundless ostentation, which makes 'em slighted by those in business. Parasites are their companions, and duns their followers: gamesters surround 'em, the seat of their ancestors runs to ruin, and their daughters have titles without fortunes. But your prodigal sort of people hurry on their fate. They are eager, impetuous, and uncontrollable, mortgage estates to sit silent in parliament, build houses, buy pictures, fine furniture, play deep, keep horses, alarm the world who never heard of 'em before, and, like lightning, give a flash and extinguish. Falsity of reports is a matter more peculiar to our sex, and a lady with two thousand pounds, that's perking up for a husband, shall have her fortune magnify'd to four. Lovers address her, she's talk'd of for several. My Lady Clack says Sir George is to have her. My Lady Joyner says Beau Straddle, and Mrs Positive swears the writings are a drawing for the Brigadier. In short, the town have marry'd her to the whole side-box. But when things appear in a true light, her sparks fly off, and she has the misfortune to be blown upon in her bloom; or, shou'd a gentleman take her fortune upon trust, who wants just that sum to clear his estate, when he finds himself deceiv'd, he must certainly make a most obliging husband, and she lead a very comfortable life.

Marriage is not a thing to be jested with, yet false reports have occasion'd pleasant conjunctions. A lady, with three suits o' clothes, gives her self out a great heiress. A beau that carries his whole stock about him talks of an estate in North Wales. Conscious of their several designs, the match is huddled up before it could be whisper'd at the tea tables. They visit in great splendour, have noble lodgings in Pall Mall – but madam's guardian is not yet come to town; Welsh tenants pay very ill, tradesmen bring in their bills; 'What's to be done my dear?' 'Why really, my dear, hypocrisy is what I always hated, and to be plain with you, I have no fortune, but your estate is sufficient to clear all and to maintain me, my mother and my sister Judy, who are just upon leaving off shop lifting'. 'Estate, the devil! An acre have I. I have made a tolerable appearance these two years, thanks to good natur'd city wives, but my father's, at this hour, a blacksmith in Houndsditch.' Their confusion cou'd not be very great. But Mrs Hurricane flying about with the news and the ladies exclaiming, 'Oh filthy, destestable creatures! Had they the assurance to visit us?'. Mr Forge marches off with a musket, and Mrs Pliant, who cou'd admirable well personate greatness, becomes an actress at the playhouse.

Letters from the country tell us that London is at present very empty and likely to continue so some weeks, that we have no occurrences whatsoever, and yet near a dozen papers are publish'd every day, which shows news writers have a very fertile brain, as they are pretty good at invention all the year round. Tradesmen grow as indifferent to their shops as to their wives, divert themselves at Clerkenwell Bowling Green, and upon an extraordinary appointment the neighbourhood is in an uproar. Mr Doodle, Mr Wise-acre, Mr Taffety, Mr Gimcrack, Mr Fribble, Mr Bisket and Mr Nincompoop, with spurs and no boots, mounting eighteen pence a side, in the middle of the poultry, very much in earnest to gallop all the way to Windsor, while their wives find a cousin to carry 'em to Hampstead Wells, and their merry prentices play at whisk in the back shop. But taverns have the most melancholy aspect of all trades. 'Tis true, the Rummer in Queen Street huffs it all the year, but other vintners are forc'd to play at hazard for their living. Drawers that have any relations may now visit them, and those airy souls the bar keepers take a ramble to Spring Garden.

The several companies have chose their masters and wardens, and spent all their legacies. Beau partners have examin'd their books and, tho' cash has been plentifully finger'd, yet new painting their shop gives 'em new credit, and they hope to weather the point one year longer. The town in general has a sort of lethargy. Decay'd gentry sigh out of sashes for want of country habitations, lawyers are dispers'd with the rooks,[99] young extravagants have hid themselves with their elder brothers, and every place is so forsaken that even St James's Park seems destitute of French folks.

99 sharpers, rogues

MONDAY AUGUST 15 TO WEDNESDAY AUGUST 17 *Number 18*

Several fellows having had the impudence in taverns and dirty eating houses to toast Mrs Crackenthorpe and wish they had her at supper: 'Prithee Jack, let's give her a pullet one night, I fancy she'll divert us,' and talk as familiarly of her as they do of Miss C—ss; one would give a shilling, and t'other half a crown to nasty wretches; a third Jack-a-Dandy cries, 'Hang her, she must be threescore, or she couldn't know so much of the world.' Another set of vain fellows, that are intimate with people they never saw, bow to coaches when there's nobody in 'em they know, pretend they are related to her – their grandmother's sister's milkwoman's aunt's god-daughter marrying into her family, and they have her at their beck. These animals think themselves safe from reflection, being below her notice. But if they persist in these airs she'll take care to have 'em shipped off in the scoundrel galley,[100] which only waits now for two prize-fighters, a cast-off lady at Kensington and a noted gamester who has made a very great figure in the world, and is flinging away his last fifty guineas at Tunbridge. However, to satisfy the curiosity of some great people, she intends shortly to give an account of her person and family.

*

In ten days will be published, as supplement to *Dr K—gs' Art of Writing Unintelligibly, The Way of Speaking Unintelligibly*, by a maid of honour to Madam Barry,[101] who lately delivered herself in this manner: 'That there was a person of kraullity of her akraintance, that belonged to the Kreen above a kraurter of a year, and he had ten wery wiolent fits, and they got him a Kraker nurse, put him on a kroif, and covered him with a krilt and he sucked his wictels thro' a krill, and they gave him krails and weal and winnegar, and a krantity of krince marmalet in a krautern of brandy, and it krite krured him.' To which will be added the *Art of Lisping Agreeably*, by a knight that plays at dice by himself, and last week, after three hours throwing, made the greatest exclamation, 'Cod bleth my thoul, ath I hope to be thaved, I have flung thixes, thix times together.

*

100 ships which transported criminals

101 Elizabeth Barry, celebrated retired tragic actress, who had taught elocution to Queen Mary

Last week Lady Betty Modish was safely brought to bed and Lady Grave-Airs is very near her time.

[The first eighteen numbers were published by B. Bragge. From this number onwards *The Female Tatler* was published by Mrs A. Baldwin. B. Bragge engaged a new writer and continued to print a rival version of this paper. It is printed at the end of this volume, as Part Three, pp. 205–217.]

WEDNESDAY AUGUST 17 TO FRIDAY AUGUST 19 *Number 19*

There are some ladies in the world who are mighty good creatures, and have no real design of being troublesome and impertinent, yet they are attended with an unlucky fate of paying visits at a time when their absence wou'd be the greatest favour they can do us. Lady Fadler has that misfortune. If you invite her, she's engag'd, if you have business with her, she's fifty miles off, but if you are in private company, or have a particular collation, Lady Fadler certainly sidles in, and, if you are in tears for the death of a relation, she comes full of Mrs Crump's wedding, that the bride look'd very silly, the bridegroom was frighted out of his wits, Lady Bumfiddle ate up a whole venison patty, Mrs Wheeler danc'd Cheshire rounds, and my poor Lady Lantern-Jaws dy'd away for a young fellow. Lady Meanwell was very eager for Mr Affable's character, when Lady Fadler, as I suspected, discover'd her fine self. She made an apology of two hours long for not having seen me two days past, that she had had a heaviness in her head, and a dizziness in her great toe, but she had a long story to tell me about a German Count and a journey-man pewterer upon Snow-Hill: Lady Meanwell was as uneasy as if she had sat upon cow- itch, but Francis, bringing up word that a chimney was on fire in Gutter Lane, Lady Fadler fancy'd her house in Bloomsbury was in danger, and mov'd off.

Letters from Enfield give so ridiculous an account of that place, one wou'd fancy the people there was distracted. One fool has lately set up a coach that's at law for his estate; three whimsical splenatic[102] affected

102 melancholic

things are pining away for a handsome barber, pretend they are out of order, and always sending for him to let 'em blood. But Mr Surplice and Mrs Mittings are the sweetest dearest creatures. He swoons at her singing; she's ravish'd at his reading prayers, and when they happen to meet their affectation is beyond trim and Mrs Fantast in Bury Fair. Cou'd he have flatter'd himself with the hopes of seeing the divine Mrs Mittings at that time, he'd have mundify'd[103] his face, comb'd out his best Bob[104] and put on his Prunella gown[105] and cassock that he might have appeared with some economy before her. She protested his surprising her in that *dishabilée* put her into so great confusion, that; 'Permit me, Madam, to say . . .' – 'One whose eyes are so constantly rolling about the church, must critically understand how a woman ought to adjust her self before'; – 'I protest, Madam,' 'Nay, Sir,' – 'till the company are quite sick of 'em. Sometimes they are a little more familiar together, trip it into the chase, dodge round the trees, laugh at one anothers' pretty sayings, and come home so tir'd with play, both of 'em having got such charming colours, that other nymphs and swains must envy their mutual happiness, tho' they think 'em perfectly cut out for one another. Yet if any body enquires when their nuptials are to be celebrated, they are frighted at the question. 'Mr Surplice and I,' 'Mrs Mittings and I,' he has profound veneration for the lady and she an obliging regard for him . . . but marriage, 'Lord! that such a thing cou'd enter into peoples hearts!' I must own it strange indeed, that busybodies shou'd make such conclusions, when they have no better grounds for 'em!

FRIDAY AUGUST 19 TO MONDAY AUGUST 22 — *Number 20*

'Tis almost incredible that ladies at so public a place as Hampstead shou'd be so far distress'd for lovers as to associate with a set of animals whose clay nature was at a loss how to form. 'Tis true at first she design'd 'em men, but the composition prov'd so stubborn that she left 'em unfinish'd to affectation, who has sent 'em into the world monsters. Amongst an infinite of these baiting insects that flutter about a fine lady, like moths

[103] cleansed [104] wig [105] clerical gown

about a candle, is Jack Medly-brain, an unhewn, unproportioned, distasteful wretch, who, by downright Irish assurance, forces himself ev'ry where among the fair sex, when he ought to be their eternal aversion. Were he handsome, had he wit, cou'd he dance, had he a voice, were he but barely complaisant, had he but one tolerable quality, the ladies might have a pretence to receive him, but when he's the reverse of every thing that's tunable, and has something disagreeable in him to ev'ry sense, he merits general contempt. And yet this Medly-brain has for several years past edg'd himself into most topping families about Hampstead and Highgate, is frankly treated everywhere, thinks himself at home ev'ry where, and the most substantial reason Sir William, Mr Sackenbottom and others can give for admitting him is that his visits are customary, and they have known him a great while.

He was formerly a seeming tradesman in Cheapside, had a front for business, but his roving temper cou'd not confine him to the narrow limits of a shop. He put on a sword, jumped from behind the counter into the side box and commenc'd gamester. But tho' men of estates suffer themselves to be bubbl'd by Sharpers,[106] there must be mien and air, wit, breeding and a fashionable appearance to engage 'em. Medly-brain they view'd at a distance. At Wills they thought him a sight, at White's they danc'd around him, and the town unanimously laugh'd him back into the city. But as men of his country are not easily put out of countenance, he thought himself sufficiently reveng'd in laughing at the town again, and went upon new projects. His Irish policy inform'd him that several deputies, church-wardens, and overseers for the poor have an uncommon affection for Whisk,[107] they have an utter abhorrence for gaming in young fellows, and their prentices are often suspected to run out their cash. Yet they'll sneak into a tavern, sit eight hours as religiously at cards as if they were upon a committee at the vestry, and lose twenty guineas each at that ingenious game. 'Why Jack Medly-brain,' says one, 'thou'rt a meer dabb, and play'st o' Sunday?' But when Jack purposely loses a single guinea: 'Have we caught you, Jack? Why, we shall ruin you; thou'lt want a meal's meat, Jack.' At other times he engages with their wives, gets 'em into deep play, which is the first step to all manner of vice, and, whatever favours he is pleased to extort from them, repays 'em with their own money. At present he's the Ganymede of Hampstead, Master of the Ceremonies, or rather buffoon of the Wells, and, some leading ladies having countenanc'd him, the multitude pay him a blind respect. 'Tis said, amongst the rest, three youthful, gay, fluttering nymphs have receiv'd him into their particular good graces, permit his private visits, supply his deficiencies, and so loosely coquet with him in public, that the

[106] rogues [107] the card game, whist

tea tables are in an uproar and several old ladies have left the place for fear of their reputations.

Lady Lisp-well, the chief of these three, who has a roguish eye, a winning pout, a fashionable waddle, and a thousand pretty taking affectations, is so entirely fond of him that she has left her family to dance after him. She thinks him a fine gentleman because she never saw a fine gentleman, as children admire small things, wanting an idea of greater, and as men worldly pageantry, having no notion of things divine; and she wou'd as much lament his absence, as her aunt does the pretty fellow that's lately gone to New York. Her Ladyship is such an upstart in public, and from the most reserv'd, precise, censorious creature, become the most airy and unaccountable, that people begin to suspect the regularity of her brain. She's dress'd, she's flown, gives airs, games, converses: 'My father's dead, my husband's a great fool, virtue's an ass, and a gallant's worth forty on't.' The good Sir Lionel, her spouse, whom ev'ry body speaks well of, and wou'd he not load his perriwig with so much powder, is as complete in his person as his understanding has, with lowest matrimonial submission, entreated her return to her children. But her Ladyship has her health nowhere but Hampstead. He supplies her with money; she wants more, has it, and 'tis gone.

Sir Lionel grows melancholy upon the matter, sends Mr Cant, Mr Drawl, and Mr Spintext to her. The upright brethren move directly forward in the work of reformation, they admonish, they are zealous, their spirit is provok'd, they are very noisy. Lady Lips-well calls for cards. They are abominable. Dice are damnable. A bottle of sack somewhat abates their fury, and when Medly-brain offers 'em a wench, they are . . . I don't know how. But the Place being too Public for religious fornicators, they shake their heads at such prophane doings, and return sighing at their unprofitable journey.

What's to be done – nothing – when a lady, after ten years marriage and prudent behaviour, shall make ridiculous excursions. She is almost irreclaimable, especially when enthusiasts are sent to tease her, whole rigid rules have from her birth confin'd her reasonable inclinations, which company have given her a sense above, and the town a taste of diversions. However, as Medly-brain is an antidote, the world malicious, and women sometimes whimsical without design, charity would still hope she has preserv'd her virtue, and when she has had her swing, that she'll return to her obedience.

*

Mrs Crackenthorpe, finding her self disingenuously treated by the first printer of this paper, thought she might take the same liberty of removing it, as a gentleman that is tricked does his tailor or perriwig maker. But such is the probity of piracing printers, that authors can't command even their names and titles, and this fellow has set up some pitiful scoundrel, whose principles are as wretched as his circumstances, to impose upon the town a sham paper, upon another person's foundation, and talks of ladies drawing-rooms, who was never yet admitted into tolerable company. But as the ladies gave the first reputation to this paper, 'tis hoped they'll so warmly espouse it as to have a just abhorrence for such base proceedings, who are the only court of judicature to be applied to in this matter. As they have hitherto found nothing rude to affront 'em in public, or immodest to shock them in private, their protection may be the more reasonably expected in opposition to the other, which at its abortive appearance in the world has entertained 'em with an odious filthy story of Mrs Crackenthorpe's man, Francis – Francis is so angry, he intends to indict 'em for scandal, to make a thief, a renegado, and a beastly fellow of him – when his mistress has instructed him with untold gold, never lay out a night without leave, and his modesty is so universally known that he never had the assurance to salute a woman in his life. As for pressing him aboard the scoundrel galley – contemptible wretches! 'tis well known he is a freeholder, has ten pounds a year in Cumberland, and gives his vote for Sir Tunbelly Clumsy.

*

Lady Circumstance at Epsom, who is a might merry, unaffected, hoity-toity creature, always at Roly Poly or the play, is desired not to stroddle quite so much, or laugh quite so loud. People speak very well of her, but several Thames-street ladies are a little angry that she pretends to lead the multitude where she pleases. If she'd but give them leave to be a little taken notice of, they'd no more envy her attractions, than they do her bulk.

*

Mrs Clack of Gossips-hall near Ludgate, who is continually prying into her neighbours' affairs, and buzzing groundless suspicions in every husband's ear, and suspecting every woman's chastity, is desired to turn her optics within herself, and particularly not to be so publicly familiar with Will Whitebread, the B——r, and when she has taken care to stifle her own shame, she may be as imperiously virtuous as she pleases.

MONDAY AUGUST 22 TO WEDNESDAY AUGUST 24 *Number 21*

r Christopher Coppy-wife, solicitor in Chancery, is certainly the most accomplish'd of cavaliers. He is so equally divided between beau and business that neither of 'em gains the superiority, having the same genius, and giving the like thought, concern, and strenuous application to both. You meet him plentifully dirty, loaded with bills, answers, pleas, demurrers and exceptions. He's a perfect squirrel in the law, skips from Westminster[108] to the Temple, to the Rolls, to the Register, is in the violent'st flutter about one pauper cause, and makes a blustering in the court as if the Council were assembl'd and the well Fee'd Sir Thomas had comb'd out his most ingenious perriwig, open'd his cherry-colour bag and study'd his quaint phrases and rhetorical ambiguities – 'May it please you, My Lord, tho' I could not be Attorney-General, I am Counsel for the Plaintiff in this Case' – upon matters of no greater importance, than to get an alms-woman twenty pounds.

He's at threescore coffee-houses three times ev'ry day, enquiring for letters and messages, and seems to have as much employment as if he were solicitor to all the litigious widows in the kingdom. Meet him in the street, he can't possibly speak to you, having a reference before a matter, affadavits to file, orders to draw up, and a subpoena to take out returnable immediate, and is as industrious about nothing, as a beau that calls at chocolate houses for letters he wrote to himself, or a decay'd sergeant that hurries to Guild Hall when he has no other business in the city than to sponge a dinner at my Lord Mayor's.

When the hurry of the day is over, as men cannot toil incessantly, Mr Coppy-wife becomes the reverse of himself. The tailor, the hosier, the sempstress, the barber are in an uproar to equip him. You see him in lac'd linen, pearl-colour silk stockings, silver long pockets, and a French night-cap. He is invited to a dancing bout, going to Spring Garden, or engag'd at cards with some fine ladies. Ask him to go to the tavern, he has appointed ladies, ladies are impatient for him, and all that you can get out of him is, ladies. His chambers at Lincoln's Inn are a perfect lady's apartment, he has his toilet, his pier glasses,[109] his tea-tables, his French print, and a fine set o' window curtains of his own stitching. Ladies admire his niceties, he makes elegant entertainments for 'em, and his collations are all in china. The Chancery Office are alarm'd at his proceedings. He has no estate, his traversing the town is but business in

108 Queens Bench Hall, a large law court, was in Westminster.
109 tall mirrors

appearance, yet they envy his happiness in the fair sex, and fancy some great lady who has an uncommon regard for him is the fund of his extravagances.

But as this prying world has an increasing itch to find out one another's intrigues, when Mr Coppy-wife had publish'd to all Chancery Lane that several ladies of the first quality were to sup with him; Ned Buisy, the impertinent of the office, bolts into his chambers, was charm'd at the number of wax lights, and began to doubt the strength of his brain, to behold in reality all the beauties of Hampton Court. His curiosity, indeed, was prettily satisfy'd, and his senses more confounded than he imagin'd; when the agreeables, the adorables, the invincibles, and the reported quality he expected to find there, were Mrs Sage-Tea, the coffee woman, Mrs Instep, the shoe-makers lady, Madam Necklock at 'the Blue Perriwig', Mrs Single mug at 'the Carpenter's Arms', Madam Stay-tape, the taylor's wife, with her two well-bred daughters and the Quality Vintner's lady at 'the Devil'. Coppy-wife was struck dumb at the discovery. The ladies rose, and desired Buisy to make one with 'em at cribbage or all-fours; but he retired between wonder and ridicule, with the greatest precipitation imaginable. The news spread, the Examiners Office took it to pieces, 'twas enter'd with the Register, and enroll'd in Chancery.

Coppy-wife, it seems, has run himself deeply in debt, and frequently entertains these creatures, that they may persuade their husbands to give him further credit; and at present, he's so much upon the totter, that if some charitable attorney don't give him one cause more, he'll be forc'd to visit Carolina with the Palatines.[110] Such a composition of extremes we shall rarely meet with. 'Tis true, this person seems to have a design, tho' with little prospect of success. A pretence to business gains a man no ill character; 'tis good to be in the way. But an old attorney wou'd no more trust a cause of consequence to a fellow that has a notion of foppery and impertinence, than a cautious lady would an intrigue to a gossiping visitor that shall tell it the whole town for a secret. These women too aim at ceremonies, nice treats, and things above their sphere, may for a while by prejudicing their husbands, bear out his false pride. But such matters are soon blown up. A consumptive person is in some measure supported by art, but nature still waiting, the party languishes and expires.

But to leave the man of business and speak a little more to the fop, what shall we say of a set of people, men of real estates, whose natures are so grovelling, souls so uninform'd, and are so very destitute of

110 The Protestant refugees from Bavaria settled not only in England but also in North America.

ambition, that they have no notion of society above tradesmen and trollops, who ask the tailor to drink tea with 'em, the spruce barber is invited to dinner, and make dancing bouts for the second hand fry; sempstresses and ladies' women, and sometimes a tragedy actress does 'em the honour of her company. These wretches pay 'em homage, and bellow out their praises; whereas people of quality pass carelessly along, never admire their furniture, and tho' Sir Tawdry has laid out twenty pounds in a fine night gown, when others praise it to the skies, they han't so much good nature as to say 'tis well fancy'd. Such persons discover more pride in associating with the vulgar sort, than those who aspire to the first rank. They had rather be the leaders o' the mob, than the fag of the gentry. But how are their understandings improv'd? Conversing with mechanics shows 'em to be but stupid beings, whereas a man of spirit and ingenuity entertains nobler ideas, his company is critically select, always with those above himself, and his modest assurance is both countenanc'd and encouraged.

*

Mrs Crackenthorpe would be glad to know how the family of Smiths came so infinitely to out-spread other names? She can't make a visit, but in comes Madam Smith and Miss Smith. What smart fellow's that? Beau Smith. Whose fine house is this? My Lady Smith's. Doctor Smith is parson of this parish. And if you travel all over England, ev'ry village has a hovel of the Smiths. The Kings and the Clerks are pretty numerous, too, but the Smiths out-do 'em by thousands. 'Tis said several people that live in mists and clouds concern themselves under that general name; so that ev'ry Captain Smith, of which there are above a hundred, may get a company of Smiths and have 'em knock'd o' the head, without the least danger of extinguishing the family.

WEDNESDAY AUGUST 24 TO FRIDAY 26 — *Number 22*

Amongst all the different degrees, ranks and orders of human species, there can be no greater object of compassion, nor any one more worthy the regard of the sensible part of mankind, than he that, in spite of natural simplicity, and amidst the frowns of an unaccountable fortune, has the additional curse of imagining himself to be a wit. Whether he is or not, is little to the purpose, 'tis enough that he thinks so, and the very notion imperceptibly hurries him into all those inconveniences, expectations, and disquietudes that usually attend on persons under that unhappy circumstance. 'Tis a condition the more to be lamented because not to be prevented, and generally seizes on a man's most sensible part, disorders his reason, and carries him out of the world before he has the opportunity of knowing himself to be a fool.

Thus it is with my friend, Tom Careless, who, tho' really an ingenious man and fit for business, (has no estate, nor ever like to any) yet thinks himself above it. His head is always full of chimerical[111] ideas of merit, he is continually disquieting himself with the fancy'd prospect of what he is never like to attain to, and at the least interruption of providence to the prosperity of his life, blames his fortune, curses his stars, and rails at the degeneracy of mankind; tho' at the same time he sees not his own error in indulging such notions, that will (if not in time prevented) be his ruin. As I know him to be a man worthy of a better fate, I have, by an application of argument, endeavoured to reclaim him, but in vain. All the answer he gives me is that he is sensible of the truth of what I say, but that the superior madness is so rooted in his soul that he cannot shake it off, tho' at the same time he sees his ruin in too visible characters before him.

'Tis not long ago that he was advanc'd to a considerable post, only on this condition, that he would refrain from those dangerous liberties he used to take in that bane of mankind, that destruction of youth, poetry. The poor man, transported with the prospect of what was set before him, took up a resolution of reclaiming his past life, and for some time kept himself in such a decorum, that if well follow'd might have conduc'd much to his interest. But, alas! such is the unaccountableness of our destiny, such the weakness of our strongest resolves against the more violent bent of our inclinations, that, like a river for some time obstructed in its passage breaks out again with the more violence, so careless after the resolution of a few months, ran on more impetuously than ever. In short, the too rigid restraint he had put upon himself turn'd his brain, so that he has not been his own man ever since. The first thing he did in one of his delirious fits, was to throw up his post and leave it for one that he thought deserv'd it better. Next, he wrote a play and at last an elegy upon himself. At present he walks wildly about the streets, rather like a spectre than a man, talks to himself, writes verses and does nothing for a livelihood. In all his actions, discourse and gesture, the motion of his eyes upwards and downwards, he plain shows himself to be out of his senses. His ill

111 fanciful

success in the adventures of love and the cruelty of the fair adds much to his uneasiness, as he himself expresses it:

> Had Sylvia been less fair, or less unkind,
> Had she been more to Constancy inclin'd;
> Had she but lov'd and not been so ingrate
> She might have turn'd the very Tide of Fate,
> And 'spite of all the World I had been great.

Thus he goes on, raving in heroics, without seeing the true cause of his misfortune, which is really nothing but misapplication; whilst his friends pity him, his enemies laugh in their sleeves, and he justly blames himself for what he thinks he cannot avoid. As he imagines his end to be near approaching, he tells me he has prepar'd his last dying speech for the press, and because he looks upon himself as a malefactor sacrific'd to the resentment of the world, he is inclin'd to take their method in haranguing the learned part of mankind; tho' with this difference, that as they generally lay the stress of their folly on Sabbath-breaking and whoring, he attributes all his failings to wit and want of money. Thus the unhappy man intends to quit the world, amidst these self disorders; and indeed I know no way to prevent it, unless some charitable friend would be so kind as to make his exit, and leave him a comfortable estate to subsist on, which I am almost positive would not only prevent his too early destruction, but restore him again to the right use of his reason, and at least make him beneficial to himself, if not to the rest of mankind. At the conclusion of this paragraph, Madam Scientia enter'd the room and would make me oblige her with the reading of what I had written, and then made this notable remark on the whole: that the greatest wits are generally the greatest fools.

*

Proposals are just publishing for the relief of old maids, great numbers of which after forty years patience are lately arrived from Gloucester, Worcester and Shrewsbury, but an infinite from Canterbury; not but they can away with a virgin state, but people do so jeer 'em, that they had rather marry the most impudent young rake than bear the continual reflection of leading apes. They intend to pitch their camp upon Hounslow Heath, thro' which many sprightly, amorous, well set sparks passing every day to Windsor, 'tis hoped they'll at least afford 'em a gracious smile, which will be doubly repaid. They do most religiously assure mankind that 'twas not pride and ill-nature in their juvenile days that brought 'em to this deplorable condition, but their cruel stars that destin'd 'em uncomfortable dwellings, where they had no gayer objects than the Dean and Chapter, unless a regiment happened to quarter in the town, which put 'em into conflicts, whether they should be kind or not, and then left the place, without so much as asking 'em the question.

FRIDAY AUGUST 26 TO MONDAY AUGUST 29 *Number 23*

Sir Charles Traffick in Mark Lane, who is not only esteem'd a man of infinite treasure, but the most polite, conversable, and best bred merchant in the city, gave me yesterday an invitation to dinner. The entertainment was so far from the grossness of a city feast that it show'd all the ease, the elegance and grandeur of the court. The company was adapted to the treat, merchants, yet men of genius, judgment and vivacity, which proves that the city, tho' a mere leaden mine, does sometimes produce a sample of the brightest ure. But as people seldom propose to themselves a happy interview, but some troublesome impertinent jarrs their intended harmony, our felicity was interrupted by the affectation of that monumental stalking, superb, and most regular piece of clock-work, Mr Stately. His conversation is really great, his notions fine, and well digested. He argues from right reason, and his assertions are plain demonstration, and his behaviour to the ladies obliging, pleasant, and respectful. But his spleen,[112] uneasiness, womanish observations, and the improper liberties he takes make the lady of every family dread his appearance, the company consequently out of humour, and servants abominate him.

He has a soft, sickly, drawling way of speech, like Lady Dainty in the comedy;[113] has his vapours, hectics, and hypochondriac, thinks the spleen as pretty a companion for a fine gentleman as squeamishness for a fine lady, and that a month's illness in great state is like a woman of quality's lying-in. He divides his sleep, business, eating, and recreation into exact proportions and, should any of 'em encroach the least upon the other, he is seized with a complication of affected maladies and the doctors are immediately summon'd to consultation, but the sight of 'em distracts him. He tells 'em, Aesculapius was a quack, and they are a

[112] bad temper

[113] Lady Dainty was a character in *The Double Gallant* by Colley Cibber.

pack of illiterate asses, that his horse is a creature of more understanding, and he'll try what the air will do, and is so very delicate that, were it not for public derision, his man must dress him in clean white gloves, hold his breath while he shaves him, his perriwig brought home in a chair, and his horse's bridle given him in a damask napkin. He complains where he's invited that 'tis five minutes beyond the appointed time and dinner is not yet upon table, enquires of everybody when dinner will be ready: 'Mr Worthy, how can you bear the laziness of servants? Mine are the horridest fellows that ever G—d let live. I'll strip 'em, faith. Come, John, set chairs, good John. You'll excuse me, Mr Worthy, if I miscall your man, one can't burden one's head with servants names; where ev'r I go, I cry John to the footman and Mary to the maid. My own servants, had I a hundred, wou'd all be Johns and Marys.' His discourse at table runs that not one family in the city understands good eating, and very rarely the dish before him escapes some correction. Yesterday Harry Wealthy dragg'd him home. His wife was as big as Cheapside Conduit, and his daughters a couple of ill-natur'd things, 'tis well he can give 'em ten thousand pounds; but the dinner was the worst contriv'd, worst marshall'd greasy medley, he wonders what he has done to people that they shou'd endeavour to poison him, and wouldn't dine with such a fellow again, wou'd he give him his estate.

Mr Stately, tho' he was bred to merchandise, and his riches are the produce of traffic, yet, having a finer thread of understanding than his brother traders, looks as contemptibly on 'em as great mathematicians do upon mechanic students; he thinks business condescension in him, and that when he over reaches a mercer in selling a parcel of silks, he does him a very great honour in dealing with him. He treads the exchange as loftily as if he came there only to gaze at the statues, and neither sees nor speaks to anybody he meets. If you have business with him, tho' it be of importance and requires expedition, he defers it till he has din'd, and then bids you call upon him early next morning; his style is haughty and commanding and he scorns to make the first proposal, tho' it be about an affair that concerns himself only; the greatest merchants and the greatest aldermen he calls Jasper Indico, Ferdinand Florence, and Peregrine Pomegranate. 'Sad Souls! I wonder, Mr Worthy, you'll muddle away your evenings with such despical wretches, the very noise of a tavern is being in a besieged town, and the company worse than common draught wine.' Yet most men court his conversation, obliviate his reflections, and buckle to his pride.

He's a mighty advocate for the county of Surrey and can't believe people can breathe freely in any part of England except Banstead

Downs; Epsom indeed he pretends to have an aversion to: 'tis all hurry and confusion, he cou'd as soon sleep in a camp – therefore his lodgings are two miles off; yet he is always galloping to Epsom and displaying himself in public, but abominates their diversions; bowls are perfect slavery, roly-poly[114] makes him giddy, raffling[115] is fit for women and children, and those noisy rascals the fiddlers, deserve to have their heads broke. He tells the ladies he has frequently set out to visit 'em, but such loads of fellows crowd ev'ry door, that 'tis perfectly running the gauntlet to pass thro' 'em; wonders what pleasure there can be in such a fluttering foppish place and is always railing at what he practices himself. In short, Mr Stately is an old bachelor, whom the ladies have lately banter'd upon the brink of matrimony. That state is seldom reckon'd to cure the spleen, but beauty has been of wonderful energy, humbl'd tyrants, tam'd savages, made fools of wise men, and given apprehensions to almost inanimate beings. However, a lady runs a very great hazard in bestowing herself on so whimsical a person. 'Tis true, a man of sense seldom abuses a woman, but when spleen, which is a sort of melancholy madness, gets the pre-eminence of reason, the same object grows tedious to the distemper'd appetite, and the best treatment she can expect is cold civility, which generally dwindles into downright negligence.

*

Whereas several conceited fellows about town think themselves wits, by using improper epithets and larding their conversation with the terms of their professions, a lawyer sends you a subpoena to meet him at such a tavern; the merchant writes – immediately upon sight hereof fail not to come, etc.; the draper cries – I'm stepp'd about fifty yards off; and the seaman drops anchor with you; the poet delivers himself – scene: a room full of good company, enter drawer with a decanter and clean glasses; the musician calls it, cremona[116] wine; the oxonian, ortholox[117] wine; the 'pothecary *Vina Anti Splenetica*; the printer desires a proof of it; and the distiller cries – with all my spirit. A mathematician wants a quandrangular French roll; an astrologer a Fortunatus's napkin cap; an antiquarian a Roman goblet of small beer; and an engineer ought to have sprung a mine to ha' blown up 'em all into the air. Mrs Crackenthorpe thinks such cant infinitely below punning, and that such fellows ought to be as much despised as your comical coxcombs that mimic squinting, imitate caterwauling, and act a drunken man, till by sipping they really become so; and when they

114 a ball game
115 game of dice
116 a type of violin
117 grammatically correct

get into women's company, think it a mighty jest to pull a snake out of their pockets, to set 'em all upon the scuttle.

MONDAY AUGUST 29 TO WEDNESDAY AUGUST 31 *Number 24*

he pride o' the city has been always the jest o' the court, and nothing can be more diverting to those of birth and education, who are always condescending, pleasant and affable, than to see a parcel of rough-hewn tradesmen swell at a little prosperous knavery, set up coaches upon being made deputies o' the ward, and put their wives and daughters into so strange a ferment that they run into a thousand monstrous affectations, are so divided between heaven and earth that servants approach 'em with fear and trembling, their old acquaintance are infinitely below their notice, and their heads are so confounded with airs and equipage, that they cannot positively say whether they are awake or not. The following account proves this assertion with a witness.

About a fortnight ago the serene company of cloth workers mov'd in graceful order to their hall in Mincing Lane, the beadle[118] showing 'em the way, and the clerk bringing up the rear. Amongst whom Deputy Bustle, cheesemonger, and reformer of manners, made no small figure; their business there was first to elect new officers, that ev'ry coxcomb might be distinguish'd in his turn, then to demolish several ven'son patties, and afterwards to puff out politics, depose the French king, commit Madam Maintenon[119] to the work-house, and send a regiment of train-bands into the Pope's territories to fright his Holiness into Quakerism and convince the cardinals that England afford as many she-saints that will confess and sin on as all the nunneries in Italy, where the fathers have free access, and the beauteous devotees are inform'd that chastity is a ridiculous imposition, caution and secrecy are the only things to be minded, and she that has the reputation of religion, has virtue in the highest degree.

The assembly that day happened to be pretty numerous, and some of the company, people of good fashion, sev'ral of the court of assistants having relations that had coats of arms, and others inviting their masters

118 a junior legal officer

119 Louis XIV's second wife

and ladies, to whom they had formerly been footboys. But amongst the women none took so much pains to display themselves as the two Mrs[120] Bustles, the fam'd deputy's daughters. Their dress was as extravagantly particular as their behaviour, their heads standing affectedly awry, their hair hanging frightfully over their eyes, for genteel negligence, their gowns pinn'd so fantastically high, that you could hardly see their heads for their tails, their under-petticoats longer than their upper, and their shifts below both. At dinner they were mightily disturbed that a baronet's two daughters set above 'em, their father being head warden, they were so crowded that their hips hadn't room to play, and their double ruffles were perfectly squeez'd to nothing; wondered how so much mob got in, and there was not one at table that they thought good enough to drink to; they reflected upon people so loud that they heard 'em, look'd scornfully around 'em, and when a gentleman very civilly gave his service to the eldest, she burst out a laughing in his face.

When the company rose from gormandising, the ladies were conducted up stairs, the two Mrs Bustles taking care to be foremost, for their father was head warden; after tea and scandal, the music was summon'd for dancing, Misses Bustle, to be sure, were the two uppermost couple, for their father was head warden, who, to show how well they understood fashionable dances, call'd for 'Damme', and 'the Parson upon Dorothy', they stood as insensibly as a couple of statues till the tune was half over, then figur'd in when they should have cross'd over, went back to back when they should have chang'd places, and ran the hay instead of giving right hand and left, yet these two butter firkins were so mightily disturbed that they hadn't room to show their parts that they made complaint to the deputy, their father, who being that day to go out of his office, resolved to do something to be talk'd of. He commanded the music to stop, and with a most insolent pragmatical air (for which he deserved to have his head broke), examin'd every gentleman and lady, what their names were, where they liv'd and what pretence they had for intruding themselves there? They told him they were most of them livery-men's daughters that had as much right to be there as himself; others, women o' condition, and the gentlemen such as gave a grace to the society, and didn't deserve to be so rudely treated; but the deputy, to gratify his daughters' pride, resolved they should quit the room, with several refusing to comply with, a knot of greasy servants took the ladies up in their arms, and carry'd 'em out of the hall by mere violence, at which disturbance the company broke up, and the music fled.

120 Mrs was then used for all adult women – married or unmarried. Miss was the term of address used for little girls, or prostitutes.

These bacon beauties have for many years been the ridicule of Leaden-Hall Street, they are the reverse of every thing that's well bred, the burlesque of every new fashion, and the gaze of ev'ry body that knows what's decent and regular, yet they pretend to wit, having perus'd the covering of several band-boxes,[121] and talk of plays and operas, when 'twould be more commendable in 'em to study weights and scales, debtor and creditor, and manage their father's shop, with an obliging and submissive carriage to his customers. But the deputy himself, whose brains are intoxicated with mock-honour and whose affronting behaviour renders him odious to all sorts of reasonable people, has set 'em such an example of pride and arrogance, that 'tis as impossible to root out a false education in such creatures, as to refine a stupid fellow, who is wholly ignorant of nature, her beginnings, growths, gifts and bounties.

The Roman Emperors never triumph'd with that presumption as some of our citizens when they rattle in their coaches from one end o' the town to the other. What difference is there between this custom and that of their ancestors: they never knew how to deprive themselves of necessaries to get superfluities, nor to prefer shew to substance; their wives had no notion of visiting-days, picquet, ombre and wax candles; nor ever rose from a cold dinner to get into a glaring chariot, but were convinc'd they had legs given 'em to walk on, and they us'd 'em and even our magistrates wou'd then walk to Guild-Hall with as good a grace as Augustus us'd to foot it to the Capitol; the pewter and brass, in those days, shone on their shelves and cupboards, their copper and iron in their chimneys, whilst the silver and gold lay safe in their coffers. Nor did ev'ry petty merchant keep a butler out of a livery, their family affairs employ'd their children, as well as their servants; and they esteem'd good houswif'ry to be the best portion a tradesman could have with his wife; every thing they did agreed with their circumstances, their expenses were proportion'd to their income, and their furniture, tables, city and country-houses all measur'd by their revenues and conditions.

They had, however, outward distinctions amongst themselves. The merchant's wife made a better appearance than the draper's, the draper's than the cheesemongers, and the cheesemonger's beyond the handycraft tradesman's, but they were less studious to spend or enlarge their patrimony than to keep it, left it entire to their heirs and passed from a moderate life to a peaceable death. In short, there was no complaint then – times are hard, money is scarce, and people are every day breaking in their debts; they had less than we have, and yet they had

121 hat boxes, often covered with attractive fabric

enough, richer by their economy and modesty than their stocks in the bank and East-India companies, and they constantly observ'd this maxim: that what is splendour, sumptuousness and magnificence in people of quality, is, in private men, extravagance, folly and impertinence.

*

As boarding schools for young ladies are very much out of fashion in this age, Mrs Crackenthorpe would admonish a certain mistress near Highgate that, unless she intends quite to ruin the character of 'em, not to trust her children's dancing wholly to their master, but to be an observator herself, appoint what entries are proper for 'em to learn, and not suffer several impudent figures that are fit only for music-houses. Information has been given that her last ball concluded with 'Joan Sanderson' or 'the Cushion Dance', which some ladies at private entertainments have refused to engage in. Girls are pretty forward nowadays, and if a dancing master's suffer'd to kiss his scholars round, the next question is what fortunes have they? And if he can steal an heiress with twenty thousand pounds, he cuts a but one caper more to his good fortune, and then adieu to jigs, minuets and fine sarabands, till for want of brains he has squandered it away, disgrac'd his spouse, and revives his profession at the plantations.

*

Whereas a gentlewoman at Chiswick with something like a paper lanthorn at the door, has been long a very great nuisance to her neighbours, her every hour being employed to ridicule her superiors, calumniate her equals, and domineer over the meaner sort; she is much such another prating thing as her neighbour, Mrs Y——g, that has sixteen lap-dogs, and beats her husband for not paying 'em respect enough, values her self upon expressions stolen out of plays and by the toss of her head, flirt of her fan, motion of her eyes, and forwardness in her behaviour, tells every gentleman she meets she's very much his humble servant. She's a brisk widow, tho' the blue of the plum[122] be off, has had three husbands, and all of 'em come to untimely ends, and is very desirous of a fourth; if any gentleman-highway-man, gentleman-housebreaker, or ingenious counterfeiter of bonds, bills or letters of attorney is willing to receive her into his arms, besides a thousand pounds she brings with her in forg'd debentures, the town of Chiswick will give a noble treat at Mrs W——k——ns the procuress to get rid of so impertinent a creature.

122 past her best

*

Mrs Crackenthorpe having invited an African prince to sup with her on Saturday next, gives notice to a certain fruit woman in Covent-Garden market, that unless she sends her in a very handsome dessert, she'll acquaint the quality with some juggling tricks between her and their servants, and the town with some other of her tricks, which won't redound much to her reputation.

WEDNESDAY AUGUST 31 TO FRIDAY SEPTEMBER 2 *Number 25*

There are some ladies in the world whose constitutions vary with their circumstances, and as their husbands, by ingenuity and application, gradually raise 'em to riches and honour, they as sensibly feel a decay of nature, and grow tender, nice and delicate, for to be perfectly refin'd is to be always out of order. A certain lady caught cold with touching a silver spoon the day her husband was made Judge, and kept her chamber upon it six weeks after. Lady Wou'd-be is remarked to be one of these, found health no burden to her, cou'd eat heartily without thinking it a fatigue, and slept so soundly that the blowing up ten powder mills wou'd hardly have wak'd her. But since Sir Politic has been preferr'd at Court, she grows hoarse at a lady's waggling her fan, is as apprehensive of her footman's coarse voice as some women are of a peal of thunder, and frequently swoon away in high colour. If she pricks her finger the surgeon is immediately sent for, who cuts a diaculum plaster[123] by a silver penny and sews it on with a bit of cherry-coloured ribbon. The doctor orders her a draught to sleep away the pain, and the next morning How-d'-ye's are sent by the ladies in town. If her head does but shoot, a blister is clapped on that moment, a stitch carries her to the Bath, and she can't propose to herself the least interval of health till she has drank the waters at Bourbon.

Yesterday her ladyship did me the honour of a visit she protested was the first she had made since Sir Politic's patent passed, having been too embarrassed with the spleen, and the hysterics so preyed upon her spirits that she didn't think nature wou'd have ever given her strength to get

123 a sticking plaster

into her coach again. I complimented her ladyship with looking extremely well, and a most agreeable colour, but she assur'd me that when she had a high colour she was very ill, and when she was pale she was at death's door. I had the whole history of her ladyship's indisposition, her accesses, ragings, intermissions, mitigations and relapses. She complained mightily of the want of appetite, that she was wak'd exactly at ten, forc'd down two dishes of chocolate, and dozed again. At twelve she had a basin of water-gruel, well sweeten'd, which went very much against her. At one she trifled with some preserves in her closet, and when she sat down to dinner at two she couldn't eat a mouthful. The doctor advised her to abate one dish of chocolate, to have her water-gruel thin and plain and instead of sweetmeats, just an hour before dinner to eat a roasted apple – but, not caring to hazard herself upon a single judgment, she sends for another doctor, who was of the same opinion, but, being oblig'd to say something for his fee, desired the apple be a golden runnet. Still dubious o' the matter, a third was summon'd, who highly approv'd both prescriptions, being according to collegiate rules, but order'd that the apple shou'd be roasted upon a clean brick, nicely washed with spring water.

The company began to titter, and I was in some pain to prevent her ladyship's observing it. I told her that plain-dealing, tho' an unfashionable virtue, was what I always valu'd myself upon, that affectation of any kind was nature's ugliest monster and only practised by vain upstarts who have a wrong notion of grandeur and wou'd fain act something to distinguish themselves from their former equals, as well in temper as equipage. That true quality have notion of spleen and vapours, they think titles and great estates ought to cure ill-tempers, and are so desirous to prolong nature and enjoy fortune's benefits that noblemen frequently dress their horses, and ladies bustle early about their dairies to preserve 'em in a state of health. I proceeded further, that tampering with a good constitution was very dangerous, and a medley of slops often brought real distempers upon people not easily to be worn off, when they might have leisure, too late, to repent the affectation of 'em; that even the physicians laugh'd at their impertinent ailings, encourag'd 'em only for the sake of their fees, and had publicly declared they got double the money by ladies that wou'd be sick than by those that really were so . . .

Her ladyship stayed supper and eat very heartily, walked a mile afterwards without being the least tired, and went home thoroughly persuaded that health was the greatest blessing of life and that a temper of mind very much contributed to a good habit of body; that to be easy with one's self is the first step to be so with other people, and that a serene, smiling and unaffected air engages general esteem, which is certainly to be a very happy creature.

*

Several good-for-nothing actresses being reduced for want of plays are desirous to be admitted into families. 'Tis true they are so far from the housewives that they are not capable of setting a stitch in their ragged head-clothes, having been altogether bred to coquetry, intriguing, revelling and taking a prodigious deal of snuff. They think themselves fit companions for noblemen's daughters, having as high a taste of breeding, diversions and entertainments. They'll call lords fellows, rail at tawdry damasks in dirty calico roppers and talk of champagne and ortelans[124] with as good a grace as e'er a lady at St James. Therefore if any person of quality, for they ha'n't their healths in the city, is willing to entertain such cattle, they hang out every Sunday night at the Birds Nest in Vinegar Square, which every gentleman that brings tea, sugar and an ounce or two of orangery,[125] will be received with utmost civility, fulsomely flattered to his face, and the moment he is gone, scandalously taken to pieces, perhaps having refused one of 'em his silver snuff-box.

FRIDAY SEPTEMBER 2 TO MONDAY SEPTEMBER 5 *Number 26*

This town does so swarm with people in masquerade that one hardly knows a gentleman from his tailor, a lady from her semptstress, or a merchant's eldest son from Dick-Dapper that sweeps the shop; and as companies feasts are generally crowded by strangers, those in authority ought to examine people's pretences, to prevent their sons being attack'd by gamesters, and their daughters drawn away by a notorious gang of fortune hunters, but in so courteous and obliging a manner, that they happen not to affront people of condition, since the same gay appearance all sorts make in public prevents distinguishing those of substance and true merit from impertinent pretenders and designing parasites. There are, indeed, a numerous set of people, younger brothers that have small annuities, attorneys, clerks and judges' train-bearers, nay, ev'n Hackney writers, book-

124 delicate edible birds 125 snuff

keepers and dancing-masters 'prentices, whose faces are as well known at city feasts as the aldermen's. They in a manner board with mayors and sheriff, very serenely share in the diversions and their constant attendance makes the beadles think they have a right to eat custard, and give 'em free admission.

Amongst the rest, Beau May-pole, the stalking Poetaster of Tom's Coffee-house, who, tho' he has neither relation, friend or acquaintance in the city, has not miss'd one Lord Mayor's Day, or Easter entertainment for seven years past, tho' he seldom goes a volunteering to pay five guineas for a fifteen shilling gilt spoon. He's a fellow that cocks his chin the most philosophically imaginable; he places him at the upper end of the table next some Deputy Grocer, talks to him about Bononcini's[126] Camilla, asks his opinion *The Tale of a Tub*,[127] and presents him with the Latin Muscipula.[128] Mr Reason thinks him a fine personage and a man of prodigious learning, like Don Cholorick in the play, who, tho' he understands not Greek, admires the sound of it, and invites him the next day to eat some white sugar-candy, and new barrel figs. He sends his service to ev'ry alderman, they rise while he drinks, pay homage to his full bottom wig, and enquire of one another who he is, but nobody knows. One fancies him to be Member of Parliament for Gostama, another remembers him at St James's talking to one o' the Yeomen of the Guard, and a third saw him in a coach with a coronet. At last by his fine complexion and graceful appearance, they conclude him no less than a Venetian Count, return his compliment and desire to know whether his honour pleases to have anything at that table. A Count! – Their wives are not able to eat a bit more. 'Dear Nincompoop, present our Deborah to the Count, I'd give any thing to have Deborah dance with quality,' and the three fantastic sisters that no body loves, with their crimped heads buried in their black hair, their broad shoulders, and short necks, were ready to fight for him.

He's as officious to serve the ladies as if he were Master of the Feast, and the ladies are as officious to be obliged by him. He tells Mrs Fribble, the haberdasher's wife, that my Lady Duchess lost fifty guineas at basset;[129] she enquires what county basset is in. When he tells her Margaretta perform'd like an angel, she asks him whether she sung panthea, for that expression, 'The Touch is all in all,' ravishes her beyond any thing she ever heard. Dinner once over, the beaus and ladies a little adjusted, and the city quality dispos'd in a formal semi circle,

[126] Giovanni Bononcini (16??–1678), Italian opera composer, very popular in London

[127] by Jonathan Swift, satirist and novelist (1667–1745)

[128] mouse trap

[129] a popular card game

Count Cock-Chin with his crane's neck and his foot set out, and Mrs Languishe with her sleepy eye, her lip dropped and one shoe unbuckl'd, begun French dances. They mov'd most regularly out of tune, were exact in one another's affected steps, and when the performance was over, 'twas pronounc'd infinitely finer than L'Abbe and Mrs Santlow.[130]

In short, the Count has a wonderful reputation there, which encourages other fellows assurance, and, as he surprises the city with things they don't understand, he diverts the court with praising city breeding and city entertainments, which proves he has no understanding himself, but his poetry is his chief perfection. He has a genius for songs, but can find no master that has a genius to set 'em. He has wrote an opera, but those senseless fellows the play'rs have refus'd it. He has indeed printed some things at his own charge, which his friends, whom he presented with 'em, may have read; he's a very great judge of plays, speaks his opinion of all authors in the public coffee houses and has declar'd that *The Modern Prophets*,[131] has a prodigious deal of humour in it, and that *The Plain-Dealer*[132] is but a heavy kind o' business.

The newest story which bears the date of the Battle of Blenheim, is of a woman in St Tuley's parish that was scolded to death, and was so reported by the ingenious company of parish clerks. This good woman, it seems, had for many years been as great a nuisance to the borough of Southwark as the gossiping parson (which, by the way, the town have not yet found out). She gave her tongue a loose to every body, and no body had lungs to contend with her, except the draper's wife, near St Thomas's hospital, who wou'd have given her a challenge had she not been a gentlewoman. At last the butchers, ale-house-keepers, and poulterers wives, people that abominate scolding, upon the advice of several eminent tongue-pads, hir'd six porters to attack her, the first she knock'd down presently, the second she in a manner played with, the third improv'd upon the matter, the fourth grew as tir'd as a court lady's running footman, the fifth did heartily vex her, and the sixth, by the assistance of the best Geneva,[133] stood so tightly to his work, and gave her such repeated vollies of defamation, that the shrew actually dropped down dead upon the spot. The gossips in Bateman met upon the matter, can't believe that talking, which is a woman's darling pleasure, can be the occasion of her death, and will maintain it that one Billingsgate[134] shall out-rattle fifty porters; tho' the men have told the story to their own advantage and the people of Southwark are in as

130 L'Abbe and Hester Santlow, dancers at Drury Lane

131 comedy by Thomas D'Urfey, played a few performances in May 1709

132 William Wycherley's successful comedy (1677)

133 gin

134 a foul-mouthed scold

great a fury if you enquire about the woman that was scolded to death as the inhabitants of Mimms beyond Barnet if you rally 'em about Parson Bellwagger.

WEDNESDAY SEPTEMBER 7 TO FRIDAY SEPTEMBER 9 *Number 28*

Lady Termigant, who is so violent an advocate for her own sex that she interests herself in ev'ry lady's misfortunes, feels her wrongs, and is as impatient for revenge as if they were immediately her own, came raving to me this morning, more like a fury than a rational creature. She had all the agonies and convulsions of an enrag'd lunatic, her words were so many claps of thunder, she blased with her eyes, and her looks and motion show'd her impetuously resolute on some fatal enterprise. She's a lady of a right understanding, strict morals and unshaken friendship, but as none are without failings, her ungovern'd zeal sometimes carries her beyond reason, as a faith too implicit often breeds enthusiasm; however, passion, which, rising to a storm, blows soon over, is a temper better to be endur'd than a peevish, fretful disposition, which gives a whole family the spleen without telling 'em why; and when I heard the cause of her ladyship's disorder I was not so much surprised at it.

It seems a certain gentleman, now a baronet, and whom we must call Sir Samuel Slender, about sixteen years past made his addresses to a very fine young lady, a relation of Lady Termigant's, whose perfections of mind as well as body, had attracted an infinite number of admirers. She had a gentlewoman's fortune, two thousand pounds, but lovers blush'd at people's naming worldly pelf[135] to 'em. She was an angel of her self and had prodigious offers, but, Sir Samuel being her first suitor, she thought honour oblig'd her to show particular regard to him, and by his insinuating behaviour and amorous protestations, he became her favourite, he visited her at all seasons, she admitted his pretences, appeared abroad with him, received treats and presents from him, and the town concluded it a match. But as the tyranny of doting relations often prevents or delays the consummation of reciprocal love, Sir Samuel had an extraordinary old uncle, whose estate he impatiently waited for, whose deity was money and whose obstinacy unparalleled,

135 filthy lucre

and should his nephew have married the most accomplished nymph with a moderate fortune, he would certainly have disinherited him.

This obstacle was no small damp to our enamoured knight, who, tho' he believed the present sincerity of Catherina's flame, yet, as her beauty was always wounding, lovers eternally pressing and youth calling for enjoyment, he doubted the constancy of her mind; for his circumstances wavering in an old man's breast, he could not entertain the hopes of matrimony till his uncle's death. But the lady having more sublime platonic notions of love than the generality of her sex, and her passion not proceeding chiefly from sensual inclinations, but being grounded on the more substantial comforts of life, thought Sir Samuel's welfare equally concern'd her self, resolved patiently to wait the event of fortune, and they were contracted in the most solemn manner imaginable. Catherina then led a most reserved life, was denied to former pretenders, Sir Samuel visited her hourly, and his conversation was to her the sum of all gallantries. Her female friends who generally meet to do a little work and have a great deal of tittle-tattle, were often levelling at her their malicious artillery of marital bliss, ecstatic joys, fading charms, and such stuff, whom she heard with temper and rallied with modesty, and tho' the old fellow had the conscience to grunt out twice seven years, she kept her faith inviolate with a most miraculous ease and inimitable abstinence.

At last the infernal powers wondering he stayed so long, demanded his appearance and the nephew possessed himself of a fine seat, a large estate, and a very ancient title, all too little a reward for Catherina's constancy. He continued his visits to her, but business now multiplying upon him was his pretence that they were not so frequent as formerly, he sometimes mentioned the contract, but with unusual coldness. Her fortune he knew to be but small and his uncle was ever against the match. In short, he slighted her by degrees and at last most inhumanly threw her off. Before the disconsolate Catherina let us draw a veil, her griefs must be inexpressible, tho' she ought to raise 'em to resentments; and as she has power yet left to prostrate millions at her shrine, she ought to summon every charm, point every glance and pursue 'em with the coquetry of smiles, frowns, complacency and disdain, all the crocodile arts of designing women, and the inveterate malice of neglected beauty, till she has revenged the injuries done her by the perfidious Strephon on his whole hated race. But as the tenderness of her sex rather supposes her dissolved in tears, we ought to soften her afflictions, reason her into calmness and muster all our forces to punish such unheard of perjuries.

Lady Termigant, would have had him flea'd alive, Mrs Romance was for exposing the monster in an iron cage like the tyrant Bajazet,[136] and

[136] In the play *Tamburlaine*, Bajazet is brought on in a cage.

Mrs Postscript would have had the match made an Article of the Peace; however, Catherina thus abandoned, Sir Samuel runs a fortune hunting, but Mrs Townly had so told it in Gath and published it in the streets of Askelon,[137] that the court ladies were as apprehensive of him as some people are of a cat. The city ladies jeered him, and the country ladies spit at him. The knight was not the least daunted at these repulses. Ill principles must be supported with a good assurance, and pursuing his fantastic adorations at last fixed Blowzabella in Charterhouse yard, a creature of that pride that she could away with anything to be a Baronet's lady. Her family was perfectly cut out for such an alliance. Her father was an apothecary, the most grabbed, crafty, covetous and fallacious of his trade who, when he had once persuaded people they were sick, gave 'em medicine which really made 'em so. He less concerned himself with the patient's death than whether there were assets to pay his bill; was ever making out his unreasonable unintelligible scrawls, impatient for the money and implacable at an excuse, yet refused to pay the least family debt he owed others. The world knowing him to be a substantial man, tho' a humourist, gave him unlimited credit for everything; and as his receipts were numerous and his disbursements few, his coffers swelled to a mighty height.

But a long series of time making people grow impatient for their money, which his soul couldn't part with and his creditors finding threats and entreaties were to the same purpose, at last threw himself into a gaol. During his many years of confinement, his wife and daughters appeared very mournful, both in habit and countenance, and their father, to give eternal proof of his probity, died in prison, rather than he would pay his debts. Mrs Julip soon dissipated her tears and changed the melancholy scene. She was now a rich widow, her daughters great fortunes, and they soon displayed themselves in their flaring equipage. 'Tis true the baffled world may rail a little, but the rattling of the chariot wheels drowns the disagreeable noise, and those that keep coaches despise the petty reflections of creatures that walk afoot. Sir Samuel was received here with all the ceremony of city affectation; preliminaries soon adjusted, the parties being eager on both sides, and they were tacked together about three weeks past. The bridegroom having abandoned truth, honour and honesty, breeding, gentility and every agreeable air have fled from him, and he appears a most awkward, tawdry, tinsy[138] old fop of fifty in white and gold, cherry and silver waistcoat and facings, and only wants a sword-knot, shoulder-knot and cravat string to make him a complete sight. Lady Bridge is perfectly the

137 'Tell it not in Gath, publish it not in the streets of Askelon', 2 Samuel, i, 20.

138 glittering

Queen of Diamonds; her necklace, pendants and sparkling nosegay, the product of her father's cozenage, show her to be Aesop's Jay decked with borrowed plumes, every bird ought to seize his own, and, leave her paramour, who has shown his judgment in beauty, and how much he prefers it to gold, by slighting the fair, the charming Catherina with no despicable fortune for the ill-turned Blowzabella, who has a larger supply, tho' of unprosperous wealth, to new rig her according to his manifest generosity.

*

Sergeant Kite gives notice that he intends to hang out his flag no more this season, till next Thanksgiving-Day, because the Duke of Marlborough has come upon him so often with repeated victories, that it is quite worn out and he must be more sparing of it for the future, unless the market women in Covent-Garden and mob adjacent will contribute to the buying a new one. Subscriptions are taken at the theatre in the Hay-Market, and the Watch-House in Covent Garden.

*

Colonel Tatalindus is pleased to direct that all whisperers, gossips, tale-bearers and scandal-mongers, do henceforth apply to him at his house until further notice, for he designs to walk under the Long Piazza in Covent-Garden no more than two hours in a day to get intelligence, till the town thickens, when notice will be given in print of his further intentions.

*

And Mrs Crackenthorpe thinks she may, without vanity, desire those who are still imposed on by the spurious paper, whensoever accidentally met with, to compare two or three of 'em with hers, and she fancies they'll be soon undeceived.

FRIDAY SEPTEMBER 9 TO MONDAY SEPTEMBER 12 *Number 29*

I consult the honour and interest of the ladies, with as much fervency, as the male Tatler does that of the gentlemen; and could wish as heartily to see pimps, panders, and bands as much humbled and discountenanced as the world has lately seen gamesters and sharpers.

But Mrs Everchat is just now come in to furnish me with materials for the present, and I shall lose her good opinion, which she is very sparing of, except to particular friends, if I'm not altogether attentive to every particular she brings. She's a lady that shows her youth only by her discourse, and being mistress of an inquisitive genius, is as communicative of what she hears as those can be that let her into their secrets. She never asks a question, but she makes a reply to it herself, before you can give her an answer, and never comes from church but has all the ladies and gentlemen's apparel as readily at her finger ends as the text. Not a ribbon to a cane, a knot, or a fan escapes her and her memory is so very good that, by running over the names of those that compose the audience there, she would be of excellent use in all probability to Mr Rich[139] (if ever he opens house again) to tell notes for him in the play-house. A marriage struck up, in or about London, without her knowledge, renders her inconsolable and she is not only perfectly acquainted with the fortunes and characters of the bride and bridegroom, but can tell you how the match came about, and by whose means. She's punctual to a second of a minute, as to the time when the priest joined their hands, when they supped, and went to bed; and, if a sack-posset[140] happens to be curdled, runs away with the notice of it to every one she sees and deals it about to the immortal memory of those that made it. But as these marriages must be between persons of figure, so 'tis the same with her as to burials, nothing under a lord's, knight's or alderman's is introduced in her memory and she not charges herself with the recital of it unless it be a subject for quality to treat of.

All her airs were copied from the court, because she is somewhat related to one that serves the Queen's kitchen, and to be thought ignorant of any transaction that occurs there is immediate death to her. In a word, war and peace, births and marriages and murders, history and poetry, plays, music meetings and balls, love and gallantries are the subjects she is always ready to talk incessantly of, and nothing comes amiss to her but speaking commendably of anybody but herself without some tokens of reserve, while she shows her ignorance in her endeavours to give proofs of her sense, and makes it appear that she understands nothing by attempting to be thought apprized and perfect mistress of everything.

So much for the description of her. Now for hers of other people. 'Dear Crackenthorpe,' says she without giving me leave to take notice

139 Christopher Rich, manager of Drury Lane theatre, whose operations had been suspended by order of the Lord Chamberlain in June 1709.

140 a milky alcoholic drink, frequently drunk at weddings

of her, 'You don't tell me how you like this suit of knots, and this cherry-coloured trimming. Lady Mary Plausible thought to win me over to a good opinion of hers by telling me they were wonderful pretty, but I had the satisfaction to know the merits of 'em so well, as to mortify her to the last degree by taking no manner of notice of what she had on. Oh! the folly of our sex to think a woman of prudence is to have her understanding biased by their commending what cannot go without all people's approbation, when I never saw anything so ill chosen and disagreeable as hers in all my born days. Prithee, what's the reason the players in Drury Lane disappointed the town last Tuesday night and made several ladies, as well as myself, dress and undress again before bed time?'[141] When without giving me leave to assign the reason, she tells it herself by saying, 'The Lord Chamberlain did not think fit to give them liberty of acting without owning his authority. Again, methinks Mr M—[142] is a charming actor, I should be glad to know what house he is to belong to now they are divided'. And immediately resolves the question she makes herself by affirming, he has turned himself over to the Queen's Theatre in the Hay-Market and shall have her for a constant auditor.

The virtuous Imoinda,[143] being now down in the straw with her fourth and last child without any father for it, declares she is resolved to observe an exact neutrality in the present war between the two Play Houses[144] till she gets up again. When that House which shows it likes her whining best may have her at his service, provided such articles be drawn up for her continuance in that station, as may be more binding on their sides that employ her than those of marriage would be on hers, had she any husband to play fast and loose with.

141 On Tuesday 6 November a performance of *The Recruiting Officer* by George Farquhar (1678–1707) was cancelled and the audience dismissed. The theatre did not reopen until November 23, when it came under the management of Aaron Hill.

142 John Mills, an undistinguished actor

143 Actress Ann Oldfield who had a succession of lovers, and had children by them, yet managed to keep a decent enough reputation to be buried in Westminster Abbey.

144 After a few years in which Drury Lane had a virtual monopoly in high-class drama, in autumn 1709 Betterton and a company of top London actors set up a rival theatre at the Queen's, Haymarket.

MONDAY SEPTEMBER 12 TO WEDNESDAY SEPTEMBER 14 *Number 30*

Mrs Windmill, Mrs Lightfoot, Mrs Butterfly, Mrs Shittlecock and the two Mrs Hoyden-tails are ladies remarked to be mighty frolicsome. They are women of quality and consequently above reputation. Scandal and detraction are diseases out of fashion, which people of rank have bequeathed to the middle sort, whose family affairs confining 'em from the world's agreements. Their sole pleasure is to pry into one another's concerns, suspect one another's conduct, and carry little reflecting stories from one house to another. But these ladies have the French taste of ease, humour and satisfaction, they talk without consideration, act without decorum, and divert themselves just as immediately fancy prompts 'em without caring two pinches of snuff what the most malicious tongue can say of 'em. They have a notion that a true enjoyment of the world does not consist in court-drawing-rooms, operas and Hyde Park, to be always displaying their tissues and asserting their quality. They are for more familiar diversions; out of their beds mobb'd into their coaches, chocolate at Bull's, clambering to the top of Pauls, a fish dinner at Billingsgate, a raffle, and a bowl of punch at an India-house, and then a ramble to Bedlam[145] – 'tis a melancholy place, poor creatures that have lost their senses, but they have sometimes observed the prettiest young fellows there they ever saw.

The downfall of Bartholomew-Fair[146] was no small chagrin to 'em, a tragic-droll by Mr Pinkethman's comedians[147] was diverting, and the cloysters[148] amus'd 'em beyond anything. However, the camp at Black-Heath has made 'em some amends, all sights are alike to those who only want a pretence to gallop. Tradesmen admire 'em, adore 'em, talk of 'em to every customer. They are the sweetest, best natur'd ladies and not a bit of pride in 'em, set a ham and chicken before 'em they'll eat heartily, they love jellies and sweetmeats too, and if you offer 'em mead, cider, wine or fine cordials they'll take of everything. Lord! how condescending they are. What a happy privilege people of quality have to put citizens to three or four pounds charge without making 'em any return and have their company too reckoned a very great honour. Their court life is to breakfast at noon, huddle on their clothes for the opera, dine at

[145] a London lunatic asylum

[146] An annual fair at which theatre companies acted in booths in the open air.

[147] actor and showman William Pinkethman ran a theatrical booth at the summer fairs

[148] side shows

midnight, away to Lady Basset's, where they ruin themselves with excessive deep play, then rattle home to bed just as their husbands rise to go a hunting.

Yesterday these six ladies, whom I had never seen before, took a fancy to visit me, their design was to divert some leisure hours, be extremely upon the ridicule, and flirt away again. But as I was never awed by titles, airs or equipage, and had too much experience to value the fleering of a few conceited, giddy young creatures, their spleen had not the diversion they expected. I took the liberty to tell 'em that the levity and unaccountable proceedings of some great people every day renders honour less valuable in the esteem of the world, that respect now was paid to true merit, and he that has wit, capacity, taste and discernment is truly noble. Honour was designed to illustrate men of valour, politic and elocution, who ought to be wise, temperate, civil, generous and grateful, and give examples to others rather than receive 'em and to distinguish ladies of more religion, virtue, modesty and generosity than the meaner sort. But greatness now very much consists in extravagant luxury, ostentation, fools and flatterers, and that there are some, who did they know their inferiors and themselves, would be ashamed of being above 'em. The ladies were a little startled at my blunt morality, but I sweetened 'em again by turning the discourse on a subject more pleasant to 'em. They afterwards behaved themselves with abundance of good humour, intend a real acquaintance with me, and I hope by degrees to contract their little excursions within the bounds of reason, decency and decorum.

*

The vintners wife near Pall-Mall, that sets up for quality, whose husband lost no more by a late fire than he has by his wife's whipping out at the back door with some of the best customers, gives notice that she is returning to her old habitation, where she intends to appear as *degagée*[149] as ever, and desires her neighbours that can't go as fine and keep as good company as her ladyship, not to be so impertinent and saucy as to parrot about her private entertainments and refined gallantries, till they are polite enough to be admitted into her cabinet council.

*

At Hockley in the Hole,[150] at the sign of Jack Adams, a very near relation to such Bear-Garden masters of defence as play the Rough Game in

149 easy
150 a lawless area near Newington Green, North London

vindication of *The British Apollo*,[151] is to be performed a concert of what they call music; tarpaulins,[152] tailors, porters, carmen, ale-drapers, basket women, costermongers, fish-wives, journeymen-cutlers, bailiffs, butchers and draymen are the principal persons that are to compose the audience. The vocal part of it by an Ethiopian ballad singer (to the tune of a late poetical description of that country, falsely styled a history) and Seignior Tatterdemaliano, an Italian rag-merchant. The instrumental by two chimney-sweepers in St Johns Clerkenwell, the C—k of St M———s Westminster and 3 Lancashire Hog-drivers; the words in the Welsh, Syriac, Coptic, Hebrew, Chaldean and Arabic tongues, by Mr Powell at the Bath's namesake and theological poppet; and Dr Pusillanimous, who upon second thoughts is set up for a great scruple-salver as well as occulist. Therefore all subscribers that have any relish for such entertainments and take in the monthly and quarterly books of this harmonious society are desired to bring their dinners with them by one in the afternoon the 16th instant, to the little box facing the street that is taken up for their reception; for the music is to begin precisely at that hour and no persons of whatsoever sex or quality from the stable to the kitchen will be admitted after it.

*

Apollo is desired to give the solution of one of the easiest of the ten mathematical problems, lately sent him by the Reverend Mr H—, which if they do not, it will be sufficient to convince the world that he answer very few questions but those of his own proposing and those too in his own commendation.

FRIDAY SEPTEMBER 16 TO MONDAY SEPTEMBER 19 *Number 32*

There being a prize comedy this winter, and Capt. Brazen[153] the chief candidate, Mrs Crackenthorpe desires the town to bestow the bays and profit on him. Nothing but want of assurance in her robs him of being the subject of half a dozen papers. We shall only touch upon some few particulars, to give the world a sample of his shining quality. What miracles has his wit not performed!

151 paper in constant opposition to *The Female Tatler*

152 sailors

153 actor, playwright and manager Colley Cibber

And, now Harlequin and Dame Ragone's children are out of fashion, his sublime, original, tender, flowing composures shall charm the pit and ravish the galleries, *Oedipus* and *Aureng-Zebe*[154] must give way to his immortal *Xerxes*,[155] and *The Double Dealer*,[156] to his judicious sprightly unborrowed *Double Gallant*.[157] Nay, that devouring monster, opera, so formidable to the theatre, sickens at the sight of him, and through his means is likely to be brought to poverty and bread and butter. I lay aside Ben[158] and Shakespeare when I but think of his elaborate piece, vulgarly called *Millers Thumbs*,[159] what will future ages say of this Terence and Euripides, this Janus of dramatic poetry? Why, that Aristotle only could give rules, and he write to 'em! But as for *Love's Last Shift*, *Careless Husband*, etc.[160] he declares 'em to be spurious and not of his own composing, wonders people can't see the difference between the style and fable, and thinks they may as well ascribe Hudibras and Bunyan to the same author.

MONDAY SEPTEMBER 19 TO WEDNESDAY SEPTEMBER 21 *Number 33*

Having received a written summons from Dr C——s, that was left at my lodgings for me, as well as the most noted coffee-houses, which runs thus, or in words to this purpose: 'Dr C——s intends (*numine aspirante*) to read upon a human body the day after the next execution, in the public hall in Physicians College, etc.' I resolved out of a natural curiosity that I am mistress of by

154 two plays by Dryden. *Oedipus* was an adaptation of the Greek tragedy and written in collaboration with N. Lee in 1679. *Aureng-Zebe*, his best heroic play, was written in 1675.

155 Colley Cibber's play, written in 1699 only received one performance despite a cast including the best actors of the day, Thomas Betterton and Elizabeth Barry.

156 a comedy by William Congreve (1693)

157 first performed in 1707, critics accused Cibber of stealing from Susanna Centlivre and Charles Burnaby.

158 Ben Jonson, poet and dramatist (1572?–1637)

159 Cibber's play *The Rival Fools*, performed in January 1709, was booed off with a chorus of 'Millers thumbs!' after a pun thought too much by the audience

160 Cibber's successful plays

my sexes charter, to make one amongst them; and, tho' I had been deceived before by an invitation of the same nature by Dr B——, who made himself a child by promising a lecture at Stationers-Hall about children's cauls,[161] put myself into men's apparel and notwithstanding I had but a slender opinion of the entertainment from the Latin he had made use of in his bill of fare, made what haste I could to the Royal Slaughter-house, where at the entrance into the amphitheatre I saw what Sir John Cutler, the Founder, would have been much more sparing of. The foliages and spikes of the gates were all adorn'd with leaf gold, and the hand that was feeling the pulse to find how the pocket stood affected, showed itself of the same complexion.

A multitude of all degrees were gathered together, some to better their understanding, and others to be thought to have more than they had; some in search of occult causes, and others whose cause of coming was to be sought for. Lawyers, apothecaries, physicians, butchers, divines, surgeons, pedagogues, painters and drugsters were the persons our learned doctor was to give proofs of his great skill in anatomy to, and the body was no sooner laid open from the thorax to the jugular, but he endeavoured to make appear by an elaborate harangue which nobody understood any more than himself, that the patient under his hands got his death for mere want of due respiration, and that the rope by compressing the jugular had stopped the circulation of the blood up to the seat of life, which was in the brain, and made him *obdormire cum patribus*, to sleep with his forefathers, an expression borrowed from the Czar of Muscovey's[162] letter. As if all the poor fellow's ancestors had gone off the stage after the same way as he did, and to suffer an ignominious and untimely death was to die a natural one. The Divines heard him with attention, that other people might do the same by them, when it should be their turns to talk, and the schoolmasters stood a tip-toe at the recital of terms that were more formidable than the figures of rhetoric which they so often fear'd their boys with, while only the butchers in Newgate-market thought much of tarrying, and swore they could have dressed three fat oxen in the time that he was opening one corpse from the throat to the paunch.

The next thing he took under consideration was the heart; whole valves and ventricles, systole and diastole was no sooner explained, but he made another learned observation from the livid colour of the blood that was coagulated in each ventricle, and gave it as his irrefragable opinion that the culprit exposed to view died very much out of

161 the membranes which surround a foetus.

162 Russia

humour, and that it was visible from its colour which was more pallid than ordinary, that he had great tokens of fear about him, and was taken with a shivering when he was going out of the world. So had poor Preston (thought I) when he was worried to death by his bear last Sunday; and, being out of all manner of patience at my coming so far to return home again furnished with no more knowledge than I brought with me, e'en left him calling over the muster-roll of nerves, fibres, veins and arteries, and giving descriptions of the lymphatic and pancreatic juices, their ducts and passages, etc. since I was perfectly convinced that if he understood the practical part of physic no better than he did the theoric, he would never be a rival for Aesculapius or a match to Hypocrates. Though I cannot well turn my back upon this edifying college, without communicating an eipgram that was made by one of the Blue-Coat boys[163] in the adjacent hospital on this occasion, and paraphrased into English by a friend of mine, who desires to be nameless on purpose that he may be the more enquired after. The verses run thus:

Ad Medicos:
Haud vexate Cruces, derrunt si corpora cultrit,
Pharmaca qui summit vestra, cadavet erit:

To the physician:
Ne'er rob the Gallows, or disturb the Place
Where P—— L—n sings Sternhold with a grace:
Your physic makes employment for your knives,
And gives you bodies, as it takes men's lives.[164]

*

Yesterday was published the seventeenth edition of *Love in a Hollow Tree*, a tragi-comedy, written for the use of all young playwrights, by a gentleman that always stands upon the stage in time of acting, and consequently must have a true knowledge of it; and printed for the judicious B—— L——[165] who gives it for his reason why the Tragedy of Phaedra and Hippolitus did not take better, that it was because it had not humour enough in it.

[163] English elementary schools established in the early eighteenth century to educate the children of the poor.

[164] a loose translation

[165] possibly Bernard Lintot, printer

*

A physicians chariot to be sold or let, at the Bear Inn in Piccadilly, the doctor having no occasion to ride in it, because he has no patients to drive to.

WEDNESDAY SEPTEMBER 21 TO FRIDAY SEPTEMBER 23 *Number 34*

The gay part of mankind, who frequent park, plays, chocolate-houses, and every little fashionable assembly, that rid away many a tedious hour in reading *Tatlers*, eating jellies, disputing on twenty different sorts of snuff, and making pretty satirical observations upon one another, must have observed Beau Maskwell, one of the walking gentlemen of the age; a person Sans Consequence, who every day makes his tour of public places with a kind of thoughtless serenity, and with no other seeming design, than the many saunterers of estate. He is what we call a clean dressed fellow, who instead of alarming people with a scarlet lace suit, tissue facings or embroidery, or elbowing thro' a coffee-house with a monstrous full-blown wig, affects pretty fancied druggets, with a gold button, or a black and silver binding, a modest French nightcap, a nice white glove, with a diamond ring over the little finger, and a colberteen[166] neckcloth. You meet him everywhere dangling after a particular set of Baronets, who are observed in public places to be very much upon the whisper, and to have a secret value for one another. He is intimate in their families, and their ladies think him a modest, sober, discreet person, that lives prettily on a younger brother's fortune, and they have a mighty value in this age for everybody that keeps within compass.

But as there are a sort of tricking people, that pass through the world without noise, and had rather pick up a moderate subsistence with security and reputation, than publicly to expose their way of living, by publishing at great matters, Beau Maskwell is not the least politic of these. He is extremely indifferent whether you call for cards or no, had as live play for sixpences as half-crowns, and if he comes off ten shillings winner, the ladies think that his company repays it, and cannot suppose such trifling play should be a gentleman's support, but, as incredible

166 lace

estates have by assiduity and cunning been raised from the most abject callings, Maskwell, who has studied Piquet more than Aesculapius ever did Physics, can slightly place the cards to his own advantage, and commit solecisms without being the least out of countenance, has for several years past genteely shuffled himself thro' all the difficulties of life. His associating with some of the better sort, makes people regard him with a kind of deference, 'tis not material nowadays, whether a man has birth, fortune, wit, sense, religion or morality; if the world stamps him a pretty gentleman, he passes current in all company. As such, Beau Maskwell has been looked upon and there's scarce a dancing-bout, basset night or collation, but he's one of the Cabal.

Sometime past he had an invitation to supper where he found a select, genteel society; amongst the rest, Hillaria, an easy, unaffected young lady of about six thousand pounds fortune, was the life of the company. Her youth and good humour made her a little frolicsome. She was equally pleasant, witty and familiar with strangers, as well as acquaintance, and the ladies were as much charmed with her gaiety, as the men were ravished with her beauty. They laughed, they danced, played at questions and commands, Hillaria romped a little. Everybody seemed wonderfully pleased with each other, and they only lamented the misfortune of being obliged to part at the break of day. Two days after, the same company assembled on another invitation. Maskwell was there, and asked leave to introduce a particular friend after supper. The vote was unanimous for cards, except Maskwell, who so strongly opposed to his darling pleasure and profession, and was so strangely eager for questions and commands, that some people began to suspect his good manners. However, the reconciling Hillaria, to make everybody easy, that she might be so herself, proposed both diversions. The company were to be first questioned and then commanded to cards. Maskwell discovered no small satisfaction at being obliged in so seeming a trifle, and when he assumed the title of King, and the bright Hillaria condescended to be his subject, he commanded her to marry him, and that the person he had introduced, should perform the priestly office. The giddy nymph, who was for Clapperdepouch,[167] or anything, readily consents, banters him with having gnawed the sheets[168] a great while; that the war has made such havoc among the men she was afraid she should have died of the pip, but that, (thanks to her better stars) she had now got a husband before her elder sister. And the stranger, praising himself for an admirable memory, repeated the service between 'em. Maskwell sends immediately for gloves and favours, Hillaria is ready to

167 a game   168 become impatient

die with laughing, the company think them comical creatures, and the romantic airs of this new married couple afforded so much of what they call pastime, that several wish it had been a match in earnest, and thought it unnatural to part without throwing the stocking.[169]

Maskwell the next morning attends his bride, was careless enough as to her person, but demanded her fortune. Hillaria laughs still, he commends her good humour and hopes his claim won't in the least divert it, but says they were actually married the night before, and that the person who performed the ceremony was a clergyman in the Fleet, whom he had introduced in lay-habit for that purpose. Hillaria then began to change, her relations were summoned upon the matter, but Maskwell impudently asserting the marriage, and being a fellow of too much craft to be bantered, bullied or baffled, the trembling Hillaria, to prevent town-talk, and the cognisance of Doctor's Commons[170] for making a jest of sacred things, gave him a thousand pounds to waive his pretensions to her. Maskwell now flourished like his Baronets, they published him a man of estate, recommended him to fortunes, and about a month past he was marry to a lady of three thousand pounds, and made her a jointure in Utopia.[171]

*

Mrs Penelope Penny-royal, a middle-aged maid, that has three thousand pounds and plays finely on the organ, having many years, to no purpose, pretended to a coach, is now willing to dispose herself at reasonable rates. She may be seen most hours in the day standing at the door, near Catherine Street in the Strand. She's a fresh-coloured lady in a yellow damask gown, her pinners[172] not above a quarter of a yard higher than other peoples, the furbelow of her nightrail[173] don't quite touch the ground, nor does her watch hang much below her knee. Whoever thinks fit to engage in her service, will have a very cordial reception.

169 always done after a wedding. Today's equivalent is throwing the bouquet.

170 law courts

171 A reference to a husband's sharing of his property with his wife upon their marriage – a rare occurrence in those days.

172 headdress

173 loose wraps

FRIDAY SEPTEMBER 23 TO MONDAY SEPTEMBER 26 *Number 35*

o Mrs Crackenthorpe

Madam,

When I came to town from the bath, I made enquiry what new papers were published, amongst the many that came to hand, two *Female Tatlers* appeared, each justifying itself the true one. I might have expected innumerable from the sex, all being qualified that way, but the difference of style and matter immediately informed me which was the spurious one, for impudence and ignorance always betray themselves, curiosity led me to detect the counterfeit.

I travelled Lime-house, Wapping, St Catherine's, and Billingsgate. Between the two last I found a person sitting most magisterially in a dirty ale-house, surrounded with porters and watermen. He pretended to universal knowledge, spoke broken sentences, nodded his head, winked with his eyes, laughed heartily at his own jests and their ignorance, (and who I found was an assistant to the spurious *Female Tatler*) 'till the gaping monsters took him for a conjurer. I modestly begged admission. He, after his manner, permitted me to approach his mightiness, who big with himself, gave me a large character of his profound skill in science, anatomized Euclid, and was fond of a worse way to erect perpendiculars. I began to interrupt him, but . . . hold . . . 'Avast,' quoth he, 'what would your little self say now?' I was silenced and he continued spouting out misapplied barbarous words, and then produced a scale and compasses. 'Good Sir,' quoth I, 'pray make no circles, for I cannot bear the sight of the foul fiend.' He laughed at my ignorance, as I at his. 'I find,' said he, 'that you have no taste of these occult mysteries, but you may thank your stars and better genius that led you into the conversation with a person of my abilities; and that you may be sensible, I am a gentleman as good natured as learned. Advance me but one Guinea and I'll show you a trick sort, a trick with a hole in it, such a trick as I assure you, is not to be despised – which nobody can deny, deny, [singing].'

He then pulled out some proposals, and thus proceeded in his Harangue: 'Besides, these gentlemen who vouch the performances, two hundred more that have travelled, painters, architects, statuaries, engravers, carvers, artificers, etc. are obliged for me the projection, nay, says he, I can draw a true sketch of your face, by means of this instrument, only fixing you in a chair, with your ears hung up two centre-hooks that you may sit steady. The thought is my own and wholly new. The universities applaud me, nay the whole world is beholden to me, not only for this but my ballads, and calculated tables, which will suddenly appear in print, as much to my honour as the rest.' Here he paused, not that he intended to hold his peace, but to fetch breath, while I took the opportunity to address him with, 'Sir, I have an extraordinary esteem for all men of learning and ingenuity, and am very forward at all times to encourage new inventions. But am not convinced yours is so, having seen the very same thing in the English Translation of the *Jesuits Perspective*, the definition in the 120th page, the book is to be had at Mercer's Chapel. That your project is new, I believe, because 'tis the project of getting the money.' Fire appeared in his eyes, and malice in his looks. He called me fool, blockhead, and all that was due to himself, and vowed he'd have me exposed in the next *Female Tatler* as a Trifler.

This made me more soft. I begged his pardon, drank to him to quench his passion and assured him I would oblige him in everything if he would condescend to bring me into the acquaintance of that author. He told me he was immediately bound thither. I compounded for my rudeness by paying the reckoning, and we passed through the city to St Paul's Church-yard, where in a dark room of a common ale-house, behind a slabbered table, sat a surly, sullen, morose, splenetic, old dotard, snarling at himself and cursing his company. I expected to have seen a glittering coquet, and such a monster should personate a young lady, it putting me in mind of Hercules with a distaff. But, composing myself, I asked him if he was anyways related to Madam Crackenthorpe. 'Madam Crackenthorpe's a B——ch,' quoth he, 'and you are an Ass. Sure I know better how to write than such a flirting queen, I, who have been an author for many years and writ poetry for Dr Saffold's-Bills and raised his fame by my pen, am not now to be compared to such a scribbling Jade as she. This ingenious gentleman knows the elegance of my style, and some of the best lines in his book, (now in the press) are the product of my brain.'

Here my new acquaintance interrupted him, finding himself exposed. 'Will,' [quoth he] 'you are impertinent. Have not I treated you for several years past, introduced you amongst the best company in Goodman's Fields and, like an ingrate, you abuse your best benefactor. I know your original, Saturn, that dull planet, was your ascendant, and Mars was in a trine-aspect,[174] which inclines you to be so Choloric.' 'You lie,' quoth he, 'my colour is owing to my father's country and calling, who was well known to be a soldier at Edge-Hill-Fight[175] and my mother, following the camp, was delivered of me then under the canopy of heaven, and thereby lost her share in the plunder. I was a very sweet baby and the pious party who always have tender consciences, believing me to be the Son of the Regiment, took care of my education, and by their charity I became so very learned as you now find me.' This quarrel grew to a height, and I, to push my curiosity a little farther, sided with the author. I tempted him to the next tavern, where a bottle or two mellowed his temper, and he was reconciled both to Mrs Crackenthorpe, and myself.

He there opened his bosom to me, declared that my late new acquaintance was a person preferred to a considerable post in the Custom House, where he might with diligence acquire a handsome fortune; but thro' false opinion of his own merits, neglected his duty and profit to catch butterflies, and, though his circumstances are very low at present, yet he spends his money freely on those who hear his tale, approve his nonsense and flatter his folly . . . That as for himself, misfortunes made him undertake that paper he thought too light a study for him, and that his fancy (for want of intelligence) was quite jaded with it. He seemed sorry for the injuries done to a lady of Mrs Crackenthorpe's character, and wished he could make some interest to tell her so. I promised to endeavour his advancement in a better sphere, in order to which, Madam, I have recommended to you the following advertisement; which if you please to publish, you will assure the world, that you treat your enemies with more honour, than any other lady in town would do. I am . . &c.

Although the persons meant in this letter are not considerable enough for the observation of some of our readers, it was thought exposing the ridiculous conceit of such wretches might yet be of some advantage to the public, which, together with some other reasons, induced me to publish it, hoping it may have the desired effect, which was the only motive that would ever have prevailed on me to set forth a paper of this kind.

*

An ancient gentleman, who is well known to be a person equally qualified with learning and good manners, modesty and cleanliness, soft and gentle

174 an astrological aspect

175 an important battle at the beginning of the English Civil War (1642)

in his expression, elegant and solid in his style, and wonderfully philosophical in his habit, is to be spoke with every day at the Ale-house in Paul's Alley, where you will find him descended from his cockloft, sitting in a common room, gnawing a hard crust, and sponging his liquor for want of the ready rhino,[176] having been so unfortunate to receive but three half crowns for writing seventeen spurious *Female Tatlers*. A friend of Mrs Crackenthorpe's, out of pure charity to his person, and respect to his parts, recommends him to a young gentleman, who has occasion for a peremptory obstinate, insolent, saucy Governor, and assures them he is in every respect qualified for that office.

*

The gentleman that gave himself the trouble of writing concerning the young linen draper in Cornhill is desired to take notice that enquiry has been made into the person's character he so much traduces, which is found to be quite contrary to what he gives, wherefore Mrs Crackenthorpe asks his excuse for not printing it.

*

The lady that sent a letter, and swore all was true by G–d in it, is requested to avoid profaneness, as much as the lady she characterises does immorality. It is heartily desired she'll mend one, and the lady she points at (if half so bad) will mend another.

MONDAY SEPTEMBER 26 TO WEDNESDAY SEPTEMBER 28 — *Number 36*

The knight that had so many irons in the fire to get an aldermanship, and burned his fingers with 'em, is desired to send his coals to Newcastle, to forward and promote his works there, since they have rendered his projects abortive here.

*

He that instanced likewise in some particulars relating to the Cross Keys Tavern is advised to remember that any vintner may refuse trusting

[176] cash in hand

whom he pleases, and it's one and the same thing with all persons that have money, or design to have it, to be sparing of their credit to those who have none.

WEDNESDAY SEPTEMBER 28 TO FRIDAY SEPTEMBER 30 *Number 37*

Before the summer season quite elapsed, some ladies proposed a voyage to Hampton Court. We selected our company and were accommodated with a nice pinnace,[177] which six mercurial gentlemen who love exercise kept for their diversion and who did us the honour to be our watermen. Resolving to be perfectly easy, we took care to have no affected things with us, no timerous frightened creature that screams at every bubble and if you mention but a sail offers fifty pounds to be set on shore; no tiresome governance that never thinks she has respect enough paid her, is reproving young people for every light expression and advises them to talk of good things, nor a covetous old bachelor, who grumbles at the reckoning, and thinks the women ought to pay their clubs.[178] We had Harry Wild-Air, that has more wit that half Will's Coffee-House, Charles Sprightly, a good natured magotty fellow, and Ned Worthy, that has complaisance without tedious ceremony, and fine sense without delivering himself in set paragraphs, Grace Giggle, whose last breath will certainly expire in a laugh, Nanny Tunable, who every night sings herself to sleep, and Betty Easy, who is not to be put out of humour and is equally pleased with every jaunt proposed provided she likes her company. 'Twas humbly hinted that we would admit George P—k[179] of the Playhouse, who would give us forty humorous songs, mimics the Italians to a wonder perfection, and behaves himself so handsomely and with so much good manners that people of the first quality are daily sending for him. I was surprised to prove miracles not ceased in finding modesty in a player, his conversation which was *bien tournée* and his expression brilliant, without being larded with oaths or the least spice of debauchery, made me heartily wish him a more reputable employment, and conclude that the ill treatment he has met with from some of the head actors is because he has less pride, better principles and more good conduct than themselves.

177 small sailing boat, with oars

178 pay their share by clubbing together

179 George Pack, a minor actor

We pass'd airily along, the sun smiled upon our progress, and freedom, which is the source of true mirth, crowned us with entire satisfaction. Mr P—k, besides his agreeable pipe, entertained us with several diverting stories relating to the theatres, their rise and progress since their original strolling with Mrs Mynns, their parties, cabals, divisions, unions, arrests, outlawries and excommunications, the birth and education of the stage ladies, their real and supposed marriages, comical intrigues, tragical lyings-in, and the disposal of their progeny.

He began with Volpone,[180] the Lord of these rebellious subjects, who, like the Turks, are ever revolting from their lawful Sovereign, has purred among them with all the craft and policy of threescore years experience to no purpose. He has deducted their thirds,[181] stopped them two days pays for forfeitures and run them in debt with carpenters and bricklayers, and yet all won't humble them. This old gentleman, says he, is the greatest original of the Age; nobody could ever yet find out whether he has any meaning in him or no, since he never gave anybody a direct answer, nor undertook a project that ever turned to any account. If a gentleman brings him a new play he asks whether he designs to call it a comedy or a tragedy, and refers it to Colly-my-Cow,[182] who formerly rejected the *Ambitious Stepmother*[183] because it was a play that had neither language nor design in it. He's as eager after a wench as my Lord Fireball is in chasing a French Privateer, will treat a nest of them with burnt brandy at the office, and if a young creature presents herself to him for the stage, he takes care to examine her thoroughly, weedles her to his purpose with a new suit to play an old part in; and when he's tired with her himself, thinks her good enough for quality. His circumstances are as mysterious as his understanding, though not quite as obscure as his person, for though he has every day fifty bailiffs after him, he has a hundred trap doors to creep through and avoid them, and though he's already head-over-heels in law, yet he is still commencing fresh suits, and maintains a regiment of disbanded players at half pay, only for the pleasure of arresting them for it afterwards. The conversation of Volpone and his slaves is more nonsensically diverting than Serjeant Kite's Mock-Camilla,[184] or Capt. Brazen's Alexander,[185] burlesqued at

[180] Christopher Rich, former manager of Drury Lane

[181] third night fees [182] Colley Cibber

[183] immensely successful tragedy by Ambrose Phillips (1675–1749)

[184] a burlesque, probably by the actor-manager-playwright – Richard Estcourt (Sergeant Kite) of Niccolo Haym's *Camilla*.

[185] Colley Cibber's burlesque of Nathaniel Lee's *The Rival Queens; or, The Death of Alexander the Great* entitled *The Rival Queans: the Humours of Alexander the Great*.

present; indeed some of them have fled from their allegiance, but he's recruiting his company again, from Greenwich, Southwark, Ratcliff and Windmill-Hill, and as soon as he can get his petition answered, will open with that famous comedy, called, *The Lawyers Fortune*, or *Love in a Hollow-Tree.*[186]

This and some other chit-chat, brought us to Hampton Court. The Giddy People diverted themselves in the maze, while Mr Worthy and myself admired the gardens, greenhouse, the staircase, and the beauties. Travellers may enlarge upon Foreign Courts, but this palace shows the British nation to be truly great and wants but this correction to equal it to Versailles: that the servants who have such large salaries (now punctually paid them) ought not to hold out their hands for money and frequently grumble if they gather not to their expectations.

As this paper is seriously to correct the vices, as well as laugh at the vanities of the age, I cannot forbear representing to the Clergy of St Pauls, that the avenue to the cathedral is become a mere exchange. The buyers and sellers were drove out of the Temple of Jerusalem, the table of the money-changers overthrown, and the seats of them that sold doves; but here, every Sunday morning, the Whetters and the dumpling-eaters meet, even in the side aisles to stockjob, do law business, talk of news, and then adjourn to the taverns who, in spite of so many proclamations and Lord Mayor's orders, have the impudence as well as immorality to fill their houses in sermon time. A careless behaviour in a place of worship, shows a trifling regard to religion itself, but when people shall make assignations there for worldly matters, just show themselves in a choir to hear the anthem and then flock out again in such shameful crowds, 'tis perfectly shocking to the few truly pious, and the House of Prayer becomes a Den of Thieves.

I have observed too at our most eminent lectures, that if the divine expected happens not to preach, half the church empties at a strange face, which is not only an affront to the gentleman in the pulpit, but to the Deity, whose Ambassador he is, for though every discourse may not be alike florid, yet there are few sermons so barren as not to merit our attention. These things are very good jests to the other sects, who are a sly-people, always picking holes, and hug themselves at the least opportunity of reflecting on the established church, but as to the walking at Paul's, if a reprimand of this nature proves of no effect, I think proper officers ought to be appointed to prevent so scandalous an enormity.

*

186 law suit

The young lady in the parish of St Laurence, near Guildhall, that lately went to the Coffee-House in man's clothes with the two 'prentices, called for a dish of Bohee,[187] smoked her pipe, and gave herself abundance of straddling masculine airs, is desired to do so no more.

*

Christopher Morose, the haberdasher, in the same parish, is desired not to affect quality so much as to have a separate bed from his wife, and though he has reported her to be melancholy mad, because his usage has been enough to make her so, yet the neighbours have sense enough to be alarmed at his brutality, and unless he mends his manners, have promised Mrs Crackenthorpe his character at large.

*

The miscellaneous ordinary in Pater-Noster Row, composed of pimps, poets, projectors, pettifoggers, stockjobbers, and custom-house officers, intend to continue their nine-penny club every day in the week, where Isabella, the fat cook-maid, who used to have a world of fire in her conversation and had a better knack of dishing out gentlemen's characters than their dinners, resolves to confine herself to her kitchen, being a little humbled with a wound she received lately in her breast, from a skewer thrown at her by an enraged Levite.[188]

FRIDAY SEPTEMBER 30 TO MONDAY OCTOBER 3 — *Number 38*

Whereas a person that underwrit himself Cross-Fortune sent a letter about a lady, with a promise of a good pair of gloves for the publication of it; this is by way of answer to inform him that it is none of my method to interfere with married people under the circumstances he speaks of, and that I do not live so far from a milliner's but I can pay for my gloves without his assistance.

*

Mrs Sleah that directed to us concerning the two twins at the Boot Ale-House, in Grace-Church Street, is earnestly begged to cease her

187 black, Indian tea   188 a clergyman

solicitations about so trifling an affair, for to descend into such particulars as are beneath Mrs Crackenthorpe's notice would give occasion to the world to suspect her guilty of too much condescension, and she's a gentlewoman of too much humanity and consideration for the failures of her own sex to take things upon trust relating to their pretended indiscretions.

MONDAY OCTOBER 3 TO WEDNESDAY OCTOBER 5 *Number 39*

he city having in so great a measure been the subject of this paper, several strangers have fancied Mrs Crackenthorpe lives at that end of the town, yet not withstanding all that has been said, nay even the noisy paper of Deputy Bustle and his daughters, the city quality from being ridiculous are now grown monstrous. Nothing can be a greater jest to the men of quality than to see a citizen coached to Windsor to be knighted, nor to women of birth, than to observe how awkwardly the title of my Lady sits upon Mrs Fribble, Mrs Bisket, Mrs Doodle and Mrs Wiseacre, and the comical behaviour of such creatures upon their being distinguished. But when Mrs Tinsy, Mrs Taffety, and Mrs Taplash arrive at gold chains, have officers to attend them, or a page for a year, victory to a soldier, gold to a miser, or fine thoughts to a poet put them not into so great a rapture. The Rhenish family, who have admired themselves for a twelvemonth past, are a merry instance of this matter. Sir Richard Rhenish, has looked bigger than he really is, the squire, whose sword and the blue apron[189] alternately graced him, and whose perfections lie in shooting himself down three pair of stairs with the dexterity of a diver, and who flourishes you out a dozen glasses of wine with the same ease a penman commands a true lovers knot, being countenanced by magistracy, stole a fortune of four thousand pounds.

But my Lady, *Libera Nos Domine*,[190] is one of the most extraordinary pieces. No stage-queen was ever finer, no city queen ever prouder, no puppet queen ever more ridiculous. At that last feast her ladyship displayed herself most wonderfully, and was only out of humour to hear

[189] a blue apron was part of a City Deputy's regalia

[190] Deliver Us, O Lord

so much wine called for and none scored at the bar.[191] She gave everybody a superb account of the management of her family and the unparalleled perfections of her children, and those that did not think Miss Sally something dropped out of the clouds were wondered at for having no business there, and asked who invited them. Miss Sally's accomplishments were this very year very prejudicial to the confectioners, for she made all the jellies; and her ladyship stalked round the hall: 'Gentlemen and Ladies, pray taste of the jellies, I assure you they are all of Miss Sally's own doing. I have bred her to the very art of housewifery. Not but she sings and dances, and is now learning Dutch and, though we are so straightened for room that Miss Sally's forced to lie in a pallet at the feet of the bride and bridegroom, which is very inconvenient, yet her father will make her a topping fortune, and I hope to see her a Lady as well as myself.' The gentlemen burst out a laughing, the city ladies crammed napkins into their mouths till they had liked to have been choked, and some of the better sort, who thought it ill manners to be kindly treated and make a jest of their hostess, almost struggled themselves into convulsion fits.

The vanity of the Rhenish Family is inexpressible. When the husband went to Windsor, the wife sat perfectly upon cow-itch[192] till his return, and, hearing some ship guns go off, concluded they were those of the tower, that her husband was just then dubbed, and ordered the servants to give her the title due to her. The husband, coming through Hounslow, called upon a relation to acquaint her with his dignity, and asked pardon for not saluting her, his lady having strictly enjoyned him that as he had her maidenhead, she should have the maidenhead of his honour. Now, would anybody suppose when *Tatlers* are daily published that people should be so horrid silly? But as the ingenious Mr Bickerstaff says – one may write to eternity, the world is still the same. Mrs Bustle brazened out the paper at the door, gives herself more airs at church than ever, and will sit above her next door neighbour, who is my gentlewoman by birth and whose husband is a hundred thousand pound man. The parson in S——k Gossips Hill, Mr Sately, is as affected as ever, and none but Sir Samuel Slender and he has had so modest a sense of his faults as to go out of town upon finding them exposed.

P.S. Sir R——, his Lady, Miss Sally, and their whole equipage and their body coach, his travelling chariot not being yet bought, have been pleased since the writing of this, to go out of town yesterday for the air, or some other considerations, wherefore it is desired of the young squire to take all convenient speed to transmit this paper to them, that is written on purpose to transmit his and their names to posterity.

191 none were paid for

192 could not sit still with impatience

*

Lady Dainty, who is extremely apprehensive of everybody below herself, paying me a visit last drawing-room night, was on a sudden taken very ill. There being a prodigious assembly I fancied the heat overcame her, but when *Sal Volatile*[193] had a little revived her, I found her ladyship's indisposition proceeded from smelling a tradesman's wife in the room. This accident gave us a new turn of conversation, and a general complaint was made that the prosperous vulgar take so much upon them in dress, air, equipage and visiting, that people of rank are hardly distinguished from upstart pretenders, nor can they propose a basset or dancing bout without an allay of such interloping mechanics, who are creatures that ought to go to bed when people of fashion rise. If they once get a knack of pleasing their betters with novelties, the business of whose life is amusement, and can tongue-pad themselves into a reputation, they immediately get estates, and pretend to look folks in the face. We have our quality midwives that keep coaches, quality mantua-makers that carry home jumps[194] in chairs,[195] nay, even quality waiting women that won't stir without a Hackney and a footman.

To visit some of these mock-genteels has given me no small diversion – their talk of what horrid company there was at the play, what an ungenteel supper my lady Fussock gave them, that salt spoons are out of fashion, and shovels are come in, and how eternally they are sent for by this countess, and that duchess, show that they are either subservient to the private pleasures of the great, or that every chariot they bridle in, the lady of it is very deep in their books. Amongst the rest of it, Mrs Flounce, the mantua lady near Surrey Street, is allowed perfectly to understand her trade, several dear creatures have been dressed and undressed at her house, she knows the nicety of the mode, and thinks herself perfectly well bred in having a mortal hatred for her husband. Poor Flatbottom, as the neighbours have nicknamed him, is so henpecked, because madam maintains him, that he's forced to ask pardon on his knees for light offences, and the gentleman that tips him half a crown to support his spirits with a glass of Burton,[196] must be truly noble, who not only generously relieves him, but employs his wife, an industrious woman that makes night gowns for gentlemen, as well as roppers for ladies. About a month past, madam turns away her maid, and honest Flatbottom has cleaned her house, washed her dishes, and been her man-cook ever since, while she, sewing on her furbelows, sings 'I was

193 smelling salts
194 ladies' underbodices
195 Sedan chairs
196 best beer

born of a Royal Race,' and quotes the following lines out of *Nature Will Prevail*:

Wise heaven in pity to our sex designed
Fools for the last relief of woman-kind;
Two married wits no quiet can enjoy,
Two fools together would the house destroy.
So providence to level human life,
Made the fool husband, for the witty wife.

'Tis scandalous for a man to use his wife ill, but for a woman to tyrannise 'tis monstrous, their virtue is very justly suspected, and if the surgeon's wife near Aldersgate Street, who beats her little husband, opens letters not fit for a woman to see and thinks her neighbours have no more modesty than herself, don't mend her manners, her character will be published at large.

*

The Beau Tradesman near Milk Street, who publicly pretends to so much virtue and sobriety, is desired to let his neighbour's maids alone. Betty the black, Mary the brown, Joan the blowze, nay ev'n the great red-haired wench in Cheapside, make horrid complaints against him. He is every night purring about the streets, hauling damsels into taverns, and has more inclination to a straw hat, or a round-about apron, than to his wife, who is allowed to be the prettiest woman in the parish. Note: Mrs Crackenthorpe desires that every woman in the parish, who will naturally think herself the handsomest, not to quarrel with her husband about this advertisement.

*

Whereas Mrs Crackenthorpe has received many letters, which are improper for the design of this paper, and has lately exasperated a very valuable person, by setting up his waste paper by way of auction: this is to acquaint those whom it may concern that she has done nothing to him but what she would allow be done to herself. Wherefore, she appoints an immediate sale, to be held this evening (for they won't bear reading tomorrow) at the Red-Cross before-mentioned, of all such notices and intelligencies she has received not fit for her purpose, and all persons studious of such inelegant requests are required then and there to attend, in pursuance of this advertisement.

WEDNESDAY OCTOBER 5 TO FRIDAY OCTOBER 7 *Number 40*

his puts me in mind of a certain lady not far from Aldermary churchyard, who has sent letter after letter to the same purpose, and is desired for the future to show less of her father's ill nature, and more of her mother's sweetness, for such a procedure as she would have me go upon may be of as bad consequence to herself as the lady she points at, and the readiest way not to get a husband herself (for she's old enough to stand a tip-toe to look after one) is to show herself ready on all occasions to seek the ruin of one that has. Let her also take this, by the by, that she is known to be a pretty little black[197] woman that cannot be much longer without a humble servant, though Mr ——— should be under other engagements, and if she persists in her obstinate resolves of exposing the person she aims at, something may be said in this paper that may turn to her disadvantage, since those would very much wrong her that durst affirm she has any enmity for mankind, and I dare not aver for my life that she is never seen but in women's company.

FRIDAY OCTOBER 7 TO MONDAY OCTOBER 10 *Number 41*

eople that have an itch at scribbling generally entertain their visitors with their happy projects, high flights, and wonderful performances, therefore 'tis to be supposed this paper is in great measure the subject of many a drawing-room. My Lady Prudence Maxim thought 'twas exposing families too much, that now, truly, a lady could not be free and gamesome, write a *Billet Doux*,[198] drink a glass of Ratafia,[199] send her jewels out when cards run ill, or be seen in a Hackney with her cousin the colonel, but the next morning the bawling fellow tells it to the whole town. Mrs Callicoe disliked it for mentioning the pride of the city. Mrs Saintly for abusing

[197] dark haired [198] a love letter
[199] alcoholic cordial

the dissenters,[200] for they do not love silver spoons. Mrs Orthodox said a clergyman had been drawn into it, and 'twas a burning shame. Mrs Whinelove, who is so fond of plays that if she is not buried under the front-box she'll walk, wondered I could speak so irreverently of her darling Imoinda, but Mrs Gaymond encouraged me to the last degree, laughed heartily at every character, and wished it had been ten times plainer, but protested, as she hoped to be saved, should anybody expose her in print, she'd be the death of them.

The major part of the world, who are the insipids, may term a paper of this kind, scurrilous, scandalous, and false, talk of it with an imaginable liberty, and affirm that the author has been drubbed, who perhaps can be even with those that say so. But the few wise, who are of opinion that people are sooner ridiculed than preached out of their follies and that more may be learned out of some plays than out of some sermons, must allow, that a Tatler alarms the world into a circumspection. And as pride, vanity and affectation furnish fit reproof, immorality and prophaneness are so strenuously exploded that the giddy sort gossip less for fear of being laughed at, and the libertines of the age sin more in private for fear of being abhorred. This discourse made my Lady Harriet Lovely hint to me to write a comedy, which was only opposed by Mrs Cavil, who asserted that no woman ever yet turned poetess but lost her reputation by appearing at rehearsals, and conversing with Imoinda, Desdemona, and a maidenhead Amintor at my years, who expect compliments for promoting their own livelihood, and would immediately fright virtue from my drawing-room, by having the assurance to visit me; and that the treatment authors meet with from the players is too gross for a woman to bear, since at the getting up of so successful a comedy as *The Busy Body*,[201] Sir Harry Wild-Air[202] in great dudgeon flung his part into the pit for damned stuff, before the lady's face that wrote it. Upon the whole, my Lady Sneak proposed that I shouldn't appear in the matter, but give the enraged Sir Harry the whole profits of the play, and then let it have neither wit, plot, sense, turn or humour; he'd bully Capt. Brazen into a good opinion of it, fourscore pounds should be laid out in clothes, and she'd warrant a prodigious Third Night.[203] But, as I had the vanity to think I could write tolerably well and could fill the boxes from my own drawing-room without the interest of the Duchess of Twangdillo, and as I positively want a hundred pounds to print a folio book, called *The History of Tatlers*, I could not see the reason why Sir Harry Wild-Air should reap the benefit of my studies, and by exporting it to Ireland the nation would want money as well as corn.

[200] Protestant nonconformists [201] by Susanna Centlivre (1709)
[202] Robert Wilks, an Irish leading actor [203] third night fees

At last it was agreed I should apply myself to Sergeant Kite, who is a person of prodigious integrity, values money no more than dirt, and we proceeded to think of characters: Sir Harry and his associate are to be two walking gentlemen, and, as they are both men of wit and judgment, I shall leave them to speak what they think proper; but, if they only move on and off, they are good figures, always well dressed, and more to be admired than Mrs Salmon's Wax-Work. Pinkee[204] is only to laugh, his face is jest enough to make the play go to six nights, and Myn Heer Van Grin, was the best thought for him in the world; the famous Jubilee Dicky[205] is to represent the figure of nobody, and Tallboy,[206] who always will be a boy, shall have just such another part wrote for him; Captain Brazen,[207] who is so fond of being in women's clothes, shall personate a finished coquet, one that jilts the men, rattles with the women, always upon the seeming trifles, though seriously grounded upon self-interest; Imoinda[208] is to be a disdainful beauty, have a world of admirers, and use them all like dogs; Lady Betty Modish,[209] a woman of quality, and plays in her own clothes, and my Lady Bountiful,[210] to talk of eating and drinking, admires a boiled pig and egg-sauce, and take a prodigious deal of snuff. The catastrophe of the play, is to be a marriage and a country dance, and Sgt Kite, by way of epilogue, to sign a ballad of his own making; the act tunes must be melancholy and moving, to keep people from laughing too much, as they play jigs in tragedies to keep them from grieving too much, and if their comedy don't gain the prize the subscribers of it must expect their characters in this paper.

Now though I have no plot to my play, I have a moral to my tale, which is that people of quality who squander away money upon such trifles would gain a public reputation, a private satisfaction, and set a noble example to their inferiors, in bestowing it upon the distressed Palatines, or giving it to such officers in our fleets and armies as do not think they are paid enough for making sinecures[211] of the posts they are possessed of.

*

The gentleman that gave me an invitation per penny post to come to his

[204] William Pinketham, actor [205] Henry Norris, actor

[206] William Bullock, frequently paired with Norris due the difference in their heights

[207] Colley Cibber [208] probably the actress Jane Rogers

[209] Anne Oldfield, actress

[210] probably either Mrs Powell or Elizabeth Barry

[211] jobs entailing no work

lodgings at Ham to have my throat cut may expect an answer to his letter at large in my next.

MONDAY OCTOBER 10 TO WEDNESDAY OCTOBER 12 *Number 42*

Well! I find people do and, write what I please, will go on their own way still. Lucilius is the very same man he was before I set up for his instructor, Cleomira will hearken to no manner of advice, but goes to church in order to be absolved of her sins, and sins again in order to go to church and be thought penitent. 'Tis none of my fault the world is not wiser, but these poor brains of mine work to no purpose. If I tell a certain new fashioned gentleman his faults, the young squire Richard, his son, makes no bones of discovering his resentment but swears by all that's good that I am guilty of *scandalum magnatum*, or if I point at a particular vice, it is always owned and laid hold of by a particular person. For shame, Gentlemen and Ladies, dismiss your follies, and bid *adieu* to your indiscretions that this Tatler of mine may have no subject to go upon and consequently be suppressed without your making interest with authority. The end of satire is reformation, and this would be of more force than your societies for that purpose, were it duly observed and hearkened to, without being misconstrued defamation. You are told your faults in order to amend them, and if characters are drawn that are injurious to your reputations, what have you to do but to disown them, since . . . every one of you might pass for wise and virtuous, would you not think yourselves reflected upon for being otherwise.

But I am under much greater apprehensions . . . and presentments and informations are not enough for me, but am threatened with mischiefs, which one would think my sex might excuse me from, and are but too destructive of my repose in the following letter. Tho' 'tis hoped he that has forgot that he writes to a woman, will not so much forget himself to be a man, as to put these threatenings in practice:

Sir,

I cast my eyes by chance upon your *Female Tatler*, No. 30, and was desired to observe an unmannerly reflection, under the character of Ethiopian ballad singer, & Co. I am too well acquainted with your humour and your person to expect a reason in justification of your actions, and therefore only think it worth my while to tell you that as I have no concern in the paper or society you make so free with, so I desire to have less with you; and if I shall at any time hereafter perceive the smallest of your sidelong glances of abuse aimed at me (I use no ceremony) I will take the readiest way to force myself a satisfaction, and cut your nose off for a decent means of retaliation.

Your servant,

A.H. Oct. 1, 1709

You may hear of me at my lodgings at Mr Hubbard's in West Ham by Stratford, and if you care not to believe my handwriting, I will tell you so by word of mouth, if you'll make me a visit.

Sweet scented Sir, your humble servant again, though you seem to point me out for a woman, in saying you are too well acquainted with my person and humour to expect a reason from me, you use me like a man, and I must tell you that I care as little to have any concern with you as you would have with me. But for your decent means of retaliation, in cutting my nose off, and your invitation to your lodgings, I bless my stars I am more of a Christian than to comply with them, for by doing so I should be guilty of self-murder, as well as yourself, who amongst other readings, have without doubt read the Coventry Act,[212] and you may satisfy yourself that I'll believe your handwriting so very much as to make it my endeavour to keep out of the reach of your dead-doing hand. So much for one letter . . .

WEDNESDAY OCTOBER 12 TO FRIDAY OCTOBER 14 *Number 43*

Some time passed I promised the town an account of my person and family, but the Bustles, the Stately's, the Slenders and the Rhenishes, having been ridiculous beyond my expectation, I was forced to defer the delineating of the Crackenthorpes till now. Our family came in with William the Conqueror, and have bounced at court in as many reigns as any race in

[212] An Act passed in 1670 against nose-slitting and maiming.

Christendom, our being taken notice of proceeded not from immense riches, gotten by sinister practices, encouraging petty factions, or flattening the vanity of the luxurious great, but from religion, probity and true politics. We were always firm to the church, loyal to our prince, and entire in the interest of our country, we never gave gold for Court honours, nor coals for city distinctions, everybody knew a Crackenthorpe was a gentleman, and the proudest Welsh families have courted an alliance with us.

The younger sons of the family were bred to divinity, physics and the law, for no Crackenthorpe was ever yet a tradesman, who, being all eminent in their station, acquired both estates and dignities, while the elder, the great Crackenthorpe, who thought that title beyond being created Lord Foppington, maintained the hospitality of his ancestors, where, instead of sashes and terrace walks, fricasees and tarts made in patty pans, you have a magnificent old structure, big enough to build forty modern quality whims, which another hurricane would blow into a different country; sirloins of good beef, and the pair pie-crust as thick as the walls of the house, and Crackenthorpe Castle, at whose gates no dun[213] ever knocked, was always a happy refuge for the poor. The sisters, which were pretty numerous, and which pert coxcombs call the drugs of a family, by marriage dispersed themselves amongst other topping families, yet, though they changed their names, their deportment and conversation still showed them to be Crackenthorpes, and their children to the twentieth generation, either in speech, gait, antipathies, or inclinations, discovered something of their Grandmother Crackenthorpe.

They were always more inquisitive about the antiquity and virtue of the families they married into than about their jointures and would never ally with any spurious issue, though of Princely blood, nor any line that had ever been tainted with a mechanic's daughter, or servant maid. They abhorred Smithfield bargains,[214] or burying a blooming young Crackenthorpe in the arms of an old dotard for the sake of his gold, but every marriage was so adapted, as probably to propagate the race, and, as a decayed Crackenthorpe has been courted by several Toms of ten thousand, so a Crackenthorpe with thirty thousand pounds has countenanced many a decaying family who could prove themselves little inferior at birth, education, plain-dealing, and popularity. The heads of the house, who were successively the pride of the county, always avoided being in commission,[215] and yet were always applied to in the greatest

[213] debt-collector

[214] marriages of convenience for money

[215] in public service

differences. They were willing to be arbitrators, to speak peace amongst their neighbours, without putting them to the charge of a warrant – for justiceship then began to be a trade, and his worship went snacks[216] with his clerk; neither did they treat away their estates to be chose Members of Parliament and hearty in their votes, and if any pitiful upstart, denominated by a monosyllable, had the assurance to oppose him, the appearance of their old Senator in the field of election immediately awed the few deserters from his interest, and the shout was unanimous, 'a Crackenthorpe, a Crackenthorpe!'

Then rivers were made navigable, taxes easy, the lightest grievance was redressed, and the greatest advantages obtained. For their representative was true to his trust, and preferred a benefit to his freeholders before a place to himself. By living altogether in the country, except when the service of it summoned him to the Senate, he avoided even the ridiculous vanities of the town, gay equipages, expensive clothes, and the extravagant subscriptions to the operas, where the syrens charms have seduced many a young heir. Then follows gaming, and other monstrous excursions. The trees are cut down, the plate melted, the house unfurnished, the next term forecloses the equity of redemption, and the following gazette tells you before what master the estate is to be sold. Instead of such courses, the Crackenthorpes were for extending their estates, and laying up portions for the younger children, not by sordid frugality, or extorting from their tenants, but from a regular, prudent, and wise method of living: in short, the Crackenthorpe's were what every true English family ought to be, and what in this age, very few are.

To give my reader now a description of my person seems to be an odd undertaking. All people are in some-measure touched with self-conceit, partial to great defects, and too opinionated of small beauties, though when it rises to gross affectation, it gives subject for ridicule. Did not some women think themselves genteel, we should seldom meet a trapes;[217] others, that they are graceful, or fat women would never dance minuets; nay, even crooked people that their deformity becomes them, or they would not wear brocade silks with a great gold flower spreading upon the very hump. Laughing at no jest, supposes white teeth; always taking snuff, a fine hand; ears should be pretty that endure holes bored through them, and a shape fine that's squeezed up in a straight pair of stays. Therefore as no person can truly define themselves, I shall only tell the town what sort of a woman I'd have them imagine me to be.

To embellish the mind rather than the body, must gain general esteem,

216 equal shares

217 a slut

though to appear decent in habit, shows respect to the persons we visit; though a woman of fifteen may be a pretty plaything, yet a woman must be thirty before she has a true management of her house, by that time she has had little experience, is at the zenith of her understanding and her little vanities and affectations contemptibly thrown aside. She then chooses a husband with judgment, manages him with prudence, and charms him more with her conversation than with her person; a middle-aged, middle-sized brown woman that's neither awkward nor coquettish, foppish nor fanatical, but dresses herself like a gentlewoman, moderately in the mode, with any easy, affable disposition, can never want admirers from such as every lady would choose, who desires to be entirely happy. The Crackenthorpes were never for marrying children together that they mightn't part beds before they came to years of understanding. They were eminent for constancy in marriages, as well as an entire friendship, throughout the several branches of the family; and, as they were never reigning beauties, so neither the men nor the women, had ever the least deformity in mind nor body.

*

On Sunday next, Mrs Crackenthorpe's man Francis begins to visit the churches of the city and suburbs, and whatever clergymen he finds guilty of spiritual lingeridge, that is taking a nap, or smoking a pipe in the vestry all prayer time, and then mount the pulpit, if they do not reform so shameful an enormity by the Sunday following, they must then expect to find their names in Mrs Crackenthorpe's black-list.

*

Mr Tiresome, the Jacobite[218] bookkeeper near Bartl'mew-Lane, who was formerly mentioned by *The Observator* for remitting money to St Germains,[219] is desired not to be so very coxcombical (which is his own word) at Jacob's Coffee House. Plays are not damned, though he cries them down, books never the sillier for his conceited banter about them, nor do accounts come even, though he cast them up; he is likewise admonished not to drink the Pretender's[220] health again, by the name of King James the Third, as he did in public, and to let his neighbour's servants alone, both male and female.

218 Jacobites were the supporters of the deposed James II (1633–1701) and his descendants – James, a Catholic, had been overthrown in the Glorious Revolution of 1688, and had fled to France.

219 the Jacobite court in Paris

220 James II's son, James Edward Stuart (later known as the Old Pretender).

FRIDAY OCTOBER 14 TO MONDAY OCTOBER 17 *Number 44*

By three letters at once, Mrs Crackenthorpe is desired to admonish the little hypocrite near Somerset House, who pretends to more devotion than her neighbours, not to be peeping, hearkening, whispering and breeding animosities among them, nor publicly to reprimand her seal-cutting husband for loving his bottle, which she hugs so in private herself.

*

My Lady Butterfield at Nightingale Hall, near Mob's-Hole at Wanstead, who has so often challenged her own sex to ride a horse, leap a horse, run a foot, or hollow, having lately buried her husband, and being apprehensive that this winter may prove as sharp as the last, does now challenge any man twenty years younger, but not a day older, to be her bed-fellow in an honourable way. Note, that this is at her own request.

MONDAY OCTOBER 17 TO WEDNESDAY OCTOBER 19 *Number 45*

There are a sort of whimsical people in the world called poets, whose delight, whose transports, nay, generally speaking, whose livelihoods proceed from satire and invective from maliciously observing the little failings of the rest of mankind, and from an unhappy genius, turned to scandal, improving them into the grossest ridicule; some do it in comedy, others by paraphrastical translations, some by downright libel, and others more by panegyric. Lady Fanciful, who had the vanity to think herself exposed in the *Memoirs from the New Atalantis*,[221] started the question, What kind of creatures are these Poets? They must be unparalleled in religion, loyalty, chastity, sobriety, all moral virtues, and correct qualifications as nice dress and address, a just and proper decorum, in different companies and conversations, but above all, in prompt payment. That they seem to take an assured freedom in lashing not only the imagined

221 a scandalous *roman à clef* by Delarivier Manley herself

vices of the town, but the pretty, pleasing, harmless affectations of our sex, which divert ourselves, and give offence to nobody.

Colonel Florid, who so judiciously penetrates into mankind, and with so much modest ease and musical eloquence, delineates not only particular persons, but any sect of people, that he bewitches our attention, entered upon the subject. His notion of poets was that they are a chimerical tribe, but a few degrees removed from madmen, who ought not be trusted with themselves, but like heedless, rambling schoolboys, have everything provided for them, their bounds set them, and their pocket-money paid them every day. They have no more concern about their passing through the world than if they were not even in it, yet have a more refined taste of dress, equipage, buildings, furniture, and entertainments than all the world besides. They have clothes regardless at what price they buy them, and, as regardless of discharging it, ride in great men's chariots, are at great men's seats, and as their wit and humour are the spirit of the table, think the greatest men are obliged to them for their company. Stepping out of the room to give some directions, I happened to hear Mrs Loveless, my intimate acquaintance, and as I thought my friend, fleeringly cry, 'Why, what is Crackenthorpe but a poetess?' The company was alarmed at the aspersion, and Mrs Wiseman wondered how a serious, reforming paper, though larded with jests, epigrams, and pleasant tales, could bring me under that denomination; but when I found the dispute growing high, I bolted smilingly into the room, and told them supper was just ready.

The colonel proceeded that poets having a finer thread of understanding, a quicker apprehension, and more noble ideas of things than the generality, they are intoxicated with sublime conceptions, fancy their bodies, where their imaginations soar, and in the heat of their poetical flights, discover the lunatic in all his shapes and postures. A poem well-finished is to them beyond settling a nice Act of Parliament, they have no plots but in plays, and seldom any there, and a comedy once brought to a full third night, is to them coming to a vast estate. They have no notion of honour but in the hero of a tragedy, friendship but for those who lend them money, sobriety after a hard debauch, nor regularity either in thought, deed, time, behaviour or habitation; therefore, when their patrons bestow preferments upon them, knowing their disposition for business, they generally take care they shall be sinecures.[222] 'And are these the creatures,' says Lady Fanciful, 'that set up for observators, that won't let one be a little particular in public places to be taken notice of, but one's character is in the new comedy, which perhaps is so beastly a thing one is not able to sit it out.' But Mrs Tire-quill, who has the

[222] jobs entailing no work

indisposition of scribbling herself, would not allow poets to be so contemptibly treated, she said they were rather Demi-Gods than men, that their thoughts were Supernatural, and, though their mortal clay over-animated for so small a tenement obliged them sometimes to terrestrial confabulation, yet they more frequently conversed with Deities; Jupiter gave them majestic notions, Mars showed them a specimen of war, Venus told them pretty love-tales, and they had rather be inebriated with Bacchus in imagination, than be really so with the most distinguished animal below the spheres. That such persons, whose writings make mortals as immortal as themselves, ought not to grovel about worldly cares, nor subject their fancies, which are always up on the wing, to any manner of constraint. That she thought conversing with an author, and perusing his works, before they were blown upon by the ungrateful world, was, next to happy conceptions of her own, the greatest felicity on earth.

Mrs Tire-quill was so zealous for the reputation of the here-and-thereian-tribe, and grew so inspired on the subject, that she would have immediately talked in verse, had not Colonel Florid turned the discourse upon a sort of miserable creatures called Would-be-Poets. Wretches! That are in business, tradesmen, petty-foggers, and notary publics, that might plod on in their thoughtless vocation, grow rich, keep coaches, and never think of the next world, yet fancying they have a genius, leave their prosperous knavery to write songs, madrigals, and damned plays, till they starve indeed, being shunned by their own tribe, and laughed at by the Kit-Kat Club.[223] These are an incorrigible crew, who, though they are punished with poverty and the utmost contempt, yet like branded malefactors who return to their old courses, they still run on in their convulsive strains, and endeavour to bring forth without conception. Upon the whole, 'twas agreed that poets were an unaccountable race, that they built castles in the air, and though they gave birth to a lady called fortune, could never make her their friend; for though they may every hour have a project to advance them in the world, yet, from a fluency of thought, things crowd so fast upon them, that they drive out one another. Sanguine dispositions can settle to nothing; whereas more sedate, considerate, and politic persons, embrace the first probable opportunity, proceed upon mature deliberation, and by a constant assiduity secure their happiness.

Lady Drivel, for we must suppose one fool in the company, wondered how poets could have such odd fancies and out-of-the-way sayings; were she to write a play, she was sure she should make horrid stuff in it, and, of all of the plays she ever saw, none frightened her so much as

223 a literary club

Macbeth, nor made her laugh so much as the *Trip to the Jubilee*,[224] but when her ladyship began to prate, the company dispersed.

Mrs Crackenthorpe has received intelligence from several people that there is a scandalous fellow about town, that makes it his business to impose on people by extorting money from them, under the pretence of producing sham letters, etc. – that unless they deposit such sums of money as he villainously demands, they shall be exposed in this paper. This is to give notice that she is no way directly or indirectly privy to or concerned in those his rascally and knavish impositions, and that she desires all persons to whom he shall hereafter endeavour to impose on to apprehend him, and, upon carrying him before a magistrate and sending immediate notice thereof to the publisher of this paper, distinguished in the superscription with care and speed, he shall be confronted and secured, she being sensible of the prejudice she has, and may hereafter receive upon these his clandestine and unjust proceedings, and desires no one to suffer themselves to be imposed on by so notorious an impostor, she being ashamed of so insufferable a practice, knowing it to be an imposition on the public, which was never the design of this paper, it being only to expose vice and folly, and to commend justice and honesty, which last, 'tis hoped she has always done, and declares she will.

Note: it is desired anyone that has been so abused, to discover the person to whom they have paid any money on the aforesaid account, and he shall be prosecuted as the law directs, without any charge to them.

*

Complaints having been made to Mrs Crackenthorpe, that a certain dear joy of the county of Tiperara in Ireland, who mightily displayed himself this season at the Bath, and wanting wit to entertain in company, grew very frolicsome, thinks he may take the same liberty with other women as with his wife, whom he every day most matrimonially abuses, foolishly offered his snuff-box to all the ladies round, which, when they opened a snake bounced out, and by the fright of it one lady was in danger of miscarrying, another's life is now actually despaired of. Teague, and several other such rattling sparks, who are fond of venemous creatures, and think it comical to do people a prejudice, are hereby admonished to lay aside those juvenile jokes, since they discover ignorance and ill-breeding, and are not only of pernicious but fatal consequence.

224 George Farquhar's comedy, *The Constant Couple; or, a Trip to the Jubilee* (1699)

WEDNESDAY OCTOBER 19 TO FRIDAY 21 *Number 46*

otwithstanding the care, pains and trouble I have taken to admonish fools, fops and knaves, yet the following account will sufficiently prove that my repeated endeavours have not yet had the desired effect, it having indeed created in me such an abhorrence for the whole race of man that I do not know when I shall be reconciled to them. Robbers on the highway, house-breakers, coiners,[225] etc. are much, I think, the honester men than the actors of such a tragical and abominable scene, which, no doubt, will create the like indignation in most of my sex. The fact is as follows:

The beauteous Almeria, who was so indisposed at the Bath, that to the heart-breaking of a thousand prostrate swains, her life was in danger. Being desirous of returning home, a physician attended her, and, at the lady's request, they went by Oxford, where the physician was taken so ill himself he was forced to remain at the university. The care of Almeria, who still grew weaker, gave him great disquiet, and he could then find no better way than to entrust her with a passenger in the coach, one of our modern Counts, who seemed to be a gentleman, and had his valet with him. The Count eagerly embraced his charge, seemed concerned for her illness, and assured the doctor what service he would do her, and how joyful he should be at the recovery of so fine a creature. When they had drove some miles out of town, and it growing dark, he began to toy with her, squeezed her hand, and ravished a kiss from her. This fright was such an addition to her malady that Almeria was dying upon the spot; nor did the Count stop here for, resolving to satiate his brutal appetite, he attacks her boisterously, the valet assisting him in the rape.

The distressed, expiring nymph, finding no house, no person near to relieve her extremity, and that prayers, tears and swoonings had proved ineffectual, she plucked up a little spirit, told him his rough behaviour had so surprised her that she knew not what she said, but if he would speak tenderly to her and use some soft expressions, perhaps she might be prevailed upon, and as she had no aversion to his person, she knew not what influence his words might have over her. The scene was then changed to gentle touches, amorous sighs, and scrapes of 'cease cruel tyrannising,' and 'O! Nymph of Race divine,' till Almeria protested she was in such a disorder that nothing but a little air could keep life in her, after which she promised him compliance. She lighted, and in the dark ran into a deep pool and rushed through a hedge, by which her hands

[225] coin-clipping (i.e. cutting off small pieces of coin for melting down) was a serious offence.

and face were most lamentably torn, and then sat trembling upon the grass. The Count not finding her return, grew outrageous and searching for her to no purpose he bribed the coachman to secrecy and bid him drive geeho-like to the next village, where each of them would get a link,[226] and the Count swore louder than at losing a fifty pound main that if he found her he'd force her to his inclinations, and then stab her.

Almeria overheard all, and being naturally desirous to preserve the few expected remains of life, made back again towards Oxford. The poor lady tottering on by tedious marches, short restings, pantings and strugglings for breath, at last reached the place of refuge. But whether providence, which brought her thither, more than natural strength, has still preserved her alive, intelligence is not yet known.

Almeria's misfortune had such an effect on the whole drawing-room that we had a profound silence. Betty Frisk who hurries to me with every story she hears, bolted in with a quarrel at St Martins Church, between Mrs Haughty and Mrs Flounce. Mrs Haughty it seems, had made a most flaming suit of clothes, and being longer adjusting herself that day than ordinary, Mrs Flounce was come before her and had taken her seat, which was the upper end of the pew. Haughty sails in and resolving to assert herself at that time, cries, 'Madam! This is my place, if you please to move lower you'll sit just as easy, and hear as well.' 'Madam,' replies Flounce, 'I shall keep this place till sermon's over, and then 'tis at your service again.' 'I must tell you Madam,' says Haughty, 'you are rude!' 'Civility, Madam,' answers Flounce, 'is thrown away on some people.' 'Madam,' cries Haughty, 'you are an impudent slut.' 'You are a vain, silly creature,' says t'other. 'Nay, Madam,' replies Haughty, 'if you give me ill language . . .' And so shoves her away with most masculine fury and squats down in her place. Mrs Flounce's devotion was quite spoiled for that day. She sat when she should have stood, and kneeled when she should have sat; her meditations were revenge, and she swelled as much with envy at Haughty's appearance as the affront she had received from her.

But as invention is seldom wanting to a woman, she found a pair of scissors in her pocket, and took every little opportunity of snipping Mrs Haughty's clothes, so that, by the time the church was done, the tail of her new gown was cut all to pieces. Haughty bridles through the aisle, with her fan spread and her streamers out,[227] but instead of peoples admiring her, she found everybody was upon the grin. When she came into the church-yard, the boys surrounded her. At last perceiving what had happened, and spying Mrs Flounce, she flew at her with all the fury of an incensed turkey-cock; 'Ay!' says she, 'you are

226 torch 227 ribbons

the Jade that have done me this piece of service, not only to spoil my clothes, but make me ridiculous . . .' Slap, slap, slap went the fan in her face. Flounce returned the blows. The congregation soon parted them, but expressions was not wanting on either side, and 'tis said their husbands are now so very foolish as to make a tawdry suit a law suit.

*

The two affected sisters, who were lately expelled from Oxford, for caballing[228] so much with the young students, have now opened a new tavern here, furnished with a variety of square tables, broken backed chairs, and other old goods, with a deaf-and-dumb drawer,[229] are desired not to carry on their frolics amongst the templers,[230] to prevent which, Mrs Crackenthorpe has ordered her man Francis, who has lately learned to drink claret, and now wears his own clothes, to frisk in there very often for his half pint, observe what enormities are practised, and prove an honest informer by not taking bribes to conceal them.

*

The enthusiastic lady, who, when Covent Garden bell rang, was in such a hurry for prayers that she snatched up a case knife, instead of her fan, and perceived not her error till she came into the pew, is desired henceforward not to be so over zealous, since she has provoked abundance of indecent tittering by so ridiculous a mistake.

*

The two old maids at Highgate, who call themselves Nuns because the men never visit them, and very rarely the women, are desired not to assume that appellation till they have relinquished all carnal thoughts, looking wishfully at every young fellow they see, and show a little more piety than to stalk into church when prayers are half done.

228 intriguing

229 boy who works the pumps in a tavern.

230 lawyers

FRIDAY OCTOBER 21 TO MONDAY OCTOBER 24 *Number* 47

Some ladies were of the opinion that this paper would gain me enemies, instead of which, since I published an account of my person and my family, lovers crowd in upon me like petitioning attorneys to be clerk of a hall: the La Fools of France, the Renegadoes of Spain, the Van Butterboxes of Holland, the O'Devillies of Ireland, the Ap Shinkins of Wales, and the Tre Loobies of Cornwall. But as my marriage is not of consequence to all Europe, I excused myself to foreign pretenders in as complaisant terms as, 'tis to be supposed, they addressed me, thinking an alliance greater with one of my own nation. The Tatter-demallions, a very ancient and numerous family, a branch of it being to be found in almost every county, perceiving that the Crackenthorpes valued themselves more upon birth than fortune, have hurried to me in great numbers, and Sir Threadbare Gentry of that line, by the mother's side, who every day walks the park from twelve to three. Duke Humphrey, dining later than the commonality, with a twisted perriwig a little upon the sandy,[231] an Oliverian black coat, with a few nutmeg buttons, mourning for the rest, a pair of stockings with here and there a stitch fallen, and something like a neckcloth, would take no denial but telling him, though I had a particular regard for the Gentrys, my old lady Gentry and my mother having the same midwife, yet my circumstances were not sufficient to raise a family, and as the pride of the Crackenthorpes was ever too great to do themselves a wilful prejudice, he walked off to petition for a pension.

One of almost every class has done me the honour of a visit on that score, which still gives me a further penetration into mankind, for courtship does certainly discover people's sense and education more than any other undertaking, though their tempers are often fatally concealed till after consummation. Some address a lady so sheepishly, and with so much fear and trembling, that she's forced to speak first; others, with so much assurance, pressing our consent at first sight, that a modest woman's confounded at the very question; some after so romantic a manner that they provoke our laughter, and others so vainly that they seem rather making love to themselves. As some people's way of courtship too gives us the spleen, I could not forbear being touched at Sir John Brute's behaviour, it proving to me the degeneracy of country gentlemen. He brought his hawk and his dogs into the drawing-room, saluted me with a hiccup, and told me he had been drinking six quarts to

231 sandy-coloured

my health at 'the Devil', that if I'd marry Brute of Brute Hall, I should have the coach when the horses did not go to plough, and if his sports and boon companions would give him time, perhaps he might get an heir to his estate. Then called for some beer, broke the glass, and reeled out again. Such a husband must try a woman's virtue, as well as patience; the ends of matrimony are no wise answered there, and she that associates with a sapless, sottish, unlicked squire, brings herself under a thousand inquietudes and, in a manner, degenerates from her species.

He was succeeded by Sir Jasper Fidget, one of those loving animals that pat and paw their wives, call them Puddy and Bunny and Tuffy, and play at Tag and Creep Mouse, with the pretty cant of 'Liva Hubby, one buss,[232] Bun do —— 'Ou be cross tit now, dood mind beat'ee and tump'ee sadly,' always slopping, and so full of childish tricks before company that they become a jest to the whole town, withal so free from jealousy, that should the husband discover a man in private with his wife, he would not for the world enter the room for fear of interrupting their business. The Fidgets, I remember, were a Huntingdon-shire family, the women were ever sprightly, witty, apprehensive lasses, but the men have been always fools, as it often happens in other families. I told Sir Jasper we should make a more unsuitable couple in understanding than Sir Dapper and my Lady Maypole do in size, who, when he hangs about her neck to kiss her, looks like a sweetbread upon a breast of veal, that my notions of love were platonic, I hated the silly toying and nauseous cooing of new married people, and, as with all my scribbling, I abominated the vulgar character of wearing the breeches, so I would choose a man that is fit to support the weakness and correct the frailties of my sex, superior in sense, and equal in disposition.

I was next attacked by a Lancashire gentleman, a man of learning, good manners, maturity and estate, his person pleased me, his addresses seemed so sincere, genteel and unaffected, and his conversation so agreeable that I immediately received an impression from him, admitted him at all seasons, and denied myself to all other pretenders. Our sentiments on most subjects were the same, nay, our appetites jumped at table, every trifle concurred to our mutual satisfaction, and I now concluded myself disposed of, till by an unlucky question, which knocked all on the head, I found him to be a Roman Catholic.[233] The surprise I was in gave him no small confusion and though he assured me he would always avoid those disputes and I knew myself proof to the most insinuating arguments or vigorous attacks, yet as in marriage a thought is to be had beyond our immediate selves, that is, our progeny, I

232 kiss

233 English Catholics were associated with the Jacobite cause at this time.

was forced to dismiss him with all the reluctancy imaginable, having observed in various families that where the parents have different religions such feuds arise about them that the children have often none.

This disappointment made me almost resolve upon dying a maid but, the matter getting air, I had the multitude again. A courtier passed often by the door and peeped up at the windows, but places are precarious, there must be some removes to give everybody a turn of preferment. A clergyman bowed to me out of the pulpit, but their progeny are but indifferently provided for, since parsons, who have the smallest livings, are generally blessed with the most children. A knight merchant sent a message to me, but could not prove himself a gentleman, and a Portuguese Jew had the assurance to write to me, but I smelled his letter at the door and ordered it not to be received. But amongst all my lovers I have had no beaux, they are sort of languid creatures between both sexes that love their ease and the opera, and their wit is turned only to make a jest of so sacred an ordinance. Upon the whole, an ingenious lawyer, a man in vogue, and business, who will not only get an estate, but knows how to preserve it, whose profession is honourable, and whose parts must be acute, is the person I would choose to make an alliance with.

*

On Saturday next Mrs Crackenthorpe intends to dine in the city, to make a friendly accommodation of all differences between her and several wealthy persons there who have fancied themselves aspersed in this paper; but that people should say characters are too plain when they are continually enquiring 'Who's meant by this lady and t'other gentleman,' seems to her a strange contradiction. She likewise informs a certain well-bred gentleman, who swallows too the ridiculous report of the author's being a man and, bouncing lately into a coffee-house, cried, 'Well, what does this scandalous rogue, this impudent scoundrel say?' with worse phrases not fit to be told again to a woman, that he never met with any such expressions in her writings.

MONDAY OCTOBER 24 TO WEDNESDAY OCTOBER 26 *Number 48*

People that set up to correct others ought to be faultless themselves, but now I must acquaint the world with a very great failing of my own.

I find too much good nature shown to those in subjection to us is more prejudicial to our interest than too much severity: that servants who are naturally ungrateful ought to be used rather like slaves, since obligations heaped on them not only make them careless of their business, but are returned like the perishing snake that, reviving by the heat of the fire, flew at the countryman that preserved it. I thought myself so happy in my man Francis that I made him rather my companion than my servant, he was my amanuensis,[234] my papers lay open to him, I allowed him money to discover enormities and, that he might be more capable of serving me in that manner, upon his sobriety, sincerity and good behaviour, I lately put him out of a livery. No sooner was he got into light-coloured drugget, with long pockets and black tabby facings to his sleeves, but when I sent him with Howd'yees to several ladies, he'd sit at the ale-house and pay a porter to go. 'Twas now no longer plain Francis, but when any of his comrades enquired for him – 'Is Mr Powder-Monkey at home?' He had a secondhand watch, a snuff box with two holes, and was steward of a three penny club,[235] and yesterday he happened to drop the following letter:

> Dear Sir,
> At seven this evening, Mr Trott, Mr Tea-kettle, and Mr Currycomb, with several other of his grace's gentlemen, are to have a bowl of punch at the cellar in Pall Mall. Mr Corkscrew and my Lord Squander's Butler will bring a dozen of French wine, and we hope to be very jocular, the honour of your good company is what we are all ambitious of, and particularly,
>
> Yours at all hours,
> Benjamin Burdash.
>
> The expense will be a trifle, perhaps three shillings a man, and my Lord's Black[236] has promised to engage us in Italian song.

The maids now may do all the work themselves, nothing less than Mr Francis can prevail with him to lay the cloth, and he takes the word 'Sir'

234 copying secretary
235 at table, each diner would pay 3d.
236 a Moorish servant

upon him from market people with as good a grace as if he were a man of five hundred a year. He thinks himself too good to wait at the table, carrying *Flambeaux*[237] is so like a skip-kennel,[238] and to be seen behind a coach is the greatest mortification to him imaginable. From the best of servants in a livery, he is now good for nothing. Plain clothes have intoxicated him. He associates with gentlemen, talks big, frequents the hazard table, and hopes to ride in his own chariot as well as several others that have wore liveries before him. Were these the sum of his misfortunes, which he reckons felicities, I should hope they were only a spurt of vanity from this change of garb, but another pleasing fate has tantalized him, by which I must conclude him irrecoverably lost.

Some ladies have thought him a pretty fellow, he that's no favour with the fair sex must be a happy man, while he continues so. My Lady Dandler plays at picquet[239] with him, Mrs Lackit carries him into her very bed-chamber, Mrs Lovejoy suffers him at her public drawing-room, and last week my Lady Brazen was seen flaunting with him in her chariot. He's at present in vogue with the women, as new beauties are for a time the toast of the men, and has so many messages, visits and assignations, that when a coach stops at the door I'm in a dispute whether 'tis to me or my man Francis. But as ladies of that character are very fickle in their *amours*, the salaries they give are but short of duration, serve only to initiate young fellows into all manner of debaucheries, and 'tis observed that the most noted rakes, gamesters and libertines of the age were originally great men's servants.

This subject occasioned my Lady Maxim to make some reflections on that ungovernable passion, love. And as beauty is not confined to quality, nay, some ill-natured critics say that great people have the least share of it, an agreeable face often deludes us into a thousand inconveniences and disgraces. A marriage ill-suited affects a whole family. How would the Crackenthorpes look to have a relation marry a fiddler, a barber or a tailor, which not only debases their blood, but brings them into a depending sordid kindred, which the wife, if she expects good usage from her mechanic, must doubly oblige though she's ashamed to own them? When a brother or sister should marry suitable to themselves, what transports appear in every face when the nuptials shall be celebrated with unusual pomp and grandeur, the bride dazzled in her jewels, relations adorned suitable to the occasion, when birth, education, sense and wit shall throughout the room; though the unfortunate of the family may, by her mien and air, show from what

237 In those days of no streetlighting, servants carried torches (*flambeaux*) to guide people after dark.

238 lackey

239 a card game

root she sprang, yet how out of countenance she must be for her pitiful husband, whom they all treat with a cold civility, place him below everybody, stare at him when he speaks without returning an answer, and can scarce endure him but out of respect to his wife. Besides, the honeymoon once over, she disputes him for a wretch, and he that has no notion of birth, values her never the more for her extraction.

The consequences of a mean passion are not to be expressed. The different reception a woman meets within company in her regular airs and after she has played the fool, shows that even acquaintance, who have no affinity, whose business is superficial, a good appearance, and general chit-chat, looks upon an intimate with a disdainful eye, when by a *Je ne Scay-Quoy*,[240] she shall degrade herself from velvet suits, the opera, the darling quality pleasure of railing at citizens, and my Lady Duchess's great suppers, that enter at six in the morning. From bespeaking plays, from swelling at India houses[241] (though now and then pocketing a fan by mistake) from doing everything that is careless, unaccountable, scornful and quality-like to fatigue herself with the management of a family, speaking to dirty servants, visiting creatures that can talk of nothing but the price of bread, and grovelling through the world . . . But as to those ladies who are so fond of Francis, my pen drops.

*

Mrs Tawny *alias* Tawdry, is desired not be so fantastically whimsical in her dress, and if she does not know, let her now remember she is told, nothing is more disagreeable and ridiculous than to see a woman of her years affect the gay, youthful airs of their daughters. And, by the by, she is reminded that if she will be so preposterously gaudy and flaunting, that if there was little more economy observed in her dress, she would not be altogether the subject of so much laughter.

*

The Duke Drab-DeBurgh, and the Marquis de Tangib in Fleet Street, who gave themselves such quality airs, and hate all their relations because they have behaved themselves so foolishly that they are despised by them, are desired, though they have entered into bonds to be each other's heir, not to be so continually arm-in-arm, since 'tis a malicious world, and the women laugh at them to a strange degree.

240 je ne sais quoi (I know not what)

241 tea shops

WEDNESDAY OCTOBER 26 TO FRIDAY OCTOBER 28 *Number 49*

Nothing can be so unfortunate to an agreeable young lady as want of decorum, since, as her beauty raises envy of the world, they pursue it by a constant prying into her conduct. The character of a coquet is sufficient to allay the passion which a fine face has kindled, and ladies are as earnest in railing at those that have more beauty than themselves, as the men are in hating those that have more wit than themselves. I would advise all the critics of fashion to turn their optics within themselves, before their spleen degrades other people, and that young ladies, though it may be thought a hard doctrine, should value themselves more upon good qualities, than good features.

*

Mr Swarthy near Aldermanbury, the heir and executor of Mr Lovebooby, deceased, who in dirty weather walks the streets with brown paper pinned to his white silk stockings, is desired not to sing *Fair Dorinda* so loud in Swan's Coffee-house at high-change time[242] that people are disturbed from their business.

*

The Bonny-Scot, the button-seller's wife, that pretends to hate all men as much as she does her husband, and declares she would not be put into the Tatler for five hundred pounds, is desired not to dance hornpipes aboard 'The Folly' with her fat acquaintance near St Clements, nor revel three or four nights together with Sea Captains, lest her character should be drawn at large.

FRIDAY OCTOBER 28 TO MONDAY OCTOBER 31 *Number 50*

Signior Pentilo, the libertine of the town, the other day fell into an argument concerning love and honour, for having a platonic wife, as he said, that valued not his corporal presence. He would maintain that, notwithstanding his liberties abroad among other women, he was of the best of husbands,

242 the busiest time

for he was always complaisant to her before company, and never troublesome to her when in private. And though stranger women might share the best of his personal performances, the better part of him, to wit, his heart, he had entirely reserved for his wife, as that which he thought most acceptable to her. Besides having been bred abroad in politer countries, he had learned how to distinguish nicely between the action and the intention, and so preserve his honour and his conscience entire, by a mental reservation, for as his affections were not alienated from his spouse, he thought himself secure and, as for his love, that was of such a diffusive nature that a man might love every woman in the world with an ardent passion and yet not love any single one of the whole with less desire.

These kind of riddles puzzled all the company, and everybody looked upon one another to see who should break the silence first, when my Lady Coquet bridled and endeavoured to suppress her choler, by bursting open her laces, sinking her throbbing breasts, and hauling off her sweaty gloves, but to no purpose, for the flesh was powerful but the spirit too weak. 'You may be ashamed,' says she, 'Mr Pentilo, to speak thus prophanely against the rites of the marriage-bed, as if you had a mind to bring them into disuse, and then palm the pretence upon your wife, because she's honest. But she's a woman, though she may be virtuous, and no more a platonic than I am, 'tis base in you to use us married women at this rate; and then lay the blame at our doors. We are too modest or too impudent, too ill-natured or too good to keep you at home. For shame,' continued she, 'Mr Pent'lo, leave off this discourse for the future, but this is the education, these the arguments you learn in Italy and at Rome, and though they make you not Jesuits in religion, they make you so in politics, to deceive your poor believing wife, or else somebody's innocent daughter.'

'Madam,' answered the libertine, very gravely, 'your Ladyship ought to speak for nobody but yourself, for your sex is a perfect medley of varieties, and he that ties himself only to one might as well attempt to live on partridge, for there is no two that can be said to be the same. You differ in so many degrees of perfections that he only knows most that knows most of you.' The ladies began to be ruffled cruelly at the continuance of this discourse, when I interrupted Mr Pentilo with the decorums of my drawing-room, which he promised not to offend against for the future, upon permission I would let him repeat the lines he made this morning upon the subjects we have been talking:

The Libertine to his Platonic Wife:
When once in bed we gently talked and played,
I well remember beauteous Cloris said
Her noble passion soared a sphere above,
The gross and brutish part of vulgar Love.

Then since my dear, said I, you're so refined,
And love affects nought but your virtuous mind,
Since you alone possess Leander's heart,
Grudge not to other nymphs, the ignobler part.

Though I've been catched in wanton Celia's arms,
And conquered by Belinda's flattering charms,
When Liberty has led astray your swain,
'Twas love of you that called him back again,
Then you, my dear, may still with justice boast,
Where e're I wander, you I love the most.

MONDAY OCTOBER 31 TO WEDNESDAY NOVEMBER 2 *Number 51*

Love has so surprising a force that the effects of no other passion can equal it. The desire of life in the fearful never made any so solicitous for themselves, as love has obliged the lover to be for others, the thoughts of glory or ambition never fired the soul with greater courage and resolution than has been shown by such who have acknowledged the power of this deity. The empire of the fair is universal, it extends as far as the remotest regions of light, and even infernal spirits submit to the Tyranny of a passion, which in some measure allies them to superior beings.

Infernal powers, uneasy at the day,
Gladly the smiling God of Love obey,
When he appears, the furies calmer grow;
Lay by their whips, and a short pity know;
The king of spectres is himself afraid,
Dreading the anger of a tender maid,
View but how close, he hugs the trembling fair,
How kind he looks, with what submissive air;

With joys and fears, alternately he strives,
As o'er Sicilian plains his chariot drives,
Thence to Hell's palace he directly flies,
Proud of his rape, and happier in his prize,
Than Jove, his brother, in the Sapphire skies.

. . . The lady who sent the letter . . . has a great deal of justice on her side, nothing can be more ridiculous than to see Belinda strip herself at play,[243] and show beauties in hope of profit, which she never would expose for her pleasure. 'Tis equally surprising to find my Lady Haughty borrow money off her footman whilst she employs herself in this unaccountable recreation. The diamond ring, pearl necklace and gold watch, the first presents of her spouse, fly away upon this occasion, and the rich merchant's lady retires as empty from a bank at Basset or a game at Picquet, to the city, as her predecessors of venerable memory came from Wales or Yorkshire to that famous Metropolis. This lady is as peevish upon losing, as a sick monkey, the other vents as many curses and imprecations as her cousin, a Colonel in the Guards.

Bellamira, indeed, is more easy. She knows a ready way to repair her losses, her person pays for the extravagance of this honour, and whatever she loses to this General and that man of quality, she pays it exactly in her own coin.[244] The good man meanwhile has a fine time of it and if his lady does a piece of service to my Lord Bellair, Colonel Generous, or Sir William Townly, be sure they return the civility to the husband, and he has the fate, of all other bubbles, to sit at the upper end of the table, have his health drank, and be adored like the rising sun, whilst he alone pays the charge of the entertainment. But if he expects the same good breeding at home he meets with abroad, he's mightily mistaken. The dear partner of his bed, whether she loses her money or her honour, is always in the same humour, and most certainly treats her spouse she has injured with ill-nature, brawlings and contempt. But I'll spare their blushes, and proceed no further on a subject that has already been touched as far as it concerns the men, where the ladies, at the expense of another sex, may see the picture of this vice in all its disagreeable branches.

*

Mrs Crackenthorpe resenting the affront, offered to her by some rude citizens, altogether unacquainted with her person, gives notice that she has resigned her pretentions of writing *The Female Tatler* to a society of modest ladies, who in their turns will oblige the public with

243 to lose at cards   244 tit for tat

what ever they shall meet with that will be diverting, innocent, or instructive.[245]

[END OF MRS CRACKENTHORPE'S TATLER]

[245] If Mrs Manley was the first Mrs Crackenthorpe, a note which appears in Narcissus Luttrell's *A Brief Relation of State Affairs* could explain her sudden resignation: 'Today the printer and publisher of the *New Atalantis* were examined touching the author, Mrs Manley; they were discharged, but she remains in custody.'

PART TWO

The Female Tatler

Written by a Society of Ladies

FRIDAY NOVEMBER 4 TO MONDAY NOVEMBER 7 *Number 53*

Emilia's Day

he conversation I met with last night was very disagreeable till interrupted by a discourse we fell into concerning a marriage of life, wherein Eudoxa railed against that unhappy state, as she called it, that made women only slaves to that tyrant, man. I opposed her with that little reason I was mistress of, and asserted, that it was in the power of women to rule if they had a mind, and that they needed not be subject to the slavery of men's arbitrary wills, if they were not wanting to themselves. This occasioned much mirth among the company at first and my adversary plum'd herself extraordinary upon my bold assertion, and asked me with a disdainful air, 'Emilia,' says she, 'I warrant when you are married you design to fight for the breeches.' 'Not at all my dear Eudoxa,' said I, 'so far from contending would I be that he should never know I had the spirit of my Mother Eve in me, for I much admire at the folly, or rather want of conduct, in the young ladies of this age, who can dissemble their passions for years together to get a husband, and yet cannot baulk themselves in a minute afterwards to get the entire masterhead over him.' The company laughed heavily at my extravagance till I begged leave of them to proceed. 'Ladies,' continued I, 'I am glad my argument can afford you any diversion, but should be much more so, could I persuade myself you would be instructed by it.'

*

A society of reforming dancing-masters in the city of London have lately set up a Civility Club, at the Salutation Tavern at Billingsgate, where manners are to be disposed by wholesale or retail to all citizens wives and their daughters. No cure, no money.

MONDAY NOVEMBER 7 TO WEDNESDAY NOVEMBER 9 — *Number 54*

Arabella's Day

No day was ever more agreeable to me than that night in which Chrisippus and Lucinda together with Violante and Emilia came to pay me a visit. Their coach stopped at the door as I was walking in a garden situated on the brink of the Thames, which is so fine that for beauty and verdure it could be compared with the most celebrated walks in Italy. The moon shined with a pleasing reflection thro' the trees, and the air was serene and calm and the flux and bubbling of the contiguous river gave me a charming tho' a melancholy diversion. The Heavens were as kind and indulgent as the Earth, the stars and planets glittered in their respective stations, and with their friendly influence assisted the light given by the moon, and made the evening more agreeable. My soul and body were equally possessed with so many charming objects and I insensibly fell to contemplate those heavenly luminaries. I considered them bodies of infinite splendour, and could not but wonder at their agreeing harmony. The sun I reflected assisted the moon, the moon did the same thing to the stars, and the Earth was obliged to all those celestial beings.

These considerations naturally led me to consider the vast advantages of mutual friendship. Friendship is that fountain from whence a thousand sweets distill every hour, and which make the sincere and generous entirely happy. Love I considered as a passion, tho' natural, yet dangerous for young ladies to be acquainted with, when as the amicable resentments of friendship inspired the mind only with such notions as to improve the mind and inspire the soul with thoughts truly great and generous. I was entertaining myself with these amusements when I saw my friends coming to me. They were told by my footman that I was in the garden, and the agreeableness induced them to follow me thither.

As soon as the usual civilities were over, Emilia demanded what could be the occasion I walked there alone, and whether love had not made me seek out retirement, which the handsome and sensible are seldom very fond of. I replied that I must acknowledge I was in love, tho' not in the way that Emilia intended, that my soul was possessed with the very tender sentiments, but that they all were turned to friendship and not to love, that I had considered the difference, and found the consequence of both far unlike the other, and that it seldom happens that any lady feels the power of love, but she loses in her reputation or her quiet, and is guilty of some extravagance or other. Here Emilia would not permit me to proceed, but frankly told me she was surprised to hear me argue against a passion which all the world paid a respect to, and to whose power all living creatures were at some time or other obedient . . .

Violante, taking up the discourse, affirmed that I had a great deal of justice on my side . . . but at the same time she very well observed that love could hardly be termed with justice a gentle passion, since most of a lover's actions are hot, rash and unaccountable; neither could be properly called a refuge for innocence, which too often gives birth to the most incestuous crimes and dismal tragedies; for this reason the God of Love she pursued was drawn, like a thoughtless infant, with his eyes all muffled to show that those who submit themselves slaves to his tyranny see little into the world, and are not yet arrived to years of discretion. She affirmed that Priam was out of his senses to let Troy be endangered for a woman that had been once married and twice ravished, but that Hector was much more to blame, who by endeavouring to maintain his brother in possession of another man's wife, made his own a widow. She continued that love was only self-interest, and being grounded on the fading beauties of the face, bloomed and withered with those short-lived flowers she pursued, that friendship only ought to be admitted to reign amongst the ladies, it being observable that no person could be a good friend without having good morals, good sense, and a soul perfectly generous. Friendship, added she, has nothing in it little or mean, it shows us once more the golden age, puts all our persons and future on a level, and is above the tenacious dictates of covetousness or interest.

Friends are always sincere partners in grief or happiness, they augment each others joys and share their sorrows, by diverting them. Petronius was sensible of this truth, and the distracted Orestes met with ease from his friend. He calmed the furies that disturbed his reason, and by such persuasions and powerful arguments found a better cure for the madness of that illustrious paracide than all the herbs or enchantments of the beautiful Circe could supply him with. Love is but a result of fancy, and the child of illness, but friendship is always the effect of choice and a serious judgment. But then the knot is eternal, and unalterable by time or accident... A thousand instances might be given of the illustrious effects which friendship has produced, but it would be too long to enumerate them. Nor do private persons and families find their interest only in the mutual bonds of friendship; kingdoms, states and empires find their account by the sanctions of friendly conventions and agreements. The united powers have to put a stop to tyrannic force, which attacked by any single nation would have been invincible. Here I saw my footman coming to tell the company that supper was ready, and I therefore desired Lucinda to proceed no further, telling her that all that could be spoken on this subject was contained in a fable of Aesops.

*

If a Goldsmith near Panton Street, in the Haymarket, has any comical designs toward a certain lady in Golden Square, he is desired to desist. Otherwise the tar[1] may have a certain knowledge of the whole affair, and he may be referred to the honest and good-natured fools in Wapping, the air of which makes some young women pregnant two or three months after marriage, altho' they were as good virgins at the time of matrimony as ever was known betwixt the Minories and St James's.

WEDNESDAY NOVEMBER 9 TO FRIDAY NOVEMBER 11 — *Number 55*

Rosella's Day

Well! Ladies, what do you think if I resume Emilia's argument, about the women's easy conquest over the men? For my part I can see no difficulty in it, since the many examples we have amongst all sorts of people makes the practice of it seem as plain to me as the theory. Lucinda, I remember, urged we were not masters enough of philosophy to subdue our passions and exercise our reason so completely as to master that unruly creature – man. But I am

1 sailor

quite of another opinion, and don't think we stand in half so much need of philosophy as we do of wit and subtlety, and we find by experience that the most sagacious and devouring beasts of the field are tamed and made tractable by the artifice of the weakest and most inconsiderable of men. The lion forgets his strength, the tiger his fierceness and the fox his cunning, the horse tamely submits to his rider and the ox to his yoke; and all this is done by management. Why then may not feeble women as easily curb the power of insulting men? Bring the great, the beautiful, the wise and the wealthy to their lure; make the first lay aside his grandeur, the next neglect his shape, a third forfeit his wisdom, and the fourth his riches to please a woman that has artifice enough to make herself every way agreeable to his expectations.

I call it artifice, ladies, I hope without offence, because 'tis seldom that we find a woman formed by nature for all the great designs of pleasing upon all occasions with the nice embellishment of dress, mien and manners, and all the culture studied art can give her. This management depends not on the rules that the grave and wisest philosophers can prescribe but on those charms that we find within ourselves most conducive to the bringing mankind under the verge of our power. 'But how,' says Arabella, 'can we discover those secret springs that will draw the men to our subjection?' 'My dear,' said I, 'that is the artifice I talk of, that's the knowledge we are to study, the language of the eyes, the motion of the hands and feet and all the little turns of seducing man to catch us. If we ward ourselves off from their snares, we surely catch 'em in our own and there the slenderest thread of art, if fairly woven, will secure them.

'To convince you of which, ladies, I'll give you a generous concession of one of their own sex, which tho' addressed to one of ours in a loose libertine way, may be very applicable in a reserved one.

"Tell me, dear charmer, in some moving style,
How you with artful looks our cares beguile?
How all your counterfeited smiles do please?
And lull us to a lethargy of ease?
Spite of ill-nature, you have ways to win
And to delude us, tho' we know the gin:
Mankind do thus like servile easy fools,
Court the deceit to which themselves are tools;
Fond to be loved, tho' at their own expense,
And proud to barter reason for weak sense,
Yet still we love those smooth deceivers more,
Then they dissemble for the glittering ore;

How mere a Bubble's man, how empty made,
That thinks himself most happy when betrayed;
Boasts most of reason, when he can impart
To some dear she, the secrets of his heart,
Who looking through the window of his soul,
Sees by what springs she easiest may control,
Then strikes her darts upon the unthinking Fool."'

'I cannot bear this reflection of the poets,' says Lucinda, 'for at this rate we suffer ourselves to be exposed and I think the conquest is not worth the purchase, if we have no other way to gain it but at the expense of our modesty, and prostituting our own virtue to collogue,[2] flatter and dissemble. I hate a woman of so mean a spirit. If I thought I had not charms enough to command a husband without that artifice you talk of, I would despise the addresses of any man that I was not assured gave me some promising hopes to expect such a rule as I would desire in a marriage life.' 'I cannot tell,' says Rosella, 'what Lucinda may expect, but I can tell what she'll be disappointed in if she trusts to her native charms and virtue without the assistance of female policy and innocent dissimulation; for I call that so which cheats a man into his own happiness. Now I beg the favour of you, ladies, to undeceive Lucinda in her false notion of those lines I have repeated, which, though they are not directly aimed at a modest virtuous woman, they may be of use to ladies of the strictest virtue, to let us know what cullies[3] men are, and how they are to be used, since we may be permitted under the closest ties of religion, to make use of politic stratagems, to engage the love and fidelity of our husbands towards us, tho' the same are made use of by bad women to ill purposes, and it can never hurt us to know what allurements are the strongest to bind our husbands in the most pleasing ties of affection and civility towards us, and the most effectually to control with them to put their utmost trust and confidence in us.' 'I doubt not, ladies,' says Emilia, 'but the happy turn Rosella has given to this argument will convince you entirely she is in the right on it, and that what I have advanced on this subject will, if pursued, be much to the advantage of our sex.'

[2] to gossip [3] fools, dupes

FRIDAY NOVEMBER 11 TO MONDAY NOVEMBER 14 *Number 56*

Lucinda's Day

FROM MY CLOSET

hloe and Celia, two young gentlewomen that are cousins, of whose affairs I knew more than either of them imagined, coming to see me this afternoon, complained that *The Female Tatler* had left off taking notice of the scandal that was sent her. They talk of dullness, hackney writing, and several other things that displeased me, for which, having a mind to be revenged on them, I told them that I had received two true stories of scandal upon two ladies, whom I knew not, that if they would give themselves the trouble of hearing them, I should be glad of their opinions, whether they were worth publishing or not. They answered by all means, nothing of scandal could come amiss to them. So, whilst my maid set the tea-table, I unlocked my scrutore and took out a sheet of paper, writ in a small character. We had hardly drank two dishes each, but I saw that the ladies were impatient to hear what I had offered, and accordingly, looking on my paper under pretence of reading it, I began the first story.

Having described a certain merchant by his size and complexion, the place where he lived and the commodity he dealt in, so exactly, that anybody who was acquainted with him might know it was Chloe's father I meant, I continued thus: 'This gentleman,' said I, 'has a sprightly young lady to his daughter that takes abundance of care to appear unaffected and gay, behaves herself with a more than ordinary freedom in all manner and company and yet pretends to be strictly chaste, and is proud of her conduct. She is very censorious upon all young people that are not of the same temper, calls modesty slyness, and hardly allows any body to be virtuous that is more reserved than herself. They had a gentleman that boarded with them, whom their daughter treated very familiarly, played at romps with him, admitted him into her chamber, and sometimes scrupled not to enter his. The father had a good opinion of his daughter, the mother doted on her, and neither of them suspecting her virtue. She was never controlled in her actions.

One morning she complained of having lost one of her garters. Search was made throughout her chamber, the mother looked in every corner of her own, the maid did the same in the parlour and the dining-room, but no garter was found. Some two hours after, the maid being come down from making the beds, held out the garter to her young mistress, where she sat with her father and mother, and smiled. The lady, snatching it away, asked her, where she had it, but being answered in Mr P——'s bed, which was the gentleman that boarded with them, she discovered so much astonishment, as well as the gentleman himself, who likewise happened to be present, that it was easily seen that whether the garter was found in his bed or not, the owner of it had certainly been there.'

I had observed that whilst as they thought I was reading this story, Celia all along had been wonderfully pleased, and continually sniggering and nodding at her cousin, who for her part looked very grave and seemed as uneasy as if she had sat upon nettles, and when I had finished, as the one called it, a silly story, and wondered Celia could laugh at anything so dull and insipid, so the other, extolling it as extravagantly, said it was the best she ever heard, and earnestly preferred me go on with the second. I wanted not much entreaty, for as these two stories, which I had ready for 'em, the first touched Chloe to the quick, so this was to be as home upon her cousin, both being literally true. Celia was the reverse of Chloe, and seemed as affectedly cautious as the other was over free. She pretended to have a great aversion to men, was very circumspect in their company, and thought ill of all women that were not equally coy and retired as herself. When I made an end of Celia's character and had been particular enough in the description of her person and circumstances to make her known, I saw that her mirth was over, and that all her good humour vanished, but on the other side Chloe, by degrees recovering from her dumps, assumed a merrier countenance, and at last seemed to feel the same satisfaction that her cousin had experienced before.

Looking still steadfastly upon my paper, I went on in this manner.

'This reserved lady,' said I, 'persuaded by her mother and other relations, relented at last and vouchsafed a more favourable hearing to one of her suitors, whom we shall call Lysander, than hitherto she had done to any, and a match was in great forwardness, when the gallant's father, who lived a hundred miles off, falls sick, and in post-haste sends for his son, who, willing to obey his father, took short leave of his mistress and went down with a promise of a speedy return. The father, after two month's illness, dies, and leaves his son a large, but encumbered estate, the troubles of which detaining Lysander longer than willingly he would have stayed, almost half a year escaped before he came back from London, where he was sooner arrived, but received the unwelcome news of his mistress being very ill and likely to die. He heard that she was gone ten miles off to a little hamlet in Essex, where her mother had a small farm of twenty pound per annum, and that her distemper was a kind of dropsy, called the Tympany.[4] He made what haste he could to see her,

4 swelling of the abdomen

but, coming there, she happened to be very bad, that he could not be admitted. But when Lysander would not be denied by the servant that spoke to him, and made several instances to see her, comes down to him at last an elderly matron, who, by telling him that the lady had been lightheaded for some days, and was that minute dropped into a slumber, and giving him a specious account of the whole state of her illness, persuaded him, tho' much ado, to forbear his visit, and go as he came.

After this Lysander expected every hour to hear she was dead, but the third day was joyfully revived with the unhoped for tidings of his mistress being on the mending hand. She now daily recovers apace, the swelling is gone, Lysander is allowed to see her, the chief of her distemper is weakness, and in a month's time she is happily restored to her former health. Everything now was got ready for the nuptials, when the day before they were to be celebrated, Lysander, just as he was entering a hosier's shop, saw an ancient gentlewoman that came out of it step into a coach. He remembered that he had seen her face, but could not presently think where, till recollecting himself he called to mind that it was the careful old lady that, with so much oratory and affection, had dissuaded him from disturbing his mistress when she was at the worst. 'Do you know,' said he, 'that gentlewoman?', looking upon the master of the shop, who, smiling, answered, 'Yes, Sir, she is a midwife, well approved for her skill, but more particularly noted for her faithfulness and discretion on all occasions where secrecy is required.' At the sound of a midwife, Lysander turned pale, and, before the hosier had quite pronounced the word secrecy, looked like a man that was thunder-struck. He asked no more questions, but, without so much as thinking what he came for, left the shop and immediately went to a physician that was his intimate friend and, having communicated to him whatever he knew concerning his mistress's distemper, as well as her cure, upon his advice broke off the match.'

I took a great deal of delight to see the different working this relation had upon the two cousins, and when I had made an end, I found Chloe in the gayest humour imaginable, continually repeating 'Tympany' and 'Midwife'; but Celia in almost as much amazement as we suppose Lysander to have been at the hosier's, till, at length her passion prevailing over her concern, she could contain herself no longer and casting her eyes full of spite and anger upon her cousin, asked her if she had laughed as much when the maid told her where she had found her garter? 'My garter!' said Chloe, 'why that upon me? I laughed at the lady that had the Tympany, what cousin is it you? I know you pretended once . . .' 'Pretended!' replied Celia, interrupting her. 'I scorn your words; it is well known that I had a dropsy, and what of that? There was no occasion to suspect me, cousin, unless my garter had been found in a gentleman's bed before I complained.' At this, Chloe, enraged in her turn, the conversation between the two cousins began to be very loud and full of quick repartee, and at last became so violent that I could understand nothing but 'garter' and 'gentleman's bed' on one side, and 'Tympany' and 'Midwife' on the other. Chloe thro' eagerness, forgetting the tea she had in her hand, her dish slipped from the saucer, and fell upon Celia's white petticoat, who, no doubting that it was done to affront her, took up her own which I had filled that moment, and flung it in her cousin's face. Then both got up, Chloe to attack Celia, and Celia to avoid Chloe. Celia being on my right, the first step she made threw down the boiling tea-kettle, spirits and all, and miserably scalded one of my dogs that lay by me, whilst the furbelow of Chloe's scarf in the pursuit took hold of the tea-table and overthrew it. The clatter of china, the screaming of one dog and the barking of another, joined to the loudness of the combatants, and the noise of my parrot, who upon occasions is used to join in the chorus, made such a hideous consort, that I was glad to quit the room and get up into my closet, to set down what had happened.

MONDAY NOVEMBER 14 TO WEDNESDAY NOVEMBER 16 — *Number 57*

Emilia's Day

FROM MY BED CHAMBER

Jenny Mowbray desires the two Welsh gentlemen that were in the town last summer to return the French gewgaw[5] they had of her, and she is willing to restore the Welsh-fiddle they presented to her in exchange; finding she had much the worst of the bargain.

5 toy or bauble

WEDNESDAY NOVEMBER 16 TO FRIDAY NOVEMBER 18 *Number 58*

Artesia's Day

FROM MY CLOSET[6]

No qualification has all along been more deservedly esteemed among the learned than the easiness and plainness with which great men are observed to express themselves and to unfold the result of their studious thoughts. It is that by which the exalted notions of philosophy have been made useful to the public. What benefit would the most excellent system of the creation have been to us in the brain of Descartes[7] if that famous man had not laid it down so intelligibly? And not only in philosophy, but in all arts and sciences, a man's knowledge can do but little good either to himself or others if nobody besides himself is acquainted with his possessing of it. This is the reason your public spirited people are so indefatigable in exposing their abilities to the world, as we may see by the crowd of advertisements that are daily annexed to all manner of newspapers, and, to find out how effectively this compendious way of writing informs our understandings, we need but consider how the whole nation, at present, seems to be persuaded of the skill and many years experience of some artists that, but a little while ago, were altogether ignorant themselves of having either.

What man or woman that knows any of the *circumforanean*[8] company would ever suspect that several of them had found out such infallible remedies for most diseases? Or what mortal that has heard 'em speak would be persuaded to believe that their knowledge exceeded that of the whole college of physicians, tho' the latter had never so little, if all the advices we daily receive from their own apartments did not so unanimously confirm it? As for my part, I can never look upon the grand occulist and the so-often-repeated story of Jones at Newington Butts, but I think on the cure of blindness, and often cry out, 'Happy are they that can see to read it!' It must be a real pleasure to those deserving men

6 examples of the advertisements discussed in this article can be found in Part Four of this volume, pp. 219–224.

7 French rationalist philosopher, known as the father of modern philosophy (1596–1650).

8 wandering from market to market

always to meet not only with such an uninterrupted series of success, but likewise patients of such grateful and obliging a temper that they'll condescend to have their names and infirmities exposed to the public, rather than suffer the merits of their doctor to remain unregarded. It is true, that those doctors commonly paying for the printing of the advertisements themselves, it has been hinted by the disingenuous (as if it was possible) that people might be hired to sign those certificates, and consequently that the truth of those cures was not much to be relied upon, and the advertising of them only a trick for quacks to get money.

But what is so just or fair that it cannot be perverted or ill construed by the malice of envious persons? It is sufficient that it is not probable, that people who were only cured of an inconsiderable cold, of hardly a fortnight's standing, should tell the world that they had been afflicted with a rheumatism that had lasted very near a twelve month; or that, if people had ever had sight enough to distinguish one man from another by it, their mothers, on the request of an occulist, should make oath before a magistrate that they could never see at all. From what I have said it is evident that to make our knowledge beneficial it is requisite we should use the means of letting others know we have it; but should it be objected that when people extol their own merit, and are always dwelling on and praising their dear selves, by all wise people they are called *Braggadocios*,[9] and counted fools for their pains, I would answer that this is only to be feared in people of ordinary capacities, but that, it holds not in those of a more exalted genius. By their excellency they are exempt from those common rules and little niceties of decency and good breeding, and, conscious of their own worth, are not ashamed to speak it.

FROM MY DRAWING ROOM

Yesterday I received the following letter:

Madam,
I am a gentleman of a very good estate, and would have made some love addresses to your nice Arabella, but my back, not being made so straight as some people's are, I have never yet spoke to her but she fell a-laughing like an impertinent fool, as she is. I desire you would not only reprove, her in particular, for so great a breach of good manners, but likewise (she not being the first that has served me so) oblige the public with some short essay against that abominable rudeness ridiculing of people, for bodily infirmities, which is not in their power to mend.
Your humble servant,
Curvino

9 boasters

Arabella is my brother's daughter, a beautiful young woman, that has lived with me from her infancy. Having bestowed a very good education upon her, I love her very well, and was sorry to hear, but could not believe, that she had been guilty of that height of incivility. When the letter came, she happened to be abroad, but having showed it her as soon as she was come in, I wondered to hear her own the charge without any hesitations, or making the least excuse for so much ill manners.

Seeing I was very angry, she, very obligingly, before I could speak, desired to be heard first. 'Curvino,' said she, 'is a gentleman that, besides the misfortune of being hump-backed, has very long limbs that are yet more remarkably slender. His body is extremely short, he has no neck, and his head is very large. So much for his shape. As to his understanding and estate they are neither of them despicable. He wears very rich clothes, but, summer or winter, never appears in sight without a loose great coat over them, with three or four pleats in the back of it, and, let what wigs will be in the fashion, he is never seen in any other than a broad Spanish one covering his back and shoulders, which like a huge fleece, he carries upon all the rest. I confess that I can't forbear laughing when I see him, not because he is crooked or ill-shaped, and I hope you don't think me so rude or so silly. What I laugh at in him is the vast concern a man must have for an infirmity for which he is no ways answerable, when knowingly he puts himself in a ridiculous dress, and takes such uncommon pains, in hopes of covering what his reason might tell him could never be hid. His misfortune being so conspicuous throughout his whole make, that, without seeing his back, whoever views him before, may be assured he is crooked behind.'

FRIDAY NOVEMBER 18 TO MONDAY NOVEMBER 21 *Number 59*

Rosella's Day

The lady in the city, who lately christened her daughter William, upon assurance from the midwife that it was a boy, is desired to be more circumspect for the future, and choose both midwives and nurses that can tell the distinction of sexes without spectacles, least the surgeons that were called in to give their opinions should publish this oversight to the great prejudice of all fumbling midwives who have lost the sense of feeling.

*

A certain gentlewoman, whose follies have formerly been reproved in this paper, and elsewhere, in hopes of her amendment, imagining this way might have some influence on her, seeing tho' she has from the pulpit in general terms heard her actions absolutely declared against as sinful, yet she will not be persuaded either to amend or alter them, so that, since nothing will do, she is given over as irreclaimable.

WEDNESDAY NOVEMBER 23 TO FRIDAY NOVEMBER 25 — *Number 61*

Emilia's Day

[The whole of this paper is a slight reworking of Paper No. 26, dated September 2 to 5 1709, in the fake series. Either Emilia was not above flagrant plagiarism or possibly the author of the fake *Female Tatler* went on to become Emilia and regurgitate their own writing. See pp. 212–213.

FRIDAY NOVEMBER 25 TO MONDAY NOVEMBER 28 — *Number 62*

This is to give notice to all idle 'prentices, carmen,[10] and able-bodied footmen, that for the encouragement of trade, the company of glaziers, during the season will cause to be distributed every Monday morning, six dozen of footballs *gratis*. Enquire of the beadle of the said company.

10 coachmen (car[riage] men)

WEDNESDAY NOVEMBER 30 TO FRIDAY DECEMBER 2 — *Number 64*

Lucinda's Day

FROM MY DRAWING-ROOM

esterday I had almost the same company at my house, that some days ago was at my sister Artesia's lodgings. They had not been with me long, but insensibly fell again upon the discourse that was broke off there. Emilia and Camilla, to ridicule what the Oxford gentleman had started, said a hundred things in praise of Caligula, Heliogabalus, Sardanapalus, and all the kings and emperors they could think on that had been infamous for luxury and extravagancy. 'You may,' said one, 'talk of the valour of Julius Caesar, the wisdom of Augustus, and the virtue of Titus, but if the example of princes has any influence on the people, Rome certainly never had a better master than Tiberius, when three thousand fishes and seven thousand birds were served at his table for one supper, the fishmongers and poulterers must have had very good business.' 'I wonder,' said the other, 'how so wise a senate as theirs, that was so watchful for the public welfare, would suffer the pernicious tenets of the Cato's, the Seneca's and other moral-mongers that extolled content and frugality, and preached against gluttony, drunkenness, and the rest of the supporters of the Common-wealth.' 'Indeed ladies,' said Arsinoe, 'I am altogether for the encouraging of trade. It is pity that we have not a law to oblige all people that are able to have new clothes at least once a month, and new furniture every year. If I sat at the helm, nobody should be counted a good subject that made not four meals a day. I would have everybody treated as a recusant that refused to take tobacco, and all gentlemen that went to bed without their three bottles should pay double taxes.' This made us laugh heartily, when the gentleman on whom the banter was designed, having said nothing hitherto, with a smiling countenance begun thus.

'I am very glad, ladies,' said he, 'that I have contributed so much to your mirth. I confess, I cannot be of the opinion that all those people who take no other worldly care than how to dress, eat, drink and sleep well are so useless to human society that they ought to be reckoned among the dead. The comical remonstrance of the upholders' company,[11] is very witty and diverting, and what I read some days ago about their interrment, pleased me exceedingly, as long as I knew that the ingenious author of them was only in jest, and had no design to bring it in fashion, and make funerals *à la Mode* of them. But if we may be serious and reflect upon all the different parts of which a potent and flourishing society must unavoidably consist, I doubt the banter will lose its force. In those that are princes born, the magnanimity, and quick sense of glory, which by care and education from their infancy they are inspired with, averts them from the mean thoughts of sensuality and private pleasure, and whenever they grow unmindful of the public, and are seen to neglect the affairs of Government, it is commonly for want of pride or ambition.

But as to subjects, to always be clean and wear clothes that are sumptuously fashionable, to have pompous equipages, and be well attended, to live in stately dwellings adorned with rich and modish furniture, both for use and magnificence, to eat and drink deliciously, treat profusely, and have plentiful variety of what either art or nature can contribute, not to the ease and comfort only, but likewise the joy and splendour of life, is without doubt to be very useful and beneficial to the public; nay, I am so far from allowing these to be dead that I think they are the very springs that turn all the wheels of trade, and if the metaphor is ever to be used, it is much more applicable to men of letters. The learned languages we'll own are necessary to all that have a mind to study any of the three faculties. But those are only counted sordid fellows that beat their brains for lucre, they are not to be styled *Literrati* – that illustrious title is only due to men of polite learning, that is, such as by reading the same books twenty times over and over, become critically versed in classic authors and, without expectation or possibility of ever being a farthing the better for it, pursue an endless study that is of no manner of use to human society. It is there, I say, that might more justly be called dead than the others, who by the solicitous care they take of their backs and bellies, make money circulate, and are the real encouragers of every useful art and science.

*

NB. Be pleased to correct a fault of the press in the Tatler of Monday last, Page 2, Col. 1, Line 28, for 'wine' read 'urine'.

11 undertakers

WEDNESDAY DECEMBER 7 TO FRIDAY DECEMBER 9 *Number 67*

Arabella's Day

milia and I having at an India house muddled away a little of our own money, were sitting to observe the variety of the company that frequent those places, and how different their fancies were in pictures, fans, china, and such fashionable impertinences. Lady Praise-All surveyed the nick-nackatory, with an amazement, as if she had received a new sense – these cups were charming, those stones unparalleled, and such prodigious jars were never heard of – everything was displaced to oblige her ladyship's curiosity, who protested she shouldn't grudge to spend an estate on things so prodigiously fine, drank a gallon of tea, and marched off without laying out a sixpence. Mrs Trifleton came so full of commissions from ladies in the country that we thought she would have emptied the warehouse, and stared at the handsome 'prentice as if she expected to have him into the bargain. She wanted finer things than were ever made, and, could they have been had, would have demanded them cheaper than they were bought. She bid three half crowns for a two guinea fan, wanted chocolate, all nut, for eighteen pence a pound, and beat down the best Imperial tea to the price of Sage o' Virtue.[12] Japan work[13] she thought at an excessive rate, China images were idolatrous, India pictures were the foolishest things, she'd have had them given her a dozen. At last, having positive orders from my Lady Smoak and Sot of Exeter, to buy her a stone spitting-pot, she shook her head at the dearness of it, and ordered them to set it down to her.

Mrs Honeysuckle was two hours pleasing herself in a paper nosegay, and Mrs Delf employed five people to match her grout[14] cup. On a sudden, stops a leathern conveniency at the door, with four fellows of the world behind it, in the gayest liveries I ever saw, out of which comes a couple of quality Quakers. They moved in, like disdainful duchesses who complain of corns if they walk but cross a room, rolled about their sanctified eyes, as if it were condescension in them to appear upon earth, and with abundance of reluctancy, one of them vouchsafed us a bow, instead of a curtsey. Emilia and I were not a little pleased to remark the pride and singularity in dress, speech and behaviour in that sect of

[12] a cheap herbal tea [13] black lacquered ware [14] beer

people summed up in these two statues. Their clothes were costly without making any show, and though they abominate profane pinners and topknots, yet, by the disposition of their locks and the artful crimping of their hoods upon wires, they showed themselves equally vain, and that they had taken as much pains to be particular as other ladies do to appear like the rest of the world, yet notwithstanding all their seeming plainness, the old man had crept in among them for watches, tweezer cases, and gold chains, and a patch or two to cover pretended pimples. When they had with secret satisfaction received all the ceremonious address of 'Ladies, your most obedient, do me the honour, etc.' which they expect from people of the world without vouchsafing any other return than a precise nod, in a sighing tone, they enquired for fine tea-tables, gilded cabinets, glass sconces, and all the richest things more proper to adorn the palace of a prince than to dizen out a yea and nay parlour in Hand Alley. Whatever bore a moderate price was trash and trumpery. 'Dost thee think my Ananias can eat his barley gruel out of such coarse ware?' But a Japan basin of ten guineas is fit for the pure ones to make gooseberry fool in, and the pieces moved as gradually out of their pockets as if the spirit had directed each in its proper place, according to the seniority of their being coined.

Susanna, having drunk too much green tea, was seized with a violent fit of the colic, so that the creature *Rosa Solis*[15] was forced to be called for. Rachel too, being an apprehensive of that diabolical distemper, by way of prevention, tasted of that tempting liquor, which they say, those carnal women called Duchesses guzzle. At that abominable rate, the demure sisters sipped up a whole quart, but their heads not being the least intoxicated with the pomps and the vanities of the world, it only made them cheerful, and being pure in spirit they were very much rejoiced.

But, as in this wicked age misfortunes will happen to afflict the upright, Colonel Sturdy, one of the greatest rakes that ever kept basset bank[16] or carried doxy[17] out of the side box, happened to reel in, seized upon Susanna, smuggled her as if she had been a beastly orange wench[18] and swore so prodigiously that Rachel staggered, and was falling into a swoon, had not the Colonel left Susanna, and taken her into his arms. Rachel, though in wondrous confusion, had the presence of mind to say, 'Dear man, who art called Colonel, do anything to me, but don't swear.' Susanna, with robust zeal, divides Rachel and the Colonel, and told him that though he had the assurance to accost her in that lustful manner,

[15] alcoholic cordial
[16] acted as banker during the card game
[17] prostitute
[18] girl orange-seller in the playhouses

he ought to have shown more reverence to Rachel, who had been a speaker[19] these seven years. Rachel accused Susanna of incivility, and said, 'What the man did to thee, sister, was blame worthy, and thou ought'st to chide him for't, but 'twas kind and tender in him to support my weakness, or I had stumbled and fell.'

In short, the sanctified sisters quarrelled so about a libertine, whom even loose women that sin with some restraint abominate for his inconstancy, that 'twas with no small struggling they concealed their enmity from the servants, and went home together in the same coach. Emilia and I were so crowded with reflections on what we had seen, that we had hardly patience to vent them without interrupting each other, but at length our sentiments appeared to be much the same, that Quakers are the most designing, deceitful sect of creatures in the world, who assume more pride and exact more homage from their seeming sanctity, than the truly pious, who are always easy and unconstrained.

Their houses are as richly and gaily furnished as those of quality, their equipages as glaring, and though they affect a ridiculous habit, a primness of air, and screw themselves up like trussed rabbits, yet they are as foppish their way, and by little and little wink at one another in those modes and fancies, which they term Babylonish, idolatrous, and diabolical. They love music and dancing, though they won't practice it themselves, read plays though they won't see them, will sneak into a tavern at the back door, fornicate with a Holy Sister, and if, by subtlety in trade, they can over-reach their neighbours, 'tis but engrossing to themselves the spoils of the wicked. The young Quakers of both sexes are so far gone from the truth, as to arrive at most libertines of the age. The men play as high at Roly-Poly and the women coquet as much upon the walks, and 'tis no novelty nowadays to see, a Fleet Street Sylvia whip into a tavern with a Damon that has no button holes behind.

*

Lost in last July, behind the late Sir George Whitmore's, a maidenhead, the owner never having missed it till the person who since married her expected to have had it as part of her dowry. If the pastry cook in Fleet Street, who is supposed to have brought it away out of a frolic, will restore it again to Mrs Sarah Stroakings, at the Cow-House at Islington, he shall be treated with a syllabub.

19 official at a Quaker convocation

FRIDAY DECEMBER 9 TO MONDAY DECEMBER 12 *Number 68*

he young gentleman belonging to the Custom-House that, for fear of rain, borrowed the umbrella at Will's Coffee-House in Cornhill last Friday night of the mistress is hereby advertised that to be dry from head to foot on the like occasion, he shall be welcome to the maid's pattens.[20]

MONDAY DECEMBER 12 TO WEDNESDAY DECEMBER 14 *Number 69*

Emilia's Day

hen the women get into so high a clack that forty tongues run together without hearing each other, the subject is certainly fashions – how they edge their heads, line their scarves, roll their sleeves, pink their aprons and cut their petticoats, as if to commit a solecism in dress were as unpardonable a crime as for any orator to break Priscian's head[21] at the university. Lady Kill-Chairman, who is one of the greatest gossips in the kingdom, and knows everybody but herself, introduced this discourse, which like wildfire flew through the company. They talked how everybody ought to dress themselves, but some of their tittle-tattle was scandal. That Mrs Prim looked like a jointed baby, Mrs Fluggins was a trapes, Mrs Frippery hadn't clothes to her back, and my old Lady Taudry dizened herself out like a girl of fifteen, and whatever lady's appearance they allowed complete, 'twere well if she had paid her sempstress, her mercer, her mantua-maker, etc. Beauty was attributed to art, virtue to want of admirers, good conduct was studied hypocrisy, religion a fit of enthusiasm, and whatever lady was the toast of the whole town, she was certainly suspected by the whole town.

20 Wooden over-shoes worn to raise the wearer above the mud on the streets.
21 make a grammatical mistake

Mrs Prudence Maxim, who loves detraction equal to her ladyship but tempers it with more good breeding, and has the happiness to have satire, general, just, and reforming, fixed the raillery on mourning *àla mode*. That the city were grown such apes of quality that the comic poets may to eternity have a tradesman's wife as a standing character, and every year vary it with new affectations, extravagancies and diverting occurrences. One lady must have her topknots from St James's, another her smocks washed in Holland, a third pretends to a visiting day, and Mrs Razor, Mrs Griskin, Mrs Tarragon and Mrs Turkey-pout are ushered in like countesses, and a fourth has an assembly for play. Many of them arrive at all, and the heads of every ward[22] would fain have a page as well as my Lady Mayoress. But what seems most preposterous is that when any foreigner of note, Count Potoski, or Count Wisnowiski, dies, every Sue Frowzy in Gutter Lane, Blow-bladder Street, and Panniers Alley, is now pressing her black-cloth, hemming her head and making herself completely dismal, when her husband hasn't sense enough to tell her whether the person deceased lived in Europe, Asia, Africa, or America. These creatures give just provocation for their husbands to quarrel with them.

I take mourning for foreign kings to be a habit as peculiar to the court as robes are to those in public professions, and what inferior classes ought not to vie with. Could anyone forbear laughing to see an alderman in a herald's coat, or a herald in scarlet and furs? Is it not as ridiculous to see a tradesman's wife in a velvet gown and petticoat? But these matters are become so great a jest that but last week a certain fine lady, having the misfortune to be deprived of Belinda, one of her favourite lap-dogs, made a mock-funeral, and the other five were put into a sort of mourning her.

*

FROM MY LODGINGS IN GREEK STREET, SOHO

This evening the ingenious Mrs Centlivre,[23] did me the favour of a visit. All the ladies concerned in this paper happened to be there and with several others of fashion of both sexes. We, having appointed a dancing bout, her business then was chiefly to have my opinion of her new comedy,[24] for that she spied me out the first night in the box. I asked her, smiling, whether she took the title for her play from the

22 For administrative purposes, towns were divided into wards.

23 Susanna Centlivre

24 *The Man's Bewitched; or, The Devil To Do About Her.* First performed by the Queens Company in the Haymarket, 12 December 1709.

characters she had drawn, or from the persons that played those characters, since a certain theatrical gentleman is often bewitched and there is a stage lady about whom there has been the devil to do.

But setting raillery apart, the whole company congratulated her on the success of her performance, and were rejoiced to see the inimitable Mrs Behn[25] so nearly revived in Mrs Centlivre. Some there, who are esteemed no ill judges, were pleased to say that they thought it a genteel, easy and diverting comedy. That it had a better plot and as many turns in it as her celebrated *Busy-Body*,[26] and though the two first acts were not so roared at as the rest, yet they were well-wrought scenes, and tending to business. The Squire outdid himself throughout the whole action, nor is Mrs Saunders, though ranked below Belinda, to be less applauded for her natural trembling and faltering in her speech when she apprehended Sir Jeffrey to be a ghost.[27] The ladies highly commended the author, as what could they expect less from one of their own sex, for the care she had taken not to offend the nicest ear with the least *double entendre*, and pressed me to acquaint the town that even dissenters may be seen at this play. And though Emilia has not the assurance of some Tatlers, to licence one man to ruin all the rest of his trade, yet she would entreat the ladies, especially those of quality, to engage her such an appearance the third and sixth nights,[28] as to show they have a generous sense of the pains she is daily taking, so wittily and innocently to entertain them.

'Twas with some difficulty that we prevailed upon this lady to stay supper with us, for though she's a woman of admirable good sense, she is still a woman, and consequently must retain a few foibles of her sex. She complained she was so horridly mobbed, that she was enough to fright people. Had she imagined the honour of so much good company, she'd have put herself in anotherguess trim, but, it being a wet evening, she expected to have found me alone and coming out in haste hadn't so much as put on a patch. But assuring her her dress needed no apology, or if it had, 'twas her conversation we coveted, she complied with our request. The Society had the curiosity of knowing the nature of introducing a play into the house. Mrs Centlivre told them that 'twas much easier to write a play than to get it represented, that their factions

[25] Aphra Behn (1640–89), playwright and poet.

[26] One of her most successful plays (1709), in the then current repertoire, and to remain on the stage regularly over the next 150 years.

[27] The cast included Bowman as Sir Jeffrey, Mills as Captain Constant, Wilks as Faithful, Cibber as Manage, Mrs Oldfield as Belinda, Mrs Saunders as Dorothy and Dagget as Num, the Squire.

[28] traditionally benefit nights for the author

and divisions were so great they seldom continued in the same mind two hours together. They treated her (though a woman) in the masculine gender, and, as they do all authors, with wrangling and confusion, which has made most gentlemen that have a genius to scribbling employ their pens another way, that to show their judgment in plays they had actually cut out the scene in the fifth act, between the countryman and the ghost which the audience received with that wonderful applause, and it was with very great struggling the author prevailed to have it in again. One made faces at his part, another was witty upon hers. But as the whole was very well performed at last, she has condescension to pass over the affronts of a set of people who have it not in their natures to be grateful to their supporters.

*

The Yeoman's wife at Sennock in Kent who, being a little purse-proud, was resolved to receive company at her lying-in, like the quality ladies, and, placing her side-saddle at the beds-head, sat upon it, dressed out in her best Farrendine gown, a plain scarf, and a high crown hat, is desired to take notice that the fashion is now altered and that the ladies now sit up in easy chairs.

FRIDAY DECEMBER 16 TO MONDAY DECEMBER 19 *Number 71*

Arabella's Day

Since Emilia took upon her last time, to vindicate Altamira's character and conduct, especially since her wise choice in one of the first mice of quality, the Court prudes are all in an uproar, and have resolved to load that deserving beauty with all the secret scandal, wit or envy can invent. To anticipate which design, I shall endeavour to draw their pictures in miniature, and find them in full employ to blot out the gaieties I have designed for them, if they like not their own faces when they see them in proper colouring or else to daub them over with varnish that may disguise the painting.

A prude is a woman who places her virtue in having wit enough to keep a man from prying in to her faults, and modest enough to hinder him from climbing into her bed-chamber. She simpers before company, as if butter would not melt in her mouth, but in private is an errant Miss Romps, and shows her teeth to her chamber-maid, as certain as she bites her lip in public conversation. Where she is so circumspect that she divides her eyes among the company, reserving always one half to herself, except by chance, she gives a glance now and then upon some gold watch, diamond ring, or other piece of finery that is before her. When she sits at her tea-table, she moulds her face into a regular figure, which vanishes away at the introduction of a dram of right Nantz.[29] And that art before which persuaded her to keep a secret, now yields with pleasure to the power of nature, which triumphs in revealing it. She consults her face every morning so long, till she goes away convinced that she is fair, and then commends her glass because it does not flatter her. She is of that reserved prim that, though her ears are guilty of hearing many things, she scorns her tongue should tell of any of them, so she cannot be censured by the world for sinning with her understanding. She seems to be bred in the stoic philosophy, for she neglects her equals and despises her betters, so that her vanity seldom can be said to exceed condescension.

She plumes herself and puts a value upon her wit if she can gain a gay lover that is remarkable for a fool that she may have the pleasure and, as she thinks, the applause of the world for laughing at his simplicity. Then the men will call her a hard-hearted and cruel creature, and the women perhaps say she is a shy lady, and too nice for a wife. If she loves at all, as it is ten to one she does, she loves not the man, but his equipage, the laced liveries and the saucy fellows that wear them. Her lightness makes her swim on the top of her acquaintance, because they visit her not in such clean linen as she dresses in. Her devotion is in a new suit of clothes that carries her to church in the top of the fashion, where she lifts up her eyes instead of her heart, to know who looks upon her, not who she is praying to. The most necessary attendants about her are her woman and her lap-dog, and the greatest curiosities she is guilty of is a better jewel, or a finer gown.

*

I was desired to tell them the story of the Law-Cats, which I had promised them, and so I proceeded. The Law-Cats are terrible monsters

29 brandy

that devour little children, and trample over marble monuments. They have claws so very strong and sharp that nothing can get from them that is once fast between their clutches. The quintessence of craft reigns among them, by which means they gripe all, devour all, burn all, draw all, hang all, quarter all, behead all, murder all, waste and ruin all, without regard to right or wrong; for among them cruelty is called justice, treason loyalty and rebellion religion. So it is plain the manger is above the rack,[30] and if ever plague, fire, famine or earthquake befall this nation, we cannot attribute them to the aspects and conjunctions of the malevolent planets, but to the abuses of the catterwauling fraternity, not to the tyranny of kings and princes or the impostures of false prophets, villainy of griping usurers or the ignorance and impudence of close-fisted physicians, loose harlots and destroyers of by-blows,[31] but charge them wholly and solely upon the inexpressible wickedness of the Law-Cats, which is less understood then the philosopher's stone and therefore not so deserted and punished as it should be.

But should they be exposed in their proper colours, not a Cicero's colloguing tongue, or a Castko's eloquence could save them for this reason, as Hannibal was solemnly sworn by his father to pursue the Romans with the utmost hatred as long as he lived, so my father enjoined me on his death bed not to meddle with that race of animals, but wait till the thunder of mighty Jove, had reduced them to ashes like other presumptuous Titans.

I cannot tell what to compare this monster to better a Chymera Sphynx, or the image of Osyris, as the Egyptians painted him with three heads – one of a roaring lion, the other of a fawning cur, and the last of a prowling wolf, twisted about with a dragon biting his tail. His hands full of gore, his talons like those of Harpies, his snout like a hawks bill, his tusks like those of an overgrown wild boar, and his eyes flaming like the mouth of a furnace. His hutch, and that of the warren cats, his collaterals, a long spick and span new rack, on top of which some large stately mangers were fixed in her reverse. Over the chief seat, the picture of an old woman holding the case or scabbard of a sickle in her right hand, a pair of scales in her left, with spectacles on her nose. The cups of the balance were a pair of velvet pouches, the one full of bullion, which overpoised the other empty, as long as it was hoisted over the middle of the beam. I am of the opinion this is the true effigies of European justice, as exercised by our antipodes.

30 a manger and a rack were symbols for lawyers

31 illegitimate children

FRIDAY DECEMBER 23 TO MONDAY DECEMBER 26 *Number 74*

Artesia's Day

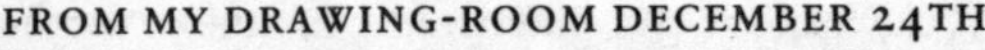
FROM MY DRAWING-ROOM DECEMBER 24TH

This afternoon half a dozen of us sat chatting together about clothes and what we should wear out of mourning, when a gentleman's coach stopped at my door and out of it came a grave matron that, immediately addressing herself to my cousin Arabella, asked her if she had performed her promise. Arabella smilingly answered that she was a-going, and presently began to speak in commendation of bridles, knots, and all manner of ribbons. 'I can't imagine,' said she, 'how they came to be so wholly laid aside, and wonder at our simplicity that we will suffer anything so becoming to our sex to remain so long out of fashion.'

Having said a great deal on this subject, the old gentlewoman that was come in her coach took up the cudgels and relieved her. She fetched a deep sigh and told us it was a burning shame that such a handsome wear should be so suddenly altogether neglected, then complaining that those everlasting mournings spoiled all manner of trades, she said nobody nowadays minded the poor, most of the ribbon weavers were out of employ, and thousands of them ready to starve. As for her part she had maintained multitudes of them for many years and could do it no longer. Thus she continued muttering and scolding for a quarter of an hour, till, seeing that nobody designed her any reply, she said if the Government would not provide for them they might see what would follow and went away in a great huff.

I asked Arabella what acquaintance of hers this was, who surprised us all by answering she was a ribbon weaver that lived in Southwark, and had for many years been used to drive up and down to the shops of her customers, begging, fetching and carrying work home in her own coach. I never expected to have heard complaints about ribbon weavers, and confess that I have never so much as thought on them. All of what I can say to the matter is I pity all that are of decaying trade, if it be honest and useful, but if the ribbon weavers have a bad time of it now, the grumbling gentlewoman's equipage shows that once they had a good one, and perhaps better than they deserved.

*

The linen draper that last Thursday had the impudence at noon-day to go into a hackney coach with his strumpet in Cheapside, is desired, to avoid scandal, not to do it just before his wife's brother's door.

MONDAY DECEMBER 26 TO WEDNESDAY DECEMBER 28 *Number 75*

Emilia's Day

My niece Sylvia, daughter to my brother Wealthy, merchant in Virginia, being sent over to be polished here under my tuition, I borrowed my Lady Stingy's chariot, who lends it to everybody because she pays her coachman no wages, and took Rosella with me to fetch her from Wapping Wall. When we came beyond the Tower, we fancied ourselves in Scotland, there was East-Smithfield, Ratcliff Highway, Shadwell Market, Execution Dock, Blue Apron Bay, and I thought old Gravel Lane would have lamed the horses and tore the coach to pieces, but they not being our own, we were extremely easy. The inhabitants ran out at the sight of a gentleman's coach, as if a blazing star had appeared to them, and the women were so boorish, so bold, and having each a child in her arms, they showed how fond the vulgar sort are of conversing with that beastly creature man.

The cries we heard were, 'sprats, mussels, trotters, grey peas and baked sheep's head'. Geese and turkeys they may have heard of, but never saw them, and for lark, teel, partridge or pheasant, they must certainly suppose them to be the names of foreign countries. Such woodcocks we imagined them to be, when we came to the place directed. We saw a thing in imitation of a house, with sash windows and a brass knocker at the door, at which impudent Will, rapping too hard, the neighbourhood was in an uproar and fancied that a great fire was broke out. Swarthy Forecastle, an amphibious creature, that calls himself Captain, who freighted my niece to England, came to the door and, having shouldered us out of the coach, he waddled before us into a place like a parlour. Rosella and I stared at one another to find that such animals have a notion of chairs and tables, but, as children strive to be men, as strollers pretend to be actors, and as players personate gentlemen, we must allow everything that is human to have a sort of pride, which prompts them to emulate their superiors, and they ought to be endured, since an awkward imitation proves a diversion to those truly refined.

Sylvia, though unknown to me, by natural instinct flew into my arms, tears of joy trickled from her, she was distant worlds from her mother, and found the likeness of her in an aunt, and the resemblance Miss had of my sister exhausted the same from me, having not seen her for ten years past. Rosella comforted her with education, company, gay clothes, plays, operas, and other fine sights, and the Tar, hanging down his head and wiping his nose with his sleeve, cried, 'please to sit for sooth. I had brought the commodity safe to harbour you see. I ne'er made any use of her, by the mass, she did what she listed, and when she had a mind to go to bed, we left her and smoked in the Gun Room.' Immediately sails in something like a woman, which the Captain gave us to understand was his dame. Her habit and her furniture of her house were all Indian, her head was as high as the main-mast, her patches were rather plasters, she had a watch like a warming pan, and her gown was pinned up to the cabin ceiling, 'Gentlefolks,' said she, 'you are as welcome as if you had been here a hundred times, and pray husband, get us something that is wetting.'

Rosella and I having repaid the compliment, and by turns affected a violent fit of coughing to stifle our laughter, in comes the cabin-boy, who, instead of a maid, tosses up the beds, swabs the house, and twirls about the sea-beef, with a swimming bowl of Rum Punch as if they designed we should have bathed in it.

The Captain, offering us pipes, and Madam Forecastle proffering to bear us company, the good nature of the beasts was (though very unwelcome) so superabundant, that we were forced to be a little sociable, or the ill-breeding had been on our side. To prevent swallowing down a filthy potion every moment, we were forced to enquire about things we did not desire to know, talk of French privateers and bear the noisy repetition of an engagement, till the Captain, fired with the remembrance of it, put himself into such a ferment that he threw about the chairs, broke the looking glass, had like to have beat off his wife's head, and had he but tumbled down his nasty punch, we could freely had forgiven him all. Madam Forecastle, the tamer savage of the two, entertained us with her acquaintance in Burr-Street, their junketting bouts[32] and how they all got foxed,[33] that truly, she thought a sneaker of punch or a can of good flip,[34] were preferable to your t'other end of the town Green tea, which was nothing but hot water and sugar, and your

32 sprees 33 drunk

34 drink made from hot, seasoned beer and spirits

poisonable Bohee,[35] which always made her bring up her dinner; and to visit where they give her nothing at all she takes it to be a very great affront, and so pray gentlefolks, drink about.

At this rate were poor Rosella and I mortified for four hours, while two strammelling wenches in the neighbourhood, had given the coachmen six-pence to sea-saw in the chariot. And whenever we rose to take our leaves, 'Avast, gentlefolks,' cries Madam, 'we never suffer Court visits at Blue Apron Bay,' and the Captain swore by the lights of Scilly, he'd hamstring us. At last having forced upon us a nauseous dram, and making us promise to visit them again and bring Miss Sylvia with us to see Miss Forecastle dance the Onion at a ball at Shadwell, we were released from these friendly monsters, the Captain pawing us out of the room, who gave Rosella such a spank into the coach that she protested she felt it two hours after.

*

Two maidenheads to be sold a pennyworth, enquire at the Cat and Fiddle in Wich Street.

*

A new totum for the use of those superstitious animals, who call mince pies popery, and cards the Devil's books, whose strongest liquor is Lamb's Wool, whose wit never soars above a harmless pun, and whose sublimest diversions are taking a sober walk, or a sculler up the river. Sold by Charles Bubble-bog, near the temple, and no where else.

*

The description of a Wapping Ball will be published with all convenient speed.

35 black, Indian tea

WEDNESDAY DECEMBER 28 TO FRIDAY DECEMBER 30 *Number 76*

Lucinda's Day

How many are the evils that are capable, of destroying our happiness in every station of human life? Yesterday, Artesia was pitying the uncomfortable condition of a young deserving lady that seemingly enjoyed all the blessings to be wished for on this side of the grave. 'Altamira,' said she, 'is married to a gentleman of a very great estate. They are of equal years, love one another to fondness, and have a beautiful thriving boy of a twelvemonth old. He is generous, she is discreet, both are of admirable temper, and neither of them guilty of any vice.' 'Indeed cousin,' said Arabella, interrupting her, 'I shall hardly be persuaded that, granting what you have said, any woman's life can be uncomfortable unless she wants her health.' 'No,' answered Artesia, 'they are both vigorous as well as healthy, and, as to their families, both are honourably descended and of an unspotted reputation. The only grievance she labours under is a mother-in-law that, doting on her son, made it her bargain when they married to be with them as long as she lived.

'The old lady, when her husband was alive, had been an incomparable wife, everybody counted her a very good humoured woman and there could not be tenderer mother than she had always been to her child. She thought nobody more worthy of her son than Altamira, before he had her, it was by her advice that he courted her, and nobody could be the more eager for the match than herself. Yet they had not lived together half a year, that every look, word or action of the daughter-in-law was misconstrued. Now Altamira is a hypocrite, all her virtue is but counterfeited, and all the love she shows to her husband is profound dissimulation. She hates him and all his family, wishes for his death and, under pretence of kindness, endeavours to make her last the instrument if it. These things the mother continually buzzes in the son's ears. She blames him for his fondness of a wife that slights him, bids him take care of his health and beware the fallacious smiles of a treacherous woman.

'The son, who is clear-sighted, knowing Altamira's innocence, strives to cure his mother of her ill-grounded suspicion, but nothing is able to convince her, and the more he defends the virtue of his wife, the more his mother is incensed against her. Altamira, entirely assured of her husband's affection, bears all the censures with an uncommon patience, which the husband would repay with a double kindness, but that he is afraid of his mother's anger. She having wealth enough of her own, he would fain have persuaded her to live separately from them, but the thoughts of it would be criminal. Could anything make a son wish to be divided from a mother that loves him more than she does her life? Altamira, could endure the frowns and ill-will of a mother-in-law if they were to affect none but herself, but, reflecting on her husband's tenderness to her, and his dutifulness to his mother, with the reluctancy he was forced to show in both, it was a constant as well as inconceivable sorrow to her that so much affliction should attend his extraordinary virtues and herself be the unfortunate occasion for all.'

This having led us to four or five stories more of young ladies who had been unhappy by mothers-in-law, it was asked in the company what reason there was to be given why the generality of women should hate all daughters-in-law, and at the same time be so fond of their sons-in-law. Arabella told us that in the first place old women seldom agreed with young ones, especially if they lived in the same house, and secondly that to lose the upper end of the table and to have the keys and the mistress-ship of the family taken from them was as great a mortification to some women, as to a Field Marshall to be commanded by one of his Lieutenant Generals. As to the fondness of women to their sons-in-law, that thinking themselves revived in their daughters, and calling to mind their youthful days, they were as grateful for every kindness their daughters received, as if it had been done to themselves.

Most of the company were very well pleased with Arabella's reasons. What she said of the sons-in-law I liked well enough myself, but the other I thought not satisfactory. 'Your reason,' said I, 'cousin, would be a very good one, if the generality of women did not hate their son's wives unless they lived together in the same house, and not only so, but likewise the houses where they themselves had been mistresses, but you see that they seldom agree, though they live never so far asunder; wherefore, in my opinion, it must be something more, generally applicable to them all, that can be alleged as a reason of that hatred with which they are so generally inspired. It is not a proverb of late date, of only five or six hundred years standing, but in Terence's[36] time who lived above a hundred and fifty years before our saviour was born, it was a saying of unquestionable truth, so generously received that he made use of it in one of his own comedies. And if I was to give my opinion about the matter it should be thus – the generality of women are very fond of their sons, in them when they are grown up they see, or at least imagine that they see, everything that was taking or commendable in the

36 Roman playwright, c. 190–159 BC

fathers of them when they were young. This makes them, as it were, jealous of their daughters-in-law, grudging them the enjoyment of their sons, because it so much resembles what once they were possessed of themselves and thought a crime in others to pretend to. This would be the first. My other reason for the hatred should be that they cannot brook strange women, as they call their son's wives in respect to themselves, should rob them of that intimacy and affection which they think they have so dearly deserved.'

I thought I had done my business very well, but was soon taken up by an elderly gentlewoman, whose son was lately married. 'I wonder,' said she, 'Madam, how your cousin Arabella and yourself, two maids that never were, and for ought I know, never will be married, should be so vain as to give your opinions in matrimonial affairs, especially such of which none can be judges but those that have known what it is to bring up children of their own. The reason for what you talk of needs not to be so far fetched. Most young women, very few excepted, are foolish and pretend to greater knowledge than they have, as they can dance a new minuet better, walk, dress, patch, and perhaps look better than those that are much older. So they simply imagine that they proportionally excel them in everything else. This makes that they are generally refractory to good council and always exclaiming against mothers-in-law, that for the love of their sons are in duty bound to advise them for the best.

As to the example your sister Artesia has given of the young lady, whom she said to be guilty of no vice, I believe it's a sad story. Was I to be as near her, as her mother-in-law is, I don't question but I should discover enough of them. Guilty of no vice! It's impossible! Some people say the same of a young gentlewoman I am acquainted with, though she has as many faults as she has hairs upon her head. It is not likely that women of prudence and experience, who generally love their sons and all what belong to them, should find fault with their daughters-in-law if they did not deserve it. And the comedy you quote is very little for your purpose. The poor woman 'tis true is blamed, and the daughter-in-law complains she cannot live with her, but the upshot of the story shows you that she had treated the other with all the tenderness imaginable, and that the daughter had only wanted an excuse to get home to her own mother's in order to lie-in privately, having been got with child in the street some months before she was married.'

I would have answered her that I did not prove that mothers-in-law hated daughters-in-law, from what happened in that comedy, but from the many instances that must have preceded to make it a proverb before that comedy was acted. But she would not hear a word, and marched off in triumph, as having obtained the victory over all the daughters-in-law in the universe.

*

This is to give notice to all news-writers, that there is lately come over a Laplander that profers to sell all manner of winds, at reasonable rates, to bring the packet boats in due time, which will spare them the trouble of inventing dull stories, and exempt the public from nauseous repetitions that may be of dangerous consequence this Christmas time, in which they are surfeited enough other ways.

FRIDAY DECEMBER 30 TO MONDAY JANUARY 2, 1710 *Number 77*

Artesia's Day

FROM MY DRAWING ROOM

Though an excess of virtue seems to imply a contradiction, yet some people are too far drawn away by good qualities that, though they are excessive, they cease not to be commendable. An instance of this is an uncle of ours that has a large estate and an ancient seat in Suffolk. He is descended of the honourable family of the Fortio's, so famous for their loyalty and zeal for the honour and welfare of their country. In every war they have always furnished our armies with heroes that have made the gallantry of Englishmen a proverb among all nations. My uncle himself served an 'prenticeship under Marshall de Turenne, and left off when that great General was unfortunately killed. He is a man of undaunted courage, but of a very high spirit, of an admirable good nature, and unshakeable integrity. No man was ever truer to his country, or paid taxes with a better will than himself. As he is a Justice of the Peace, he serves the Government faithfully, and is very severe against all Grumbletonians.

Some time ago, a fellow, after reading the votes, wished the Queen and Parliament took as much care to keep the poor from starving at home as they did to keep their armies abroad. My uncle heard of it and bad him be whipped for speaking seditious words. He is a prodigious admirer of soldiers, and whenever they are quartered near him, his house is the general *rendezvous* of the officers, and nobody in a red coat was ever unwelcome there.

Once a year he brews half a dozen hogsheads of incomparable strong liquor, which he calls his triumphant ale, of this he is very saving, but, upon the arrival of some good news, he has a large tankard that holds two gallons, which is called the Helmet of Mars. Whenever our own forces, or those of the allies, have obtained any advantage over the enemy, this huge piece of plate continually kept filled with triumphant ale, walks around among the country people, conquering as it goes, as long as anybody is able to hold it, whilst the old gentleman, crying for joy, hollows and capers about like a stripling, and throwing everything he can lay his hands on into the bonfire. If he sends anybody into the service, which happens very often, he calls it making him a man, and gives him half a piece out of his pocket to drink the Queen's health, which at night is the last thing he does himself, and his morning's draughts always begin with prosperity to all our forces by sea and land. He has such a respect for everything that belongs to the army that two years ago he turned away his chaplain for advising one of his maids against marrying a drummer that was going for Catalonia. His eldest son, my cousin Alexander, who made a campaign before he was sixteen, a very hopeful gentleman, was killed at Blenheim.[37] Caesar, the second, was wounded in the trenches before Mons, and is since dead at Lille. He never had more than one daughter, who died of the smallpox about half a year ago, and all the children my uncle has now alive are my cousin Pompey, who is bound to one Mr Mohair, a turkey merchant.[38] Pompey it seems is an extravagant youth, has debauched one of his master's maids, and is run away from him. What he has writ to his father I do not know, but yesterday Lucinda received the following letter from my uncle:

Dear Niece,
In my last I wrote to you how your cousin Caesar, after having partaken the glory of the most famous victory that ever was obtained, had the honour to be wounded with a grenade before Mons. Three weeks ago I had a letter from his Colonel, to acquaint me with his death. He gives him a very great character, and assures me at the same time that his brother Alexander, that was shot at the Battle of Blenheim, would have been made a Captain if he had lived out the battle. The simple woman, your aunt is hardly to be

37 Events in the Low Countries Campaign of the War of the Spanish Succession.

38 trader dealing with middle eastern countries

pacified, and does nothing but lament his loss, not considering that they might have lived till four-score, and not found an opportunity of dying so gloriously, or in so just a cause. I design to erect the valiant couple a noble tomb, and shall be obliged to you if you would think of an epitaph for them in Latin.

I confess, niece, that I can scarce speak of them without betraying more weakness than in justice I ought to do, and if I do not value my children's fame above my own affections, I sometimes could freely wish them alive again. I ordered Mr Mohair if he could find out the surgeon that attended Caesar to make him a present of five-and-twenty guineas, but I hear the villain reports that my son was as well of his wounds as any man living, and accidentally died of a fever. Pray, dear niece, enquire into this matter, which is of the highest importance of us all, and, if you perceive that he has ever said so, let the rascal not have a farthing and be forthwith prosecuted for defamation.

I have had some complaints of Pompey, and hear he has grown a loose spark, but last night I received a letter from himself that has wholly reconciled me to him. I was always afraid the boy was of an abject low spirit and would have chosen a pitiful unactive merchant's life, but by this writing I am in hopes that he is not entirely lost. He talks of five hundred pounds for a company, but pray dissuade him from those mercenary ways. Let him deserve it by treading the same path of honour as his brothers have done before him, and assure him from me that if he shall go to the army, he shall want for nothing, have as handsome an equipage and appear as well as any Captain there. In the meantime, I have desired his master to let him have money and treat him like a gentleman.

Your loving Uncle, etc.

P.S. I have strictly charged Pompey to leave off keeping the wench company, of which his master complains, but rather than that should be an obstacle, you may privately insinuate to him that I would not be very angry if he should take her along with him, for upon second thoughts, as he was always a great sloven, she may be serviceable to him in keeping his things tight abroad.

By the same post my sister received this letter, I had another from my aunt, who is a very good woman, a tender mother, and an obedient wife. She is of the family of the Sapientio's, who always contented themselves with being good, peaceable subjects, and never hunted after blessings but what were to be had in England. She writes thus:

Dear Artesia,
You have heard without doubt that my poor Caesar is dead too, first my eldest son, last summer my daughter, and now my Caesar. Poor Caesar, too, whom I so fain would have kept at home when his brother was killed. O niece, I am distracted for the loss of my children, and my grief is daily aggravated by the insensibility of my unnatural husband! Whenever I tax him with it or lament the miserable and untimely deaths of my unfortunate sons, all the answer I get from him is that they sacrificed their lives to their Queen and country, to whom they owed it. Sometimes he thinks to comfort me by talking of tombs, inscriptions, and what he'll pay to their memories. But heavens! What recompense is all this to a mother for the loss of her children!

Another great vexation I have is to hear that my Pompey, my all that I have left, is grown a wild ranting blade. Dear niece, if my husband should entice him likewise to the war, I am a dead woman. His father writes to him tonight, but what it is about I don't know. He seems pleased with him. I know his humour, and I am in a thousand fears. To have three sons with so much care and tenderness brought up to men's estate – how can a man be so bewitched and then to throw away their lives as if they were of no kin to him? Fifteen hundred a year, and of three as lovely men as ever the sun did shine on to my children, shall I not have one to inherit it? If it was by sickness or . . . O, disconsolate woman that as I am. Dear niece, excuse the incoherence of my style, my head is much disordered. Pray deliver the enclosed to my son. Remember, Artesia, my only son! And tell him that if he ever leaves England, he stabs me to the heart. Then tell him that I am his mother that brought him into the world, but so I did his brothers . . . I can no more. Adieu.

My sister and I are yet divided about the course we ought to take, but whatever we agree upon, you shall have at another opportunity.

MONDAY JANUARY 2 TO WEDNESDAY JANUARY 4 *Number 78*

Lucinda's Day

Far from the thronged luxurious town[39]
Lives an enchantress of renown,
Called HONOUR, who, by secret charms,
Pulls swains from yielding virgin's arms:
For her husband leaves his wife,
Despises pleasure, health and life;
For her the Trojan Refugee
Forgot the cave and went to sea;
By her the daughter of the sun,
Ensnaring Circe, was out-done;
From whose bright looks, from arts unknown,
She drew Ulysses to her own.
The silly sweethearts she bewitches,
Admire the rods for their own breaches;
Many (is it not a thousand pities)
A Lover's brain so void of wit is?
Their limbs shot off, imagine charms
Where sleeves hang dangling without arms.
Others t'a leg of flesh and bone,
Prefer a sorry wooden one,
Some lose an eye and say it's no matter,
A plaster on the hole looks better.
In bloody fields she sits as gay
As other Ladies at a play;
Whilst the wild sparks on which she dotes,
Are cutting one another's throats;
And when these wild folks, for their sins,
Have all the bones broke in their skins,
Of her esteem the only token,
Is t'have certificates they're broken;

[39] By now, Artesia and her sister, Lucinda, disagree about what should happen to Pompey. Artesia now agrees with their uncle that he should go to war, whereas Lucinda takes their aunt's side, and to dissuade Pompey she composes this poem in ridicule of honour, entitled *Grinning Honour*.

Which in grave lines are cut on stone,
And in some church or chapel shown
To people that, neglecting prayer,
Have time to mind who's buried there;
Till some half-witted fellow comes,
To copy what is writ on tombs,
And then to their immortal glory,
Forsooth, they're said to live in story;
A recompence, which to a wonder,
Must please a man that's cut asunder!

'Tis strange that any other woman,
By supercilious men's called common,
Whose generous loves of that extent,
As to 'ore spread a regiment:
Whilst in this sorceress it's no crime,
To love whole Armies at a time,
But then they say, the ill-natured Jade,
For all her sparks, is still a maid,
Because none e'er lay in her bed;
Unless they first were knocked o' th' head.

WEDNESDAY JANUARY 4 TO FRIDAY JANUARY 6 — *Number 79*

Emilia's Day

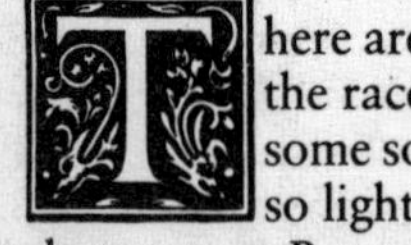

There are certainly as many unaccountable humours amongst the race of mankind as there are complexions and features, some so superciliously grave no jest can force a smile, others so light and thoughtless that the most tragical story can not draw a tear. Between these there is a medley competition, creatures that laugh and cry by turns, that pull pity on and off like a glove, and find subject of mirth from the wave of a fan. Of this sort is Camilla, whom I accidentally met at my lodgings yesterday. She no sooner entered the room, than she burst out into a violent fit of laughter. 'My Dear!' said she, 'I'll tell you news.' Then she laughed again. 'The fine lady that lodges over against me, Oh! I shall die with the relation. You know, I told you, went for a great fortune, and Beau Scentwell of Lincolns Inn was her conquest. I shall certainly swoon if you don't ease my lace a little, Mrs Dresswell. Bless me, I wonder what makes me so merry, I'm sure. I have a dreadful story in a letter from my cousin Betty in Norfolk of the sudden death of a new married couple, the best bred people in the whole country. Lord, it has given me the spleen to the last degree. The gentleman, it seems went into Leicestershire, to receive his lady's fortune, where he stayed about ten days. Sure I'm the most tender-hearted fool breathing. He writ her word he would be at home such a night. She, in expectation of her charming spouse, dressed herself to the best advantage, and paid a thousand visits to the gate of her courtyard, having been a voluntary prisoner to her chamber from the moment he left her. Bless me, how my head aches. I am not capable of relating to the rest, nor will my tears give me leave to do it.' Then down she sat, pulled out her handkerchief, then wept and sobbed like a cunning widow at the grave of her husband whom she had wished there seven years before.

My lady knew her temper, and said everything upon that occasion which a real grief might have expected. But I, who thought it the most ridiculous whimsy I ever saw to hear a woman begin two stories of such different natures, touched with the humour of both yet make an end of neither, could not forbear saying it would be very happy for some of our eminent players could they attain to such command of their passions. 'But for Heaven's sake,' added I, 'dear Madam don't let us lose the conclusion of two tales so admirably well begun. If you find yourself too tender to finish the last, give us leave to read the letter, and, if there be any secrets in it, fold down that part and pursue the thread of your former.' 'With all my heart, Mrs Distaff,' said she, 'for these melancholy relations always give me the vapours most intolerably.' With that she gave me the letter. As I opened it she burst out into a second fit of laughter, crying, 'Hold good, dear Mrs Distaff, I must beg your pardon for one moment, till I inform my lady how Squire Foxbound treats his wife, I protest I am not sorry for her neither, when I reflect how ill she used all her adorers in this town, preferring a clownish country-booby to men of sense and figure. Well, but go on Mrs Distaff,' said she. 'My dear Madam, finish this one, I beseech you,' said I, 'or we shall have so many ends, 'twill quite spoil the whole.' 'Phough,' says she, 'I hate your formal way of beginning and ending with a breath, but for once, I'll try.'

The Squire pursued, she lords it most tyrannically – 'His house is a kind of Seraglio,[40] where, for want of Eunuchs, he discharges the office himself. They say he had some thoughts of entertaining Signior Gri——dy,

40 harem

but the matter of the opera out-bid him, and secured the thing for the stage. Ha, Ha! Well thought on, now we talk of the opera, don't your ladyship design to be there tonight? Well!, there is something so ravishing in the sound.' Here I could hold no longer for my soul, but, smiling, asked her what charms she found in the sense. Then re-assuming her Te-hea sense – 'O, my stars! Who cares a patch for the sense!' 'So much for the opera,' said I, 'now for the story. How does the Squire treat his wife?' Here she paused a little, as if she had forgot where she left off. 'Ho! The Squire, yes,' said she, 'true Sultan like, he revels without control, every day he has a new doxy, who fits in his coach at the door, till his wife be decently locked up, who is become so tractable that as soon as she hears the coach stop, she presents herself on the head of the staircase with the key in her hand, which the courageous, prudent husband soon turns upon her, then marches his Cleopatra into his bed chamber, where he often keeps them for two or three days, during which time the conjugal prisoner has her penitential allowance turned in through a window.'

Here my Lady Modish expresses some concern for the misfortune of her friends, then commanded me to make an end of the letter, which I readily obeyed and read as follows:

> The charming pair, dear cousin, you so admired when you was here, are dead; the gentleman died in Leicestershire, whither he went to receive his lady's fortune. She neither dressed, received visits, nor left her chamber from the moment they parted till the day appointed for his return, but distinguished that by all the marks of a sincere joy. She dressed that day in all her wedding clothes, invited all her neighbours to dinner, gave a barrel of ale among her servants and workmen, and took a thousand turns to the door to watch his arrival. But oh! 'Tis shocking even to relate, in the midst of all her hopes, his body was brought to the door in a hearse, with all her relatives mourning around, at the sight of which she gave a great shriek, and dropped down dead. They let her blood, but all in vain; she never breathed more. So they buried them both in one coffin, not thinking it fit to separate those bodies whose souls the God of Love had joined.

'Here's an example of true love,' said I, giving her the letter. 'This story is very moving and really has a melancholy effect upon me,' said my Lady. 'Therefore, dear Camilla, give us the remainder of your first, to raise your spirits again.'

'I vow that story is diverting enough,' replied Camilla, 'though had it ended in matrimony it would have pleased me better, for I would have all fortune hunters perished in their own way. You must know his elegant speeches, fine shape and gentle mien snapped the heart of the lady, as he thought, so the happy day was set, and the joyful bridegroom all in new, repairing to his adorable bride. But, passing through Temple Bar, met a friend of his, whom he beckoned and took up into the coach, telling him his good fortune and desiring the favour to receive his wife from his hands. Away they drove to her lodgings, but as soon as they entered the chamber, the lover was surprised to see his friend salute his intended bride something too familiarly, and hear him say, "What, is it you, Molly, that has catched this gentleman? This must not be." Whereupon, the lady flew into a violent rage, and discharged a volley of names interlarded with curses for her disappointment, but the gentleman only laughed, and carried off the lawyer, who was so confounded that he had not one word to say for himself.'

*

The reader is desired to take notice that (to use the famous Bickerstaff's words) when he supposes we are dull, we have some hidden design, though that great man has his happiness that, when he really is so, he has admirers enough that will not believe it.

*

Emilia, taking into consideration the great rise of bread and wine, at the same time desires all good husbands to do so too, and those that did not come home till eleven, not to be out after nine.

MONDAY JANUARY 9 TO WEDNESDAY JANUARY 11 — *Number 81*

Lucinda's Day

FROM MRS BALDWIN'S

I am come hither in hopes of meeting with something worthy to be taken notice of. Here are abundance of letters full of scandal, and malicious stories, most of them very ill-spelled, and I believe, worse designed. Some of them contain nothing but home scandal, where people are too plainly pointed at, which I hate; others again seem to be writ with a good intention, but are very trifling, so that, of the whole heap before me, I shall only insert but one, which I don't think much to be found fault with, and is writ thus:

Ladies,
I am a young gentlewoman that takes great delight in plays and operas, and read the *Tatlers* both male and female as constantly as they come out. I generally understand everything I read, all but what's Latin, and that I skip, but there is one cramp word, for which Mr Bickerstaff has an extraordinary value, that puzzles me abominably. Now I am used to it, it sounds very well. Everybody seems pleased with it, and yet I can never meet with it anywhere else but in the Squire's papers. The word I mean is 'Lucubrations'. I read it a hundred times before I could remember it, and for a good while used to call it 'lubrications', for which I was horribly laughed at by a gentleman of my acquaintance. Sometimes I have thought that it was smutty, and blushed at the hearing of it; but what is really meant, I ingeniously confess I don't understand to this day. I know several of whom might be informed, but everybody having it so current, I was always ashamed of appearing more ignorant than others. I would write to Mr Bickerstaff himself about it, but I doubt he is too high to take notice of such blockheads as myself. Methinks I am satisfied that it is something very comical, and yet I perfectly long to know what it is. Wherefore, pray Ladies, honour me with an explication of it, either by way of advertisement, or in any other part of your papers, you shall think fit yourselves, and you'll infinitely oblige,
Your humble servant,
T. G.

This letter confirms me an opinion I have had a great while, that most people are more ignorant than they care to appear. The word is not so common, but a young lady might read plays and romances for ten or a dozen years and never meet with it, I confess, and I don't think it strange that anybody should not understand it, but I wonder how it should come in the young gentlewoman's head to ask us to explain it, unless she thought that Tatlers were to be understood after the same manner as they catch elephants, by the help of females, according to that of 'Hudibras',[41] wherein he says: – The Tame Female . . . Of Elephants inveigles the Male.

I am altogether against resolving of questions, though they were never so lawful, and declare that I will always leave it to those that make it

41 One of the most popular poems of its time, by Samuel Butler (1613–80).

their business. However, for once, and not to make a custom of it, I'll satisfy a young lady's longing that prays so heartily. The word 'Lucubration', in its large signification, comprehends all manner of work that is done by candlelight, whether it smells well or ill; but in its stricter sense, it is by excellency applied to the works of the learned only, from a supposition that when people are hard at study they do it by night as well as by day, and consequently that they want some artificial light, or other to see by. Hence it was that elaborate books were by the Latinists, proverbially said to favour of the lamp. 'Lucubration', like 'work' in English, signifies both the labour itself and the product of it. The word has always been a very serious one, and has never been ridiculed before Mr Bickerstaff happily attempted it. As to the reason of his making a jest and appearing to be so fond of it, the Authors differ.

The better sort are of the opinion that the Squire, being an airy, facetious man, that writes with strength and spirit, and would make the world believe that his papers are writ off hand, has called his Tatler's 'Lucubrations', and derision of those sour, laborious pedants that have taken such wonderful pains and yet not been so diverting or instructive as himself. But others think that having used the word too often in the beginning, before he was aware, as soon as he saw it and found that others did the same, to prevent our thinking that he had been in error, he purposely seemed to grow more fond of it, and endeavoured to persuade the world that he had all along designed it as a jest, and, by this stratagem they say that his incomparable genius of turning everything which way he pleases, he has gained our applause for what was in reality at first a fault of his inadvertency. I know some Rosicrucians[42] that will have it that there is a secret charm in the word, understood by none but the Adepts,[43] and that, in his way of conjuring by the magic force of it, the Squire has wrought very strange things. Several people again hold to the contrary, that there is nothing in it and that he only keeps it at his fingers' ends as jugglers do their sticks to amuse the crowd.

Speaking of all these different opinions, I can but think on the strange interpretations and various constructions that are always made of the words and sayings of great men. From the writings of Homer the sagacious critics have gathered that he was a perfect master of all Arts and Sciences, and yet to outward appearance they only look like bombastic poems, full of ridiculous epithets, furbelowed similes and nauseous repetitions, which has often made me suspect that most commentators took more out of books than the author ever designed to

[42] A secret society founded in the 17th century, who claimed to possess esoteric wisdom handed down from ancient times.

[43] those who have discovered the secret of the philosopher's stone

put in them. As for my part, I take everything in the sense it most naturally seems to imply, and believe that Mr Bickerstaff calls his papers 'Lucubrations' for no other reason but because the generality of them are so. A man that exercises his body all the morning in the noble science of defence, and spends the afternoon in his chair of judicature, can't be supposed, at least at this time of the year, to write much in Sheer Lane without the assistance of candlelight, and, as I was writing this, I received the following letter directed to Lucinda and Artesia:

> Ladies,
> I am a very impatient fellow, and a mortal enemy to all things that are of any long continuance. I walk in the park every day, and never went the whole length of the Mall at once in all my life. I should take great deal of delight in your papers if you would not dwell for so long on a subject.
>
> I am a great lover of tobacco, and foul above twenty pipes in a day, yet I don't remember that I was ever so well pleased with one as to take it off, and I am commonly tired before they are smoked halfway.
>
> I generally dine at the Tavern, but I can't endure to go twice to the same house in one week. I believe I am a tolerable good judge, and yet I can much better endure nonsense, so it be short, than the best series of continued sense.
>
> Variety of matter I know is chargeable, and if you can't afford too much of that, forge letters, steal off others, put in stale verses, draw lines and make etc.'s, or anything in the word that makes a disturbance in the paper, and diverts the eye. Where *primo intuitu*[44] I see nothing of that kind, I never venture upon *Tatlers*, or any other paper whatever.
>
> Nay, if ye all writ like angels, (I think the Devil is in me) I should never be able to reach the bottom of the second column if there were no breaks by the way.
>
> Yet I can bear with an ocean of ink if it be filled with isles of blank paper, for which reason nothing in the map is so diverting to me as the little bits of dry land that are crumpled in the Archipel.
> Your humble servant,
> Vario

This letter came in very good time, for I should have filled my whole *Tatler* with Lucubrations, if I had not been prevented by it. I own the gentleman is in the right. It is a courteousness in my nature that I don't know how to part with a thing once I got hold of it, and I often serve my

44 at first sight

arguments as I do my tea, which I make pretty strong at first, but because I would have all the goodness out of it, I generally drink it weaker at last, than really I love it.

WEDNESDAY JANUARY 11 TO FRIDAY JANUARY 13 *Number 82*

Emilia's Day

ell! 'Tis a difficult matter to distinguish what will and what will not please the town best, since two or three leading ladies are led out of their way, though not without some censure of them being too fond of some of the parrots of a poet, which to oblige, they possess themselves enemies to wise learning. Witness their ungenerous proceedings with the Virgin Poet, 'tis barbarous to engage a party against an author's third day. Had the famous Ben[45] met such usage in his time, the Haymarket would have wanted the *Fox*, *Alchemist* and *Silent Woman* now. Our sex, formed for modesty and innocence, ought to encourage tragedy, whose well-wrought scenes raise the soul to glory, and stamps the notions of true honour in it; whilst most comedies draw conscious blushes from the cheek, and covers the face with scarlet dye.

I happened into a sort of medley conversation t'other day, yet every one a masterpiece of wit in their own fancy; one cried up the admirable plot of *The Careless Husband*,[46] another that diverting farce, called *The Emperor of the Moon*,[47] a third the connection of *The Tender Husband*,[48] and a fourth, the inimitable diversion of a puppet-show, and protested that Punch's conversation was an engaging as any player of them all. Now I could not for my soul distinguish whether she meant upon the stage or in the bed-chamber, whether she thought Punch a player, or all players sticks and clouts. A fifth, strangely admired the

45 Ben Jonson
46 by Colley Cibber
47 by Aphra Behn
48 by Richard Steele

performance of the most famous Mr Higgins,[49] a sixth extolled the Scaramouche,[50] and thought him a miracle in nature. The debate grew warm between these two which was the prettiest fellow, till a seventh stepped up, and protested that she had rather see Sir Harry Wild-air[51] cut a caper than either of them. Now I leave my reader to judge, which of these seven had the most refined taste.

The following letter comes from an Officer in the army, which we received just now:

Ladies,

For since your names are unknown to me, I am obliged to direct you all, my request is, that you be pleased in your next *Tatler* to inform the public, consequently including your humble servant, whether your society be maids, wives or widows? If maids, how old and wealthy? If wives, how your husbands are qualified, if they are sufficiently patient to be admitted in the citizens credit of cuckoldom? And if they are, how well their coffers are lined to pay for the honour? If widows, how handsome, and what jointure? Now if you would know why I am thus inquisitive, you must understand that this day I received letters from some of my friends in Flanders, that gave me the dreadful account of an approaching peace. I command a Regiment at present, keep a handsome equipage, wear the best lining, and have a mighty passion for embroidered clothes. Now I have an aversion to retrenching and can no longer descend from Burgundy and Champagne, to Derby, Yorkshire or Nottingham ale, than I could be content to shoot myself through the head, to prevent being eaten up with the spleen, when reduced to half pay.

As affairs stand, I find it absolutely necessary to fence against the levelled danger, and I think no expedient better than a wife with a good portion, especially in land, for then I may come to be a Member of Parliament. If so, I'll lay my life I'll make such a noise in the Senate that they will be glad to give me a place to silence my roaring, and then I'm provided for of course. If any of you happen to have this comfortable ingredient in matrimony, you can't do a more generous act than to secure a soldier from the desperate condition of peace. Remember Ladies, there are all the temperal

49 A contortionist who turned himself into 'such variety of amazing shapes and figures that the particulars would be incredible to all persons who have not seen him'.

50 The dancer Layfield, who not only danced the pantomime character Scaramouche in theatrical interludes, but also performed vocal imitations of horn, huntsman and a pack of hounds.

51 Robert Wilks, an Irish leading actor

works of mercy in such an act, and gratitude to the highest pitch, for you feed the hungry, and clothe the naked, etc. and reward the brave. For who ought to possess that virginity and wealth but him who has ventured limbs and life to preserve them? This much for maids and widows, one word to the wives, and I have done. Now, according to your age, I shall abate or enhance the price of your pleasures.

But first I think it would not be inconvenient to give you a slight sketch of my person. I am not quite six foot, well-shaped, clean limbed and a good rakish air, and, without vanity, have the best teeth and soundest body in the whole army. My complexion's good, and though I take a cheerful bottle sometimes, I have not the least sign of it in my face. Now, if any private objection should be started, I can bring five hundred laundresses, Corporal's wives, and Sergeant's ladies, besides servant maids, Burgher's daughters and smiling hostesses, to vouch for my ability, and so forth. But to what I was saying before, a woman of twenty, with a tolerable forehand, for as many guineas, shall enjoy all and every single part of me for the space of twenty-four hours. I'll not stand for the odd four, but generously throw them into the bargain. If she draws near to thirty, I'll overlook that too, for I'm a man of honour. The same sum shall suffice, but if she's arrived at forty, the purse must be double, and so on to fifty, though I doubt I shall do but single duty upon those years; but be sure none of you exceed, for I have a mortal antipathy to threescore.

We desire the Colonel's patience till next week for an answer, not having leisure to give it this.

To Mrs Rosella,

Madam,

It is to be supposed a person so nearly resembling the knight inhabitants above as your Ladyship must be endowed with every qualification in nature. I take it for granted then, that you are as conversant with the stars, and know all their conjunctions and houses as perfectly as their next door neighbours, and can read the fate of us mortals as readily as the alphabet and know what company Charon[52] shall have over sticks[53] this new year, as certainly as the waterman of a Gravesend Tilt-boat can count their passengers. How many virgin martyrs will fall a sacrifice to the blind God, and what number of happy cuckolds will be landed on

[52] name of a horse [53] horse racing with jumps

Elysium? Therefore I desire you would give me a cast of your art. I am in love, confoundly in love, and though I talk tolerably well in a chocolate house, or over a bottle, yet the Devil a word can I get out to my mistress, nay, though I have tried Mr Bickerstaff's prescription of Lilly's best Spanish,[54] renowned for it's admirable help to discourse, yet I am dumb still.

I look at her, cross my arms, shrug up my shoulders and sigh, but that's all. Now I can't find that this way of proceeding is at all intelligible to her. She laughs, talks, sings, and drinks her tea as unconcernedly as if she had not shot one of the prettiest fellows in the kingdom quite through the heart. Therefore, madam, I would gladly know whether she is really ignorant of my pain, or only seems so; whether I may with hope pursue her, or apply a pistol to my ear out of pure despair. For, faith, I find I can't live without her, or somebody else as exactly like her, and if you are sure the Gods have made her a twin sister be pleased to signify in your next (that is if you find by the figure that the other will never be mine) where she resides. Be pleased to observe that I was born upon Childermass Day, '84, about twelve at noon.

Yours,
A.H.

*

Lost: The second instant, from under one of the modish petticoats of twelve yard circumference, in a new-fashioned hackney coach, a gem called Honour, supposed to be taken by some of Higgins Scholars, who, whilst the lady was descending from the balcony of her coach, very dexterously cast himself into one of the folds of her coat, and lay concealed till Jehoe whipped forwards. She was ashamed to cry out, and the darkness of the night favoured his escape. Whoever gives notice of the person to the East-India Company, so that the jewel may be had again, shall be well rewarded.

*

Lost out of a gentleman's scrutore, in the Middle Temple, some original copies for a general correspondence, by way of love-letters, suspected to be taken by a certain lady, who is desired to restore them by the end of the month, and to keep the secret entire, to prevent having her name in print, with the place of her residence, and the cause for which she retained him; and he promised upon receipt of those papers, to restore

54 cheapest snuff

her back to her fee in *specie*,[55] and with it a small pot of complexion[56] to keep her in countenance, which she dropped out of the bosom of her stays.

*

A gentleman that frequently reads his *Billet-Doux* in the Chocolate House, is desired to keep a secretary to prevent his own hand being known, when he writes to himself.

MONDAY JANUARY 13 TO MONDAY JANUARY 16 *Number 83*

Rosella's Day

This day has afforded such variety of company and discourse, so out of the way from what a reasonable person might imagine, that it gave us abundance of diversion, though for my life I cannot reconcile such contradictions as a lion to have the nature of a lamb, and the lamb, that of the lion. Here was a gentleman of the army, whose post brings him forty shillings a day, (a very pretty income) bewailing the hardships of his country, and pitying the distress of the poor occasioned by the length of the war, who protested that, though his sword was his only fortune, he had rather apply it to his breast, and Curtius-like,[57] sacrifice his own life than those of his countrymen by exhausting their treasure too much in a foreign war, and that way reducing their charity unable to support the indigent. Therefore, though he knew half pay would be annexed to peace, yet for the considerations above, he declared solemnly it would be the welcomest news that could be brought him. All the company knew him to be a man of honour, and as much courage as any man that ever took the field, so that none could object he wished this out of fear, and they also knew he was no philosopher, no despiser of money, but a man that

55 in cash 56 make up

57 Curtius Lacus leaped to his death into a chasm which opened up in the Forum to fulfil the prophecy that one more life must be sacrificed to save the city.

keeps up his port, and admires a fine appearance, even in all he converses with, as well as in that of himself. From whence we conclude him a person of excellent principles and a hearty lover of his country, for which he had ventured his life out of a pure zeal for her welfare and not out of any mercenary end.

Emilia told him he was a miracle of a soldier, and 'twas pity he did not help to fill the senate, or what was yet dearer, the order of religion. He bowed and begged her to believe he were not the only soldier of those principles. She replied it was a pity that there was not a draught made of them then, to supply the deficiencies of church and state. Here she was interrupted by the appearance of a man in black, but a man of this world every way, properly distinguished, a high-flying clergyman. You might read his principles in his air, for he frisked about the room like a whirlwind. After civil ceremony had passed on both sides, Lucinda asked him what news. He said there was nothing new, at least nothing strange, in suffering persecution for the truth's sake. The generation that stocked this nation in forty-one[58] will never be entirely rooted-out. But had the citizens foreseen what is now coming upon them when they laid the foundation of St Paul's, they would have chosen to petition the Parliament for leave to pull down the rest of the churches which escaped the fire,[59] and convert the stones and timber into conventicles, to settle upon their posterity, and, rather than have contributed to the building of new ones for no other use than to drive bargains and observe fashions in, since a man's conscience must not dictate to his tongue.

I observed the honest swordsman bite his lips, and gather up his brow, and therefore would have turned the discourse, but the parson went on with it. 'It is a burning shame,' said he, 'that the whole body of the clergy don't interpose their authority, and do that worthy member of our cloth, Sacheverell,[60] justice.' ''Tis pity,' said the red-coat warmly, 'that the Government don't whip your coat above your ears, and his head from his shoulders. I am sure if all such sowers of sedition were twice a week to number the kennels from Newgate to White-chapel with the rod of correction at their backs they would have the justice they deserve.' 'No doubt Sir,' replied the other, 'but if we return to an Olivarian Government, we shall have martial discipline, vice in laced coats that will swinge off honestly in rags.' 'O!' said the officer,

[58] before the beginning of the English Civil War, 1642–9.

[59] the Great Fire of London, 1666.

[60] Henry Sacheverell: political preacher who in 1709 delivered two sermons opposing the Revolution Settlement and the Act of Toleration which led to his impeachment by the Whig government.

'would I had your whole party in my company, I'd make you run the gauntlet six times a day, but I'd jerk you into obedience. You should have marks of the beast you worship in abundance, and you should have just title to the Chevalier de St George's favour.' 'You are a soldier, Sir, you talk like one of your cloth.' 'That's more than you do,' replied the other briskly, 'for you are a scandal to yours, and I hope the patriots of my country will take care to cashier all such as you and your worthy friends out of the pulpit. I dare say that the university that nursed you is ashamed to own you for her son.' 'That's your mistake, Sir,' said he, 'for you'll find both Oxford and Cambridge interest themselves in the affairs of those you treat thus scandalously.' 'Yes, Sir, and to justify what he has asserted, they design to have that book burnt, which a certain man much commended by some people wrote against the sermon of a worthy prelate to show religion has not lost all her champions, but that there are men left that dare die for the truth.' 'D'ye call vanity, ambition, ostentation and treason, the truth?' said the hero. 'O impudence! 'Tis well your cassock and the presence of these ladies protect you, or I should endeavour to breath a vein to let out the poison in your blood.' With these words, he quitted the room, much to my satisfaction because I feared the heat of their passions might have produced some ill-effect.

I desired the doctor to sit down, and hoped we should fall upon something more agreeable than the last discourse, but I immediately found it was not to cease so soon, and heartily I wished the black coat had gone instead of the red. For by chance a Bourignian[61] was here, which is related to one of our society, who immediately took up the cudgel, and told the doctor that the universities were schools of debauchery, nurseries for Satan and the destruction of youth, where their bed-makers and laundresses were more examined than their books, except when they told them to get drunk with the money; that the foolish things of this world was given to confound the wise, and that the spirit of truth never came in the colleges, therefore no danger of martyrdom for religion, when there never was any such thing in either university. This stung home, and set the doctor in a flame, which cost me five quarts of Imperial tea to keep within the bounds. These two made such a din, that we women, whose prerogative it is to be noisy, could not be heard. Some expressed an uneasiness, others laughed, but none would venture to interrupt their jargon, which grew louder and louder, and as confused as that of Babel, till a Quaker passing by (the door being upon the jar) and hearing some of the young

[61] One who believed that religion should follow inward emotion rather than outward practice.

fellows puritanical expressions, took it for a meeting house, and entered without any manner of ceremony.

At first he sighed, and his spirit groaned exceedingly, but lifting up his eyes upon the company, and discovering his error by our dress, and turning quick upon the doctor, whose black gown made him jump from the place where he stood, he roared out – 'Avoid Satan! Though enemy to the spiritual man, avoid, I say, and come not near these corporal parts of mine.' Then suddenly caught hold of the parson's antagonist, crying, 'What dost thou, taper of light, do in the tabernacle of the wicked? Why dost thou vex thy religious spirit, in preaching to the congregation of the whore of Babylon?' With that, tugged him quite downstairs, and the company burst out into a fit of laughter, that the other was ashamed of the disturbance which he had occasioned and took the opportunity to sneak off. We all rejoiced at his good breeding in that point, and after a few observations on what had passed, we all concluded that it was the most extraordinary company that ever filled the circle of a visiting day, but such as we have no inclination to see a second time.

*

Lost in the gallery of St James Church, on Sunday the first of this instant, a thought, supposed to be taken up by a lady in Piccadilly, of twelve thousand pounds fortune. She is desired to restore it to the owner to prevent atheism, for the gentleman has never said his prayers since.

WEDNESDAY JANUARY 18 TO FRIDAY JANUARY 20 *Number 85*

Emilia's Day

To perform our promise and answer your letter of Friday last, we must tell you, Sir, we find your inclinations are very extensive, and there is something particular in your address that points directly on Hibernia,[62] and shows us what country we are obliged to for the production of such an able bodied warrior. Had there been so many infallible marks of the incomparable

62 Ireland

Homer, there had been no room left for dispute. You desire to know if we are maids, wives or widows, to which I answer, we are all maids, but I doubt out of the latitude of your pretentions. Some of us are young and handsome, but no gold, dear Sir. Some well shaped and witty, but horridly proud, and could no more live upon half matters than yourself. Some very rich, but very cunning, not part with a shilling without a valuable consideration. Now if you could have brought five hundred acres, besides fine country seats, with gardens, parks, and manors, instead of laundresses, sergeant's ladies, and burgher's daughters to vouch for your abilities, you had done your business effectually. For everybody likes your picture, and we could let it rest in the frame of levity too, were there gold enough to set it off, but the mischief ou't is we are all a little whimsically inclined to like that shining metal in our pockets more than upon the outside of a husband; nay, some of us are so tasteless as to declare openly that the plainer the man the finer the wife, and have taken the resolution not to marry anything with a lacked coat, or full wig.

Really Sir, I pity those brave men of the sword whose fortunes depend on a fan; and to take the air upon Hounslow, or Bagshot Heath, for ought I know would be the best resolution of the two, since hanging and marrying are twin-sisters of destiny, and 'tis but a cast of dye which is the happier fate. Pray do not think I give this advice out of spleen or contempt of your person or parts, but on the contrary I assure you I am noted in our society for my liking a soldier, therefore, when they all declared their minds, they gave commission to me only to return you this answer. I would have declined it for I hate to be the messenger of ill news, especially to a handsome man, and I must own I have formed such an idea of you that it was not without some reluctance that I obeyed. But e'r I begun, I took an opportunity to visit all my acquaintance and read your letter wherever I came, hoping some lucky chance might offer to do you service, but I found the widows, throughout of your class, still in the same lesson, jointures and settlements!

I pleaded the services you had done abroad. They answered the taxes they had paid at home were sufficient. I enlarged upon the merit of your person, they upon their estates. So that one might as soon reconcile contradictions, as bring them to a right understanding, they were all mere pagans, except one, who indeed was so generous to desire me to let you know she felt a tenderness for you, and I confess, I believe she was real, for she melted into tears as soon as she heard your letter, and cried, 'Poor gentleman, he deserves our pity, he shall not languish, I'll relieve him. Pray Mrs Emilia,' says she, 'let him into the particulars of my mind with those of my estate. I have you know five hundred a year besides ten thousand pounds in the Exchequer and some old bags in the bottom of my coffer, which, according as he behaves himself, may fall into his share. My age is but seventy-seven, but you need say nothing of that, for I think you will own that if I had but a new set of teeth, which upon this occasion I design to get, that I do not look to be above fifty, and you see the gentleman has no aversion to fifty by his letter.'

Here I, in favour of you again, objected against a salt rheum which fell continually from her eyes, which she kept wiping away with a piece of green silk, but she assured me that Sir W—— R——[63] had promised to remove that in ten days time; she has a kind of palsy on one side too, but Dr G——[64] prescribes a husband just about your years, as an infallible ingredient to prevent her shaking. But though I remember you declared against threescore, yet, to oblige the widow and leave you to the choice of making your fortune, I have faithfully given you an account of my proceedings thus far. It rests now in your breast, whether you will lay a help in hand towards her cure. A soldier in his life must have done a duty against his will for a Brown George[65] and a cup of water. Then if you refuse a post which will bring partridges and burgundy to dinner every day in the year, you have too much philosophy to fear a peace. Weigh this matter well and know me for your friend. Let me have your answer, and I'll quickly send you word where the lady lives. In the mean time let me interest you not to think of wives, it may be of evil consequence and very pernicious to the good of the Commonwealth. By sowing the seeds of war that may rise up a mutinous generation, to the utter destruction of that peace we now hope for, tho' according to Dryden – *Absolom and Achitophel* [1681] – bastards are always to the bravest men, yet it has been observed never to bode England good. Thus far by way of advice, and now I am Sir, your most humble servant.

*

Mr A.H., we have but one in our society that understands astrology well enough to calculate nativities, and she has been in the stars up to the elbows, but I cannot feel any good fortune for you. First, she drew a scheme, and erected the figures in the usual form, thinking the common way might do. But finding her mistake, immediately called for a

[63] Sir William Read, Her Majesty's occulist, who regularly advertised in papers like *The Female Tatler*. See advertisement section, pp. 219–224. He was self taught, and a quack, but became very rich.

[64] possibilities include Roger Grant, another quack occulist, or Samuel Garth, a famous doctor and poet.

[65] a military provision of a coarse brown loaf

telescope and levelled it right upon the Milky Way, supposing that place the most likely to trace the footsteps of love and discover the inclinations of our sex. But of a sudden she said a thick wrought sullen cloud, which she is positive proceeded from your bashfulness, screened it from her view, and left her in the dark. She is sometimes of an opinion that your birth was unlucky, and it is impossible to remove the curse that one brings into the world. Wherefore, her advice is, since the planets refuse the solution of your fate, that you would apply yourself to some well skilled in necromancy to see if their art can fetch it from below. But if you should not approve of that, then she councils you to pluck up a courage, go and visit the lady, and boldly tell your pain.

You seem to hint that you understand the language of the eye. Join to that the language of the tongue, talk much, no matter what you say, so that you do but embellish it with flame, darts, uneasiness awake, and dreams of her when asleep. Ply her with these when present, and with letters when absent. If your genius don't lie to writing, there are those that do, and for a couple of guineas may be procured to furnish you with *Billet-Doux* for a week. Toast her in all companies, and be sure to bribe the chamber-maid as well, as the readiest way to the heart of her mistress. If this way fails, there are several ways out of this world besides that of a pistol. You may take your choice, for we cannot positively tell whether there be any parallel to that beauty you so much admire, without you had sent her name and the hour of her birth; though this we dare affirm, that if these methods does not gain her affections, she has not her fellow on this side of the Alps. Therefore, you may prepare for travel as soon as you please.

*

There is now in the press, and will be speedily published, the *Art of Keeping a Secret*, very useful for beaus and women, especially some that have lost the retentive faculty, and drops their copies of their clandestine works out of their pocket on purpose to discover the author accidentally.

*

Lost from behind a gentleman's coach, four footmen. Whoever finds them are desired to send them into the service, the gentleman to whom they belonged having no farther occasion for them.

MONDAY JANUARY 23 TO WEDNESDAY JANUARY 25 *Number 87*

Sophronia's Day

A young gentleman who I'll distinguish by the name of Philaster, was born to a noble fortune, the heir of an ancient family, who valued themselves more upon their titles than the virtues of their predecessors, and would not have consented to his marrying without a long scroll of heraldry to have proved his high birth. He lived in the neighbourhood of a young virgin that had nothing to boast of but innocence and beauty. He had seen her at her window and at Mass, for they were of that persuasion, and felt the bewitching softness of young love. He watched all opportunities of being heard privately, and in a fatal hour succeeded. The lady was an orphan, ill used and helpless. He sued, he swore, he languished and despaired, and was possessed of all the artillery of love, a graceful person, an agreeable wit and the most prevailing eloquence of eager passion. She listened and she was lost.

He showed her the impossibility of marrying without being disinherited, which would not only ruin them, but condemn their posterity to servitude and sorrow, if ever it come out whilst his father lived, and there was no depending on the secrecy of a third person; that he must live in perpetual apprehension, if not discovered, and that was sufficient to blast his hopes of greatness and dash the joys of love. But whatever was sacred, whatever was solemn, should bind the contract between themselves, which he would confirm the first hour he was his own disposer, as the Church required. Thus the unwary innocent was caught, and he, by the assistance of a friend, had her conveyed to lodgings, where she lived unknown, and so by his management remained wholly unsuspected. His passion abated not with possession, he doted to excess.

Some years rolled on, and a son crowned their wishes. He thought himself the happiest of this kind, and held it impossible to be false; but alas, how little do we know ourselves. A lady of equal birth and fortune, not sixteen and extravagantly handsome, was invited by his father with her relations to a ball. The old gentleman had a design to ensnare his son's heart, not knowing of its pre-engagement, and to that end surprised him that he had no time to arm his soul against the invincible charm of superior beauty. He gazed and sighed, fear, desire, remorse at once distract him, duty, interest and inclination urge him on; but gratitude and honour keep him back. At last he flies to his first choice in hopes to lose in her dear arms this wild ecstasy. But all was tasteless and insipid and so palled, that he cannot counterfeit a joy.

She soon perceived the change, wept and begged to know the cause. He would have concealed it, but moved her by entreaties, and having the bear of nature to sincerity, he told her all his heart, assured that he had strove against the encroaching mischief, but strove in vain. This was thunder to the poor dismayed. What did she not say, inspired by love, jealousy, and despair? He pitied and advised, but love was fled, nor could his utmost endeavours recall the fleeting boy. After some time past in fruitless strugglings, between a growing and declining flame, he came to the unfortunate and bid her prepare to leave the town with her son, for the marriage was agreed and she must not be heard on. He would take a particular care of them both in some remote place, which he would find speedily for her, and in a few days was as good as his word, and ordered her to be ready for her journey on the next morning.

She being well resolved what to do, told him she submitted to her hard destiny without complaint, that all she asked for ruined virtue and for injured trust was leave to take her last farewell. She begged he would sup with her that evening and constrain himself to suffer a few hours, since he knew they were the last she ever should make tedious to him. This was obliging a request that he readily granted, viewing her still with pity and imperfect gratitude. At night he brought his friend and confessed his shame and regret for what he was about to do, and wished there was a power on Earth could snatch him from the tyranny of the ungenerous passion that destroyed him. She had prepared the wine he loved and gave it to him often. About the midst of the entertainment, he complained of sickness and unusual heat, upon which she fell onto her knees, implored his pardon, and bid him think on Eternity, for he was poisoned. 'Tis not easy to conceive how many different passions agitated his mind, at the same minute he heard the dreadful sound – 'I have not done it for revenge' said she. 'I was no more able to outlive you, than to bear your being another's. I have pledged the fatal draught, and shall go with you on the gloomy way. Send for a priest, and for your father.' He conjured his friend to fly for both. In the meantime he looked with melancholy concern on their unhappy offspring, by turns caressing and condoling his infancy.

With incredible haste, the father and the confessor came, they sent the friend for a physician, though she assured them the poison she had bought of an Italian no antidote could expel, nor had they an hour to live. On this the confessor approached, and, as she owned her crime with Philaster, said she should die with horror unless in these last moments of life, for both their souls eternal good, the Holy Father might make them one. Philaster joined in the petition, truly satisfied that what she had done was owing to her excess of love, and just punishment of his ingratitude and perjury. He earnestly recommended the care of his son to his father, and then desired the priest to join their hands and pronounce absolution, which was as much as they had life to hear. This done, the friend returned with a doctor and apothecary, who were for pouring down oil. But the lady, clasping the knees of Philaster, and shedding tears of joy, besought him to forgive her honest artifice, for he had drank nothing but a large quantity of gorge-stone,[66] which aided by imagination, 'has assisted to make me blessed'. The father, the friend all applauded her pious cheat. Philaster embraced her with more tenderness than till that moment he had ever known, nor lives there a happier pair.

WEDNESDAY JANUARY 25 TO FRIDAY JANUARY 27 — *Number 88*

Artesia's Day

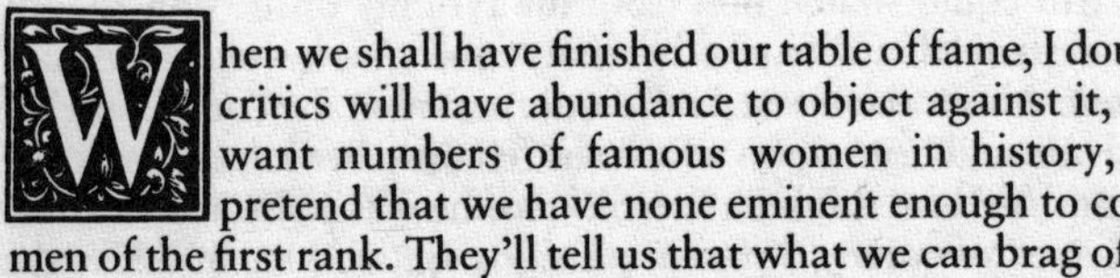

When we shall have finished our table of fame, I doubt the male critics will have abundance to object against it, not that we want numbers of famous women in history, but they'll pretend that we have none eminent enough to cope with the men of the first rank. They'll tell us that what we can brag of in our own sex consists chiefly in particular actions and single instances of virtue, but that we can show but few women whose lives were made up of a series of heroic deeds, as those of Alexander, Caesar, and many others which the men can produce. As I foresee this objection so I shall take care that those of my sex may have an answer ready whenever it shall be made. First, it is to be considered that virtues are never more conspicuous than in great persons, and therefore in the male table none are admitted among heroes of the first rank but mighty kings and emperors and such as have attained to a superlative power.

Secondly we must mind that the writing of history has been all along engrossed by the men, of which the most cunning have always been so

[66] an emetic

careful to pick out the most remarkable subjects, never endeavouring to render any name immortal, whose greatness was not able to perpetuate their own. From what I have said it is evident that the women, unless they had enjoyed an equal share of power and greatness with the men, will not be found upon record for their excellencies so much as the latter, though they had exceeded them in every virtue. Since men have enslaved us, the greatest part of the world have always debarred our sex from governing, which is the reason that the lives of women have so seldom been described in history. But as this is only to be imputed to the injustice and tyranny of the men, so it ought not be of any disadvantage to the women.

Speaking of this, I can but wonder that, in a nation detesting the tyranny of the Salic Law,[67] all women that are not born to be sovereigns should be made slaves, so much more than in other countries. Why should we be treated almost as if we were irrational creatures? We are industriously kept from the knowledge of arts and sciences, and if we talk politics we are laughed at. To understand Latin is petty treason in us, silence is recommended to us a necessary duty, and the greatest encomium[68] a man can give his wife is to tell the world that she is obedient. The men, like wary conquerors, keep us ignorant, because they are afraid of us, and, that they may the easier maintain their dominion over us, they compliment us into idleness, pretending those peasants to be the tokens of their affection, which in reality, are the consequences of their tyranny.

But what enrages me most is to see our sex so stupid as to believe themselves better treated than the women of other nations, because we are more egregiously cheated out of our right and liberties than they. A man is called prudent for not trusting anything of moment to his wife, and makes her believe that to be his co-partner in the management of his estate would be an insufferable trouble to her; whilst by his neglect, folly or extravagancy, she is often made a beggar at the same time, when she thinks herself a wealthy woman.

*

How can people in their senses think that the fine clothes, and all the trinkets that are given us are bestowed upon the sex any other ways than playthings are given to children, to amuse, keep their thoughts employed and their hands from doing of mischief? Does anybody believe that rich

[67] Certain monarchies in Europe adhered to the Salic Law of Succession, which originated in France. By this law, the throne can pass to male descendants through women, but women themselves cannot rule.

[68] high-flown praise

men are at the charge of sumptuous liveries, because they love their servants, or bestow fine harnesses upon their coach horses, because they value them.

FRIDAY JANUARY 27 TO MONDAY JANUARY 30 *Number 88 [sic]*

Emilia's Day

I had no sooner laid down my pen, but in came Melanthe in her usual precipitate way. 'My Dear,' said she, 'I am infinitely glad to find you at home. I should have been the most disappointed of wretches, had I missed of you.' 'What news, my dear intelligence, then,' said I. 'Nay, not for that,' answered Melanthe, moving forward to the great glass. 'I'll but mend this patch and tell you: Belinda, the gay, the lovely, the adored Belinda! Monstrous! How I look today! She that reigned in every heart, the wonder of our sex and the wish of mankind! My dear, how do you like my handkerchief? Don't you allow that lemon helps my complexion more than cherry? She that sung and played, danced and talked, and writ, and almost distracted us with her perfections, is now so lost a thing, that I can scarce forbear pitying the poor creature. I called upon her just now, and found her crowd of admirers vanished. She sat pensive at her table where she had writ these lines:

> Attend ye fair, who boast of wit and youth,
> And learn from me, this melancholy truth:
> 'Tis fruitless all what you so highly prize,
> Depend not on your shape, your voice, your eyes,
> All charms but wealth can sordid man despise.

Well, I have stayed an age with you, but you have not looked upon my muffs. 'Tis wonderfully becoming this new way of wearing one upon each arm. They are as graceful as bracelets, and but very little broader. I fancy they'll keep in all summer, and that will be new, and French, Adieu.'

. . . Here she disappeared, and the boy brought me in the following letter.

To Emilia,
From this time you will know me as your friend, since I put it in your power to prevent the oddest catastrophe that ever ignorance occasioned, love. Waving all other pretences, I have the reputation of being a fortune, and that has drawn me a large retinue of ogling, sighing, whining, lying things, commonly known by the assumed titles of eternal, eager, despairing lovers. One of them, deep red in romance, has been at the expense of many follies to disguise his better reasons. He has accused his innocent destiny, my imaginary charms, and arranged every power above and below, but the right, dear irresistible gold. He has sent me one acrostic,[69] two anagrams, and many epistles, in which he has gone through the experienced regiment of poetry, the disinterested passion, the distant hope, the humble request, the importunate perseverance, and the voluntary despair, and I would not have him go off a loser. He has taken into his head of late to pass the night in amorous meditations under my window, often looking up with steady regard and suitable ejaculations, no doubt, and by the unluckiest accident imaginable, my father has observed him.

My father, who never understood these methods, but married out of pure compliance to his honoured parents, and does not know love though he should meet him in a full light! Alas, misled by doubtful appearances, he has mistaken him for a gentleman thief and accordingly taken measures to have him secured the next time he loiters there at that suspicious hour. I had no way left but this: to advise him of the danger he was threatened with, for though he has been very communicative to state of his heart, in that of his abode and circumstances he has shown a strict discretion, and let me see he can keep a secret when there are such pressing reasons he should. The first opportunity I shall convey his ingenious papers to your hands, where he may call for them at leisure. They may serve another time with better success. But should I have suffered matters to come to that extremity, and produced them as proofs of his honour, what had acquitted him and condemned me, and my father's country house had been my prison during life, from whence not prose nor verse, could have retrieved me from savage gardens, etc.

This would have been of unhappy consequence to the assiduous, and by the way may serve for warning to all night adventurers, a sort of lovers

69 a word puzzle

that have been frequently observed about July and August, but seldom or never taken at this season of the year. A man must be strangely unprovided of an answer that is surprised in the middle of a fine simile or a soft unbraiding and examined in the severe tone and harsh terms of a constable. An unhappy bias to his customary way of expression would undo him. The least slip of the tongue concerning silent night, blazing fires and certain death, would all be taken in a wrong sense and be understood as relating to robbery and murder. I shall take care to give the gentleman notice, as soon as the manuscripts are in my possession.

WEDNESDAY FEBRUARY 1 TO FRIDAY FEBRUARY 3 — *Number 89*

Sophronia's Day

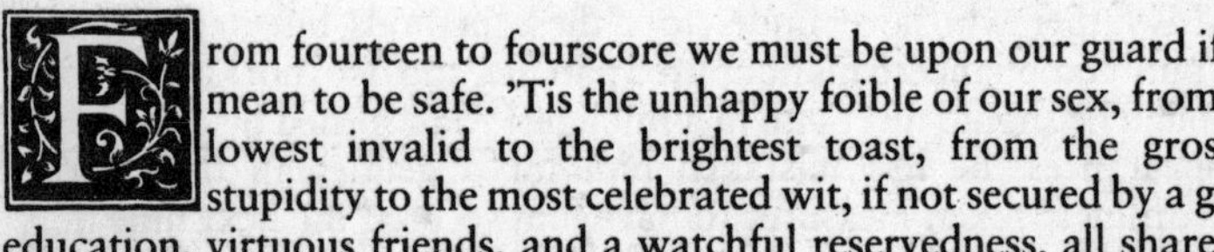

From fourteen to fourscore we must be upon our guard if we mean to be safe. 'Tis the unhappy foible of our sex, from the lowest invalid to the brightest toast, from the grossest stupidity to the most celebrated wit, if not secured by a good education, virtuous friends, and a watchful reservedness, all share the anxiety with Delia, or expose themselves by the ridiculous affectations of Lesbia, yet though the cause be pretty near the same in all, *viz.* an over-weening opinion of our own perfections which gives credit to flattery and desire of sovereignty, which makes us careful to gain and preserve the most despicable adorer, yet the choice of the favourite lover, and manner of expressing ourselves, make a whimsical and infinite variety in human actions as well as conversations. The very same chagrin that makes Delia resolve to quit the town and withdraw to privacy and thought, so books and groves urges Alinda to appear first at all public places, that she may miss of no opportunity to discover who it is her inconstant has preferred before her.

That zeal to please which displays itself in Lesbia's exactness, the low-pinned handkerchief halfway down the back, the happily fancied bordure[70] of her headcloths, and the comely farthingale[71] lurks under

70 trimmings

71 a padded petticoat

Chloe's negligence: the tumbled pinners,[72] the careless tie and the artless pleats of her Marlborough gown. Gloriana, by reading, has formed herself an Oroondates,[73] and believes wandering around a wood, climbing up a craggy rock, or leaning over a spring the sweetest enjoyments of time, whether she praise or rail, fondle her monkey, or quarrel with her maids, 'tis all in blank verse, and the first languishing admirer that approaches, with a soft voice and judicious cadence, and speaks of murmuring rivulets, warbling choristers, of their radiant charms and inestimable favours, may from that minute become the darling object of her vowed affections.

Now this would be Arabic to Mrs Lettie-blowze of Shadwell, yet she's in love too, or at least has an instinct for swill. But she desires her suitor may drink fair and speak plain, a can of flip, a sea song and a roguish tale hits her taste, and she believes no pleasure beyond them. Love, in a weak capacity and strong imagination, unusually explains itself with fits, and requires a large quantity of cold water to regulate the blaze of youth and keep the fire from exhausting its force and fuel at once. But, in the decline of years, 'tis generally observed to call for cold tea, to feed the expiring lamp of life and love. 'Tis strange that so different effects should flow from the same original. Mrs Clumsey it has refined to a polite coquet, and Mrs Simper it has metamorphosed to the greatest romp in nature. I have a cousin among Her Majesty's servants[74] in the Haymarket that it has converted to a prude, and an acquaintance near Pewterers Hall, that plays at cards on Sunday at the command of that tyrant, but 'tis endless to enumerate examples of this kind in favour of my sex. I'll say no more, but conclude with an observation an ingenious critic made of that inimitable player, Mrs Barry – that as her perfections were ever new and charming, so her very mistakes had something in them which prejudiced us in their favour – which I think very applicable to woman-kind.

*

The true, famous and approved cosmetic, being a composition of ingenuity, truth and modesty, very admirable for both sexes, and may be used constantly with great safety. It takes away all blemishes whatever, and renders age and deformity desirable, preserving youth and beauty in an eternal bloom. It has been often and long experienced, and never failed. It gives a lustre that cannot fade, and is the greatest secret of this kind, to be had gratis of those three worthy sisters,

[72] Headdress

[73] boy whose love for Statira, Alexander The Great's mistress, drove him to dangerous activities

[74] the actors

learning, justice and humility, of whose abode, I hope none want to be informed.

FRIDAY FEBRUARY 10 TO MONDAY FEBRUARY 13 *Number 93*

Sophronia's Day

In the new street leading from the Strand to Covent Garden, lives a famous artificer in paste and butter, either singly or together as ordered. He forms images in which shall be expressed not only the symmetry of the features, but the passions of soul, composed of nothing but butter. Whoever doubts the truth of this advertisement, if they please to go to his shop, they may see his mourning widow, infinitely beyond whatever the wax-work in Fleet Street can produce, and with this advantage – that when you are weary of the curiosity you may melt it down into sauce, a frugality to be considered in these hard times.

MONDAY FEBRUARY 13 TO WEDNESDAY FEBRUARY 15 *Number 94*

Artesia's Day

Last Sunday night I supped at relations, where we had the company of four gentlemen that were officers in the army. I stayed till almost eleven, and, there being no coach to be got, one of them whose name was Captain Weakly would by all means wait on me home. It was no time for compliments, and I was glad to accept of his civility. Being come without the least disturbance from

Fleet Street as far as Bow Church, in our way to Fenchurch Street, we had the most unpleasant encounter that I ever met with in the street in my life. But that the adventure I am going to relate may seem less strange to you, I shall give you a brief description of the gentleman that was my guard. Capt. Weakly's stature is somewhat under the middle size, and can be called no otherwise than short. He is a small boned man, but admirably well shaped, mettlesome, nimble, and understands a sword very well. By what I have heard of his actions in Flanders, he must have the courage of Hercules, though by what I have seen of them in Cheapside, he wants somewhat of his strength.

When we were advanced a little beyond the place I have already mentioned, a great looberly[75] fellow very rudely pushed me from the wall. The Captain, in great fury, struck him with his cane a swinging blow over the head, which he accompanied with such expressions of anger and confidence, as I thought, considering the man they came from, might have been sufficient to frighten half a dozen ordinary fellows. But this sturdy rascal, as void of fear as the Captain was of compliments, came to ill language in his turn. This, I confess, was very provoking to a gentleman, and an officer, that had often signalised himself. But the Captain, seeing that I was for making the best of my way, told his adversary very succinctly, that if he added one word more, he would cut off his ears. Perceiving him at the same time to lay his hand upon his sword, I was under no other apprehensions than that he was going to execute his threatenings, when, the very moment his brutish, antagonistic, who was at least as big again as himself, with an unmerciful fist, knocked him down at a blow, and immediately seizing on him with his gigantic paws, broke his sword into several pieces and treated him most inhumanly.

I was in such a fright that I have forgot whether I shrieked out or not, neither can I tell what became of the unmannerly rascal that had made all the mischief, all I know is that the Captain, in a miserable pickle of dirt and blood, was led into a tavern, and myself carried home in a coach that waited at the door.

*

FROM LUCINDA'S DRAWING ROOM

When I told the company that was here today the story of what happened to me last night, it occasioned abundance of discourse. One gentleman was of opinion that the captain ought to have run the fellow through at first of all. Another blamed him for not jumping back and drawing his sword as soon as he had struck him again over the head. A

75 clumsy

third had thought that considering he had a woman to look after he had done well not to come to that extremity as long as he could help it. Yet most of them agreed that seeing the fellow's bulk he ought either not to have hit him, or at least immediately after the blow secured himself from the reach of his iron clutches. But the more they talked of it the greater difficulties they found in the case, and nobody could determine what a man should do upon such an emergency; for if a gentleman suffers every rascal with impunity to abuse the woman he pretends to protect, he may depend upon it that he shall never remain a great man in her esteem, and if he draws his sword tho' for no other reason than to keep the impertinent aggressor at a distance, the mob will certainly be against and fall upon him for drawing his sword upon what they call a naked man, without ever enquiring into the provocation he has received.

When they had said as much upon it as the subject would bear, my sister told the company that she could blame the captain, who without doubt kept a servant or two, for nothing more than walking with a woman and no attendants in the streets of London. That since drawing a sword was both against the law and prudence, and the rudeness often met with in the street insufferable and not to be passed by unregarded men of honour, especially in the presence of women they have a respect for, she advised all gentlemen, if ever they were forced in town to walk on foot with one or more women, to provide themselves of a sturdy fellow, one that knows how to use his hands and feet and is able either by his presence to prevent or with a cudgel correct the ill manners of abusive fellows.

Having said this by way of moral, she cautioned the Weaklys in general to be more reserved in their expressions when they spoke to people of ten times their strength. 'Ever since gunpowder,' said she, 'has been in fashion, a man may make a very good commander in our wars without much bodily strength, but he ought to remember that where this levelling composition is not to be used the case is altered. I know that cutting a man's ears off, slashing him into stakes, knocking off his head and beating him into mummy, attended with "Sirrah's", "dogs", and "slaves", are the usual threatenings of injured gentlemen to inferior scoundrels, with bitter imprecations against themselves in case of non-performance. This I could bear in the West Indies, for a man to do it in his own plantation, among wretches he is sure will not resist him, but to hear a tender diminutive spark deliver those words, of course with a serious look and an air of assurance, to a great bulky rogue that is able to crush him to death, is very ridiculous in England, where a gentleman has no greater prerogative than a porter. I have often thought that these hyperbolical threats were a remainder of

Paganism, and generally attended with the same fate of the haughty language in old romances, where those that gave it always came off by the Lee; but with this difference, that there the giants spoke it to the knight errants, and here the knights errant often say it to the giants.'

FRIDAY FEBRUARY 17 TO MONDAY FEBRUARY 20 *Number 95*

Lucinda's Day

'Both my daughters are married and have children, and if they had admired learning as much as you do, ten to one but they might have been maids still, and as far from husbands as yourselves. Depend upon it, no prudent man will ever take a wife that knows more than himself. Everybody loves women that are gay and witty, but solidity and learning are no more becoming of them than breeches; and Latin is as ungenteel a furniture for the inside of a woman's head as a beard is for the outside. Young women should only study how to get husbands.'

WEDNESDAY FEBRUARY 22 TO FRIDAY FEBRUARY 24 *Number 97*

Artesia's Day

ucinda told you in her last what I said of the design and usefulness of *Tatlers*, but forgot to tell you that when I had done, the company voted for the plurality of them, and several were of opinion that if the male had not been so old, we might have increased and multiplied before now. But it is impossible to please everybody.

FRIDAY FEBRUARY 24 TO MONDAY FEBRUARY 27 *Number 98*

Emilia's Day

had no sooner concluded my letter, but in came my sister Rosella with a city lady, an admirer of fashionable wit, one that could no more smile at a sentence than like a handkerchief that was not of the newest invention; one that drinks Mr Bull's coffee and Mr Shepherd's tea, but because they are well spoken of. She had no sooner seated herself in the elbow chair, but she begun. 'Pray, Mrs Emilia,' says she. 'What news do you hear? Will these French headclothes take? Is the lottery[76] full? Does the trial come on next Monday? Is there any certainty of a peace?' To all this answered as brief and as satisfactory as possible, and then questioned in my turn, 'Pray, Madam, how do you like *The Female Tatler*?' 'Like?' said she. 'I should like it well enough if the authors would not be so much upon the reserve. There was once scandal sufficient to have pleased our end of the

[76] In 1709 the government started a lottery to raise a million pounds towards the cost of the war.

town, but why should I confine myself to that. The Court dotes on scandal, and, should they not, we should quickly hold it in disgrace.

'But of late the authors of *The Female Tatler* set up for morality and are as insipid as anything in print. Well! This morality is a wicked mistake in writers. 'Tis monstrous and abominable to pretend we want their monitions. Mrs Emilia, we want diversion, instruction apart for our children. Pray who would give a half a penny to read what they know already, or what they are certain they can never be the better for. Yet, if they are severe, 'tis on some general vice. They give one very rarely to know who they aim at, and that is what we hate. I love to find an acquaintance exposed or a neighbour ridiculed. It is not a farthing matter whether they deserve it or not. There is my intimate Mrs Friendly and her two daughters. They are as good people as ever lived, but so awkward that they would make admirable figures in *The Female Tatler* and oblige the town for two days. Mrs Emilia, if you know any of the Tatlers, I'll give you their descriptions. They are creatures would oblige everybody in a clumsy manner. They are brimful of good nature, without one regard to ceremony and they'll entertain you a whole afternoon with housewifery and family stories. If you offer them any snuff they hold out the back of their hands, and then make you deaf with sneezing. Coffee and tea they count slop tawdries, but as soon as you appear they call for a tankard of ale, and before you go it is ten to one that they bring you a glass of surfeit water.[77] They know just as much of the fashion as if they lived in Greenland, but very inquisitive concerning taxes.' 'Sure,' said my sister Rosella, 'this family contributes greatly to your mirth.' 'O,' says she, 'since my father will still live at this odious end of the town. Cheapside had been the death of me, but for the pleasure I take in laughing at these dear creatures.'

'By your description,' said I, 'I know the originals. I visit there sometimes and have ever remarked them for sober, hospitable, worthy friends, ignorant of the vices, and guiltless of the follies of the town, and should they read this paper, might take an honest pride in seeing their pictures, even as they are drawn by yourself. But thus it is we all laugh at one another and believe everything a folly or a fault that differs from our own opinions or manners. The gayest wit, though never so bright, among a company of prudes would pass but for a ridiculous scene, and it was the advice of an admirable pen, "Not to value ourselves upon our judgments, nor flatter ourselves with reason, a brisk buffoonery will run it down, and the false glittering of a youthful fancy will turn to ridicule our most delicate conversations." The ingenious Mr Rose-hast mistook his way into a coffee-room dedicate to stock-jobbing, and there said

77 a cordial to relieve indigestion

things would have been set down in every commonplace book[78] at Whites. But for an unlucky error as to time and company, he has by all those solemn and misunderstanding politicians been despised for a shallow half-witted person, and made the subject of their heavy mirth and harmless railing of the rest of the week. What pity was he had not prevented their scoffs by taking his own infallible rule not to pass for a fool in one company, who is sure to be regarded as a philosopher in another.

'It is easy to secure ourselves by sorting with equal capacities and agreeing opinions, but public papers must share the common fate of the reverse. You, Madam, want scandal. Another cries out for the liberty of the press that dares encourage anything of that kind. One says they are the improvement and diversion of the town, others that they are a tax upon public houses and invented to ruin them. A lady assured me yesterday that *The Female Tatler* was the best paper extant, and, not knowing I writ any of them, advised me to take them in, and this evening another seemed to hint that there was nothing at all in them, who shall I believe or which should I oblige, 'tis the old story of Aesop's travelling family, and I think to follow my own measures, to do as little mischief and as much good as possible, and endeavour to entertain all that are foes to vice, and friends to virtue, to lash guilty follies and criticise on the failings of all who imagine themselves perfect.' Here the lady rose and took her leave, and because I think her own picture would be more diverting than what she drew for her friends, I intend to give it another opportunity.

78 notebook in which to collect witty sayings and epigrams

MONDAY FEBRUARY 27 TO WEDNESDAY MARCH 1

Number 98, [sic]

Lucinda's Day

here is now in the press, and will shortly be published, *The Art of Impudence*, with plain directions of how to attain all the advantages of study and experience at a very small expense; without loss of time or hindrance of business, very useful to all lazy and ignorant people, especially such as in less than a month would make miraculous improvements in the mysteries of physic. To which is added a true and wonderful relation of an eminent tinker that, by the help of the aforesaid art, became first a dissenting preacher, and afterwards, with only one receipt[79] for sore eyes, a great bushy wig and a secondhand blue coat trimmed with silver, a famous occulist. Originally written in Billingsgate,[80] and Englished by Shameless Front M.A. fellow of Brazen College, in Newgate Street.

WEDNESDAY MARCH 1 TO FRIDAY MARCH 3

Number 99

Rosella's Day

f another species is the *fantasque*[81] of Julia. She has such a passion for conversation that she receives all that can bear with hers, from stupid chaff[82] to insipid brisk, with open arms and repeated welcomes. When you visit her, she is overjoyed you are come, but she's ashamed to see you. She excuses her dress, complains of her daughter-in-law, and the colic, irreligion and ingratitudes, she speaks much of experience and piety, she thanks her stars she has reached the summit of human knowledge, and she has lived

79 recipe for a cure

80 foul language

81 fantastic person

82 *badinage*, humorous ridicule

up to its divine dictates from her cradle. Should a profane jest interrupt this modest account of herself, she is sure to laugh the longest and the loudest in the company, and then re-assume the thread of her discourse. Would you be acquainted with understanding, examine her capacity; do you seek perfection, consider her virtues. Is anyone in distress, pity tears her mind. Is anyone in prosperity, envy eats through her heart. When she praises, she takes to let you know that she speaks altogether her own imagination, for, to confess the truth, the person she is talking of has not one good quality. When she rails, which is not seldom, she introduces her business with some necessary phrase, as 'I speak without any design of doing the smallest injury, for my part I wish everybody well, I am in perfect charity with all the world,' etc, then proceeds to the blackest detraction malice ever whispered.

She is a great prophesier of events that are past, but has a very imperfect guess as to futurity, yet has a constant apprehension of the worst. To all this she is a designer of mirth, and a proposer of assignations, a worker of public good offices and private ill ones, an aggravator of misunderstandings, and a suspecter of friendships. Music, company, love and poetry are her delight, but discord, ill-nature, hatred and dispute are her business: I have seen a volume where sermons, plays, pamphlets, and hymns were bound together by a capricious hand, with some scurvy animadversions and applications, and this comes the nearest a description of Julia's mind of anything that occurs at present to my memory. She is a collection of mistakes, an assembly of contradictions, and an abstract of vanity.

Hypocrates next claims my regard, who wears his ingenuity so concealed, 'tis doubted by many whether he has any or not. That common maxim of suiting ourselves to our conversation, he rejects, and behaves himself by a rule altogether odd and new. He is wise with beaux, and talks of the ancients, of language, and sciences, and twenty other learned masters they are ignorant and innocent of. Then leaves them to their snuff and their canes, greatly satisfied with his absence. From these he goes to the adepts, and entertains them with elegant discourse on dress and tea, and wonders why they make him no answer. He visits virtuous women, and there repeats the guilty scenes of his ungoverned youth, and with ladies of known liberty he is reserved as to a stoic, but to young libertines he tells endless stories of platonic love, and to old men that have one foot in the grave, he dwells upon the nature, and remedies of amorous distempers.

With the softest humility, he grants the request of avarice, but with insolence and indignation passes by entreating indigence. He is generous to profusion, where he knows they are above being obliged, but sordid to a proverb, where misfortunes ought to excite his humanity. He knows perfectly well what is for his interest in the practical part, which makes so many speak well of him that do so of nobody else. And yet he seems wholly unacquainted with agreeable manners and good morals, which is the reason he has so many foes amongst friendly dispositions. Today he often smiles on you, and promises to do you all the service in the world, much more than you ask or want, but tomorrow, persuade yourself to forget it all, for, if you attempt to remind him of what he said, he wonders at your presumption, and has so much forgot it that he does not know your name. Thus qualified, how could he miss of being great, and thus true to his idol gain he can never be less, and need not regret being spoke against.

MONDAY MARCH 6 TO WEDNESDAY MARCH 8 — *Number 101*

Emilia's Day

Why should a book or a pen be more appropriate to a man than a woman, if we know how to use them? I can see no reason why they should be denied us in any degree. 'Twas the tyranny of mankind that condemned us to the glass and needle, or we had sat in parliament long before this time, and perhaps without the assistance of a pack of cards to shorten the time.

*

Broke loose from the chains of Cupid and the apprehension of matrimony, a tall slim young man of strong will but weak intellects, apt to shut one eye and open his mouth when he would be attentive, in an edged hat and a yellowish wig, a blue coat faced with defiance, a large sword and dirty linen, very pert and slovenly. If anyone can discover him to Mrs Band-box, in the New Exchange, they shall receive a pinch of plain Spanish[83] out of the lady's tortoise-shell book, and a dram of Rosa Solis Gratis.

83 cheapest snuff

MONDAY MARCH 13 TO WEDNESDAY MARCH 15 *Number 105*

Artesia's Day

FROM MY CLOSET

f there be no real happiness without content, it is demonstration that no one can be truly happy who has the least ambition. Then why should that restless grasping of the mind be counted one of the necessary ingredients to make up the felicity of the great ones? Seneca and all the moralists may say what they please, but there is no general definition to be given of happiness unless all mankind has the same aim, and agreed in their wishes.

WEDNESDAY MARCH 15 TO FRIDAY MARCH 17 *Number 106*

Emilia's Day

e that distract our minds and exhaust our inventions in serving the public voluntarily have undertaken the hardest task of any of any mortal scribblers, confined as it were to strike fire every time we stand in need of it, and not permitted to spread the embers we find remaining of the brightness of others. Though you must give me leave to deviate from this, as often as I shall find myself inclined or necessitated, since it is allowed we are come too late after seven thousand years that human thought has traversed the flowery paths of knowledge, to pluck one daisy that has not been worn before, much less a rose. Scandal, which is at the moment the very life of the press, that without it would be still and motionless as death, can no more than follow in the tract of ancient malice, shade good actions with suspicions of their motive, and wrest honest meanings to their own black purpose, lessen virtues and magnify mistakes, which has been the practice of envy and discontent, since they first gained admission in splenatic minds.

Then for praise, does it not still flow in the usual channel of interest? Though if any topic will admit of innovation, 'tis certainly this of commendation, which I presume all will agree with me has hitherto been sparingly handled, and never attempted but from the powerful impulse of self love. I have been designing for some time to turn over the vast products of wit to find, if possible, one Panygeric that confessed not in its dedication this is to be its great beginning and end. But finding it a truth universally subscribed to, I'll save myself the labour and take the first opportunity of showing myself a disinterested admirer of worth, wherever I find it, though in an enemy.

FRIDAY MARCH 17 TO MONDAY MARCH 20 *Number 107*

Lucinda's Day

ature is contended with little' is philosophy for swines. If they can't meet with chestnuts, acorns, peas, or what they like, they'll eat guts or garbage, grains or green leaves or anything they can get. Belly full is a bully full. I would not ridicule or disprove the validity of so ancient a saying, but I could wish that those interpreting it with all the rigour it is capable of would recommend it to us in this world, were to take up with the dress, diet and habitations of the golden age, and look for the innocence of it where they could find it. Whoever delights and is satisfied with unpolished nature, without wishing or endeavouring to partake of the improvements which art and industry have made upon her, is so far happy that he may have his wants almost as soon supplied as the beasts of the field, but withal has no great reason to brag of a fancy much exalted above them, and therefore, in order to enjoy the world, those that are not born to a large estate are not to be discommended for devoting a considerable part of their time to the slavish drudgery of acquiring what is only able to purchase the delicacies of it. Nay, I would not blame even those that, already possessed of the comforts of life, dare likewise aspire to the elegant conveniences of it, and spare no reasonable pains to obtain 'em.

But he that spends his whole life in the fatigue of scraping wealth together, without ever endeavouring to enjoy it, and with his estate only increasing the desire of enlarging it, remains insensible to the happiness it might procure him, is like a man that sets out about earnest business, and, forgetting his errand, tires himself to no purpose. I count the degrees of felicity to be had on Earth so considerable that I would allow everybody to slave part of his life, to make the rest more happy. But he that, neglecting the aim which can only justify his labours in the pursuit of happiness, falls in love with the chase and slavery itself, must have a wretched taste of pleasure. What would you say of a man that should seem to be very hungry, make great provisions, and be all the day long a-dressing of his victuals, if after all his care and trouble he went to bed without his supper? And is he less ridiculous than seeming to have great occasion for money, hunts after it with uncommon eagerness, and yet makes no use of it when he has got it?

MONDAY MARCH 20 TO WEDNESDAY MARCH 22 — *Number 108*

Rosella's Day

I have received very loud complaints of irregularities still practised, notwithstanding all the care we female moralists take to root them out of the human kind. Clidamira still invites, and is denied. Lesbia continues devout and implacable, and Fulvia has encouraged a new lover to expose himself to her scorn. But what more nearly afflicts me is that yesterday, hearing a young lady give a loose to invention and amuse the company for some time with that art which is vulgarly called lying, I took the occasion to observe how careful we ought to be of reporting improbabilities, if we would be thought tolerably of ourselves; what constant graces accompanied truth, and how easily we were persuaded to believe all other virtues were established in that mind where we found unshaken veracity. The young lady confessed by a blush she understood me, and watched her opportunity to retire with me to the window, when, finding ourselves unobserved: 'Why really Madam,' says she, 'I am convinced of my error, and yet I'll produce you a great authority for this latitude of discourse.'

Here she took a copy of Saturday's *Tatler* out of her pocket and showed me where Squire Bickerstaff joins with Old Homer not only to excuse, but to recommend a lie, a lie twice told. I could scarce believe my eyes to see a crime palmed upon us for a moral: Juno partially seeks the destruction of the Trojans, and, that she may gain Jupiter to her purpose, deceived Venus out of the Cestos, inspires Jupiter with indecent ardour, and gains her ends. Here's revenge, subtlety, falsehood, and a fault not proper for me to explain to you, proposed for imitation. But lay it by, you will be never the worse if you should wholly forget it. Sincerity is an armour never to be left off on any pretence whatsoever, lest unregarded virtue receive such injury as can never be retrieved through a long life. What is not convenient for me to own, let me conceal by prudent silence, not dissemble with unnecessary fraud, and, however merry lies may divert for an hour, they seldom escape the censure even of those that laugh most at them. 'Tis a despicable pleasure we take in such conversation and we are ashamed and angry with ourselves that one scene of our face should have encouraged it.

I have known many we should have esteemed and loved, had they not claimed, both by a feigned genealogy from some great family and a tedious account of their generous education, which only served to awake our curiosity to trace them to their primitive dunghill, and there leave them with deserved contempt. 'Tis strange to hear how far this vice will carry it's proselytes. I knew a merchant, reputed worthy fifty thousand pound, that to heighten his industry into getting a large estate, used to exercise his invention perpetually in aggravating the poverty he rose from. Whilst some are vain on the perfections they never had; others boast the vices they have not had opportunity to act. Delia[84] is bad enough in any account, but infinitely blackest in her own, ambitious of the first place in iniquity, she relates of herself incredible abominations, which, if true, were a scandal to the age in being passed unpunished. But this good use she serves to – vice appears in her so loathesome, that to converse with her a day makes a convert.

I have been often importuned to try my skill in advising Sonoria to observe half-an-hour's silence every day, for the relief of her family who, like the mortals condemned to dwell near the banks of the Nile, are deaf with the continual sound of her complaints. Call what hour of the day you please and you shall find Sonoria in a passion. Her husband is ever in

84 Probably a reference to Mrs Manley, known as Atalantic Dela, who spared no detail in the description of her own rather florid life in *Secret Memoirs From the New Atalantis*, 1709.

the wrong. She has the most provoking children and the worst servants in the world. She ordered her head to be dressed with two wires and the milliner has sent it home with but one. Cithrone, the dear animal, is lost, and not one creature in the house seems inclined to go distracted. Everything contributes to her sorrows. Her chocolate is made too sweet in the morning, and she waits two minutes and a half longer than she designed for her tea in the afternoon. What can I say to such an unfortunate? Is it in the power of language to assuage such griefs? No, I decline the fruitless attempt and agree with Sonoria, that she is the most miserable of the human race; that there are but few can vie with her in wretchedness, and none more unhappy than her domestics, friends or relations that are confined to bear with her.

Ocyroe did me the honour of a visit this afternoon. Ocyroe far gone in learning and intimate with the classic authors, who advances nothing without a quotation and strengthens all she says with a Latin sentence, wonders at the idleness of the clergy who have in a manner banished from the pulpit what is superior to the understandings of the multitudes, and holds nothing orthodox that is not incomprehensible. She pities all her sex that are bred up in English, and maintains the Latin grammar to be the original of all the arts and sciences; who knows not that knows nothing, according to Ocyroe. 'Twas well for me that I was not expected to answer, or I should have been at a loss to have matched her style. She talked of a parenthesis in the weather, of the privilege of ratiocination, of the pleasure of discussing a problem and the precocity of ignorance. To all this I smiled and bowed so apropos, that she left me greatly satisfied with my natural capacity, and confirmed that I wanted nothing but the languages to render me the boast of my family. This lady now lives in defiance of modern gossiping. The intrigues of Old Rome employ her memory altogether. 'Tis not what Lady Credulous and Lord Plausible does that concerns her, but whether Ovid and Julia were as great as some authors have insinuated to posterity. But I leave her to her beloved antiquities.

WEDNESDAY MARCH 22 TO FRIDAY MARCH 24 *Number 109*

Artesia's Day

FROM MY CLOSET

I remember that I was a good big girl before I could be persuaded, but that they were all fools that did not love cheese. Such wise-acres as I was then are all people that esteem others less for not loving and hating the same things, and in short, for not being of the same opinion as themselves.

FRIDAY MARCH 24 TO MONDAY MARCH 27 *Number 110*

Emilia's Day

Preparing for the press, and will be speedily published, a treatise on anger, showing its mistake and pernicious consequence, seriously addressed to the ladies, where it ought to be rejected as an unnatural vice, but has been observed to possess their hearts, distort their faces, falter on their tongues, and menace in their eyes, to the astonishment of those near, and if not soon prevented, will hurry them in an instant to vain remorse, and wrinkles.

MONDAY MARCH 27 TO WEDNESDAY MARCH 29 *Number 110 [sic]*

Rosella's Day

he ladies having lately been so involved in politics, as to rise sooner than they used to go to bed, and having neglected cards, Tatlers, plays and operas, and that surprising entertainment the Puppet Show, our Society have been less studious than formerly finding everything lay dormant, but the important affair then in agitation. But now parties begin to take a little breath, to converse without heat, servants not to wrangle in the kitchen about what was debated in the parlour, and the common people not to abuse one another in the streets, we intend to renew our usual gaiety, and give the town such entertainment as in Mrs Crackenthorpe's days seemed pleasant and familiar to them. The season of the year being now come when the plump country ladies with their squelch husbands and their hoydening daughters gallop up to town to buy fine clothes. Emilia and I once more borrowed our Lady Stingy's chariot, which was every day seen at Westminster with different ladies in it, to ferret the India houses, exchange and the mercers, to hear North country language, smell West country breaths, admire Welsh gentility, and observe with how much judgment and fancy the ungain part of the world dish themselves out, that they may not appear like other people.

At Mrs Japan's sat my Lady Hogstie and her progeny, drinking pint dishes of chocolate in the afternoon, who never rose at our appearance because they were not acquainted with us, but whispered the India woman to know who we were 'for truly in London nowadays every proud minx that can but stick herself out in painted callicoe, squats down as familiarly as if she were as good as a Justice of the Peace's wife'. Her ladyship showed particular good breeding in buying everything we cheapened out of our hands, which Emilia presently perceiving, called for Old Fashion images as tall as my lady's daughters, jars for her ladyship to make powdering tubs of, French flowers for the young lady's chair, chocolate with more sugar than nut, and course Bohee tea that the strength must be boiled out of. So that we helped Mrs Japan off with her unsaleable trumpery, furnished my lady's house suitable to it's antiquity, and hugged ourselves at being revenged on the creature for her ill manners.

We drove next to the mercers, where we found the family of the Widgeons buying everything as fantastically showish as if they were rather to turn players than alarm a country church and put their tenants into fear and trembling. Madam Widgeon chose a sumptuous garden silk, designing to distract the country, and Emilia was so ill-natured as to persuade her husband to have a waistcoat and breeches of the same, who sat whistling of want of thought, and every now and then had his mouth full of prog[85] to show that the country gentry are not ashamed of good stomachs. And the two Miss Widgeons had pretty persian linings to their grandmother's wedding suits, which was divided between them. They talk how dear provisions were that they thought they must have laid down their coach, which they never use but on Sundays, the horses going to plough all the week; that the roads were extremely bad between Exeter and Plymouth, and that their youngest daughter had a chin-cough.[86]

At the door stood sheepish Jereboam, who was coachman, footman, butler, groom, gardener and what-not, who, hobbling ten yards lower to listen to a knotted ballad singers, had like to have been lost, had not our servant Rowland re-conducted him, which occasioned a sort of chat rather than conversation among fellows of their class. When one cried, 'I hope we shall have a good crop this year,' the other asked, if he had seen *The Fair Quaker of Deal*.[87] When the country booby spoke of tulips and sunflowers, our coxcomb talked of two pretty mantua makers in Durham Yard. Rowland wondered that how anything human could be so impolite, and looked on him with as much contempt as the horse-guards do upon the city trainbands, and Jereboam stared as much to find one of his own tribe could afford watches, snuff boxes, amber headed canes, and shirts of six shilling an ell,[88] when his very master Squire Widgeon wore shams.[89] However, London is a place of negotiation, and a pretty fellow in a livery has not been the aversion of some ladies, who come sooner than ordinary to sit by them in the front box.

But to return to our superior animals, who were as ridiculously complaisant as the Hogsties were pragmatically rude, asked our opinions with as much reverence as if they had asked us our blessing, invited us down at first sight for a whole summer, and when we took our leaves, made us courtsey so extravagantly low, that we left them squatting, and can't positively say whether they are up yet or not. We grew almost tired with this sort of diversion, as the most monstrous jests cloy the soonest, but having occasion for some fresh ribbons, gauze handkerchiefs and gloves, which we women for the sake of dear variety, and to set off an ordinary suit of clothes, do most abominably confound,

[85] food [86] whooping cough

[87] A new play by Charles Shadwell. It had received its first performance on Saturday 25 March.

[88] one and a quarter yards [89] fake shirtfronts

we hurried to the exchanges, where we saw my Old Lady Youthly buying plain deep scarlet knots for her daughter, and cherry and silver for herself. The Widow Lack-it chose a silver gauze handkerchief, and a coster-mongers wife laid out forty guineas in a laced head. But the affectation, impertinence and assurance of the sempstress and her two journey women, who are Lambeth Wells[90] dancers, were so shocking and tiresome that, finding ourselves a little splenatic after so farcical a ramble, we drove away to my Lady Tattle-tongue's, to divert ourselves with a little scandal.

WEDNESDAY MARCH 29 TO FRIDAY MARCH 31 *Number 111*

Lucinda's Day

FROM MY STUDY

From those dear companions in whom is neither falsehood nor forwardness, my few honest counsellors, my books, I begin today's advices. Here 'tis I can differ in opinion without exposing myself to the storms of dispute. Here I can be instructed calmly and at leisure in truth and knowledge without being despised for my ignorance, or blamed for my curiosity. What an advantage have mankind had beyond us from the first dawn to the meridian of learning? This apartment has been wholly appropriated to their use, and the cares and impertinence of human life were the generous portion they allotted us. The first ages of the world found us the servants of imperious mankind, keeping of sheep and kneading of dough were our ordinary employments. After that we were condemned to the distaff or the Seraglio, elder and chaster monasteries than those founded on better pretences; one, while we were educated in a strong desire of being blind by thirty that our names might live in a point Cravat and posterity, be witness how much time we took pains to throw away, then embroidery was introduced, and a waistcoat finally worked saved

90 The Great Room at Lambeth Wells showed speciality dancing acts.

the beaux of those days many a pot of complexion, which they find themselves under some necessity of using in these, for want of proper ornaments to divert the eyes another way.

Letters were denied us lest we should see and claim our great prerogative, and equality with haughty man, to whom we were created friends not servants, and designed to advise and assist them in the Government of the Earth. By length of time and negligence of our tyrants, the enclosures of learning wore away, and capacity and inclination led many of our sex to venture on that forbidden ground, and bright examples the rest that at present I believe, should Apollo require a list of the names of those authors now in being, to the great joy of his impartial goodness, he would find his female votaries of almost equal number and industry to his male, and put in as good a claim to immortality as those who endeavour to disappoint their purpose, or divert their pursuit. The needle is justly quitted for the pen, and the spice box removed to make room for the scrutore; ask a lady for a receipt, she knows nothing of the matter, 'tis probable her servant may, but she desires you to read such a pamphlet, and give her your thoughts how it is writ, and what you think is meant by those letters and dashes. The first question in a morning, is not what conveniences the family may want, but if the Tatler be come in. What commendable alteration is this? How lofty and superior to the little drudgeries of life are we now grown?

The poor gentlemen whose stomachs were so weak and nice they could eat nothing but of their wives dressing, have fasted themselves into better appetites and can make shift to get down a little of their maid's cookery, and find it begins to digest with them pretty tolerably. Many have been so tenderly fond they would not wear a stitch of work but their spouses dear fingers have wrought. What ragged linen would the husbands of this age have been obliged to appear in, should they have proved dotingly obstinate in that point? How much better do arts and sciences becomes a lady than salves and potions? What a figure does *The Tale of a Tub*[91] make on a toilet[92] beyond a herbal, which, with a book or two of devotion, used to be our allowance? 'Tis true indeed there are some accidents not altogether so advantageous as might be wished attendant on these privileges we have taken. Fond of arithmetic, we have given a loose to gaming, that we might know it thoroughly, in a practical as well as speculative way. It must be owned the Dutch women have far better method to attain that art by counting their gains and confining it to trade, but, when English husbands will give a sincere account of their affairs and consult with their wives and confide in their friendship and diligence, I dare believe they will soon overtake their neighbours in the

[91] Jonathan Swift's satire, published in 1702

[92] a dressing table

use of that commendable science, and those whose conspicuous fortunes and boundless treasures have placed above such limits can (if they please), I make no doubt, find business enough for numbers in summing up their good actions, and by that employ keep arithmetic alive, though there were neither cards nor counters in the nation.

Then acquainting themselves with astronomy they are grown so intimate with the stars, and have contracted such strict friendships among them that they cannot live a day without enquiring to know, their resolutions. So observant of their wills, that they would not buy a pair of gloves if the moon were out of humour with new things, nor venture out of doors if Mercury gave them the least twinkle to the contrary. They dare not pay a farthing but when the planets order them, though sometimes they are prevailed on to receive it against the opinion of their celestial guides, which they remember with great remorse, and expect to be punished for by finding the treasure vanish without doing them any good.

This remote correspondence carries them something too far from home, and not being skilled in the Chaldean tongue,[93] interpreters are very apt to impose, as they may conclude from many events they meet with, the reverse of what they were ordered to expect. Chloe was to have been married the Thursday before the last eclipse to a gentleman under Mars, and a coach and horses described by Mercury. She prepared everything necessary for the park and the opera, and put on a prudent coldness. Before those acquaintance she held it convenient to drop, when all that happened remarkable to her at that period, was that her necklace broke when she neither coughed nor laughed, and that her left shoe unbuckled three times between one o'clock and ten that night. Again they inform themselves so fully of the force of reasoning that no argument escapes them. They are tempted to maintain the plainest falsehoods and deny the most apparent truths, that they may display the strength of contradiction.

But what are these trifles in comparison with invincible ignorance? Who would not rather mistake sometimes than never think at all? All that I have heard of the woman of our family, as worthy memory, is that they looked upon the ground when they spoke, were frightened at the appearance of a stranger, and fled to their several recesses. But if compelled to stay by the authority of parents, they sit confused, blush if they were spoke to, and answered nothing. This was called modesty and discretion, and often preached to me by way of example, but for their fear I ever looked on it as proceeding from their opinion of themselves, their blushes from conscious guilt, and their silence from a perfect

93 language of soothsayers

stupidity, not knowing what to say. Therefore I ventured to take my own way. My shame I keep for my faults, which but too often require it; my silence for instruction when wisdom or virtue speak, and my fear for that doubtful hour when I find it difficult to discern between good and evil, least I should blindly choose the last.

[END OF *THE FEMALE TATLER*]

PART THREE

The [Fake] Female Tatler

By Mrs Crackenthorpe[1]

Aliter vitium vivitque tegendo[2]

WEDNESDAY AUGUST 17 TO FRIDAY AUGUST 19, 1709 *Number 19*

Mrs Crackenthorpe acquaints the public that her man, Francis, has of late deserted her service and carried away with him several letters and papers of moment, which he is required to return; and if any person can give notice of him to her, they shall be gratefully rewarded. He is a pretty fellow, as times go, middle-siz'd, a pleasant aspect, fitted for ladies company, (which made way for this temptation, for he is suppos'd to be seduc'd by a scandalous lewd wench, a cast-off miss to a quondam quack doctor in the city, who has been seen in his company very lately). If any person light on him, they are desir'd to give notice to Mrs Crackenthorpe, or have him press'd aboard the scoundrel galley.

[1] The 'Fake' *Female Tatler* published by Mrs Crackenthorpe's former printer, B. Bragge, appeared concurrently with the genuine paper, beginning with issue number 19. See introduction, p.vii, and p.viii.

[2] Otherwise the error survives by its concealment.

FRIDAY AUGUST 19 TO MONDAY AUGUST 22 *Number 20*

avour me with one word, my good Lady Carper,' says Mrs Undermine, 'I think you might as well spare some of your reflections to bestow upon that sullen piece of mortality, Mrs Sensible, who not only then, but at all times, whatever company she is in, always thinks herself too good to open her pretty chops, but sits screwing of her mouth, turning up her snout, and tossing up her empty noddle, as if all her words were too good to be spoken in such company. From such a pink of pragmatical formality, good God, deliver me! I am sick at the very thought of her, I know nobody living that is more my aversion, and yet I'll warrant you that she, forsooth, passes with some for a discreet, prudent ingenious person, when in truth she is nothing but a composition of pride and ill nature.'

Thus for some time these two ladies continued their severe reflections by turn, the Lady Carper against my Lady Fiddle, and Mrs Undermine against Mrs Sensible, though for quite different reasons and upon two opposite accounts. Dear Madam, thus we see that scandal and censure will fix hold on anything, and that there is no person to be found that cannot be made a proper subject for them to enlarge upon, who employ their time and talent that way only, but more especially, whenever it happens to be accompanied with envy and emulation. Few of the nobility and persons of best quality, are yet come amongst us, their presence will afford more 'riety of intrigues and diversion, and when anything particular and extraordinary shall present itself worthy of your cognisance, it shall be speedily and faithfully communicated to you by,

Most engaging Madam,
Your devoted humble servant.

E. Findout, Tunbridge Wells[3]

3 Is this letter the first ever from 'Disgusted of Tunbridge Wells'?

MONDAY AUGUST 22 TO WEDNESDAY AUGUST 24 *Number 21*

An antiquated widow near S——H——S, who has a jointure of three hundred pounds per annum, and a considerable value in cash, plate and jewels, having lately patched up a match by the assistance of a female manager of such affairs, with a very brisk and handsome young spark of the town, equips herself with a new set of teeth, plumpers,[4] etc. to repair the defects of old age. Having not made sufficient trial of them, whether they would be pliable as her former and as well adapted for the exercise of the organs of speech, but being very tedious in dressing that she might appear as amiable and as charming as possible in the eyes of her bridegroom. The Gallant also being desirous to make sure work of it, less anything might fall out betwixt the cup and the lip, came somewhat of the soonest with his friends and very much importuned her to be expeditious that the company might not wait.

She was not very avers'd to his request, but immediately rigged out of hand, and so, coming to the last finishing stroke, the aforesaid implements were in all haste applied to their proper places. Madam was led into the coach and driven to the church with all the speed imaginable. When all things were ready and the ceremony came to be performed and she to pronounce her part of the responses, it is not easily to be conceived what a consternation she was in, for her new gear being too stubborn and stiff, she could not move her jaws, but was gagged, and not able to pronounce one articulate word. Her confidante only, as is supposed, imagining the real occasion of it, whispered the parson to withdraw with her to the vestry, whilst she went home and brought others to whom she had been more familiarly accustomed, and then matters were completed.

My Lady Simpleton's eldest son, who is as like his mother as if he were spit out her mouth, had a month's mind for[5] her maid Abigail, and having for a long time made his addresses to her, at last it came to my Lady's ear. She broke the business to Sir Simon, he was immediately for turning her away. Quoth he, 'My dear, we must not suffer this saucy baggage to stay one moment longer in our house, who has been so presumptuous as to make our son and heir, and the eldest branch and hope of the family of the Simpletons, fall in love with her. Impudent Queen for her pains. As I am a justice of her Majesty's Peace, though I have not done one act of justice since I was in commission, I have a great

4 Pads inserted into the mouth to give the appearance of full cheeks.
5 fancied

mind to try to make her mittimus,[6] and send her to be severely chastised in the House of Correction. 'By no means, my good Sir Simon,' replies my Lady, 'we must have more wit in our anger for Si is so pestilently in love with her that it would go to the very heart of him if he should hear that any harm came to her. We must keep her in the house whatever comes of it, if we intend to have poor Si Simpleton alive. But leave it to me, and I'll try what a woman's wit can do.'

My Lady immediately sends for Mrs Gymcrack, her mantua-maker, and after many grave debates pro and con, it was resolved to marry Abigail to their Chaplain, and that they should live in the house together. The matter was communicated to Sir Simon, who wonderfully approved this project of her, broke the business to the Chaplain and my Lady to Abigail. Everything was agreed upon, the day appointed, and the young Si by father's and mother's direction was to be father.[7] The Chaplain was a young smirk much about his age, so, going to the church, the squire and he, as was agreed on before, changed habits, and the parson gave his intended spouse to the young squire, for which he was well rewarded, the squire being at age. They returned home without the Chaplain related, how matters were managed. So Sir Simon and my Lady, after their surprise was over, said it was too late to repent but they must make the best of a bad market, but their comfort was still that they more plainly saw that their son Si had more wit than all the rest of the Simpletons.

*

The Printer of the first *Female Tatler*, is at present out of town, but upon his return will sufficiently clear himself from all false and malicious aspersions laid to his charge. The author does not in the least think he ought to be concerned at the spitting such venom and rancour in regard his reviler is altogether as much a stranger to his character, principles and circumstances, as he is an enemy to truth, wit, sense, and civility, and does not esteem such scurrilous ribaldry deserves any other reply.

*

Mrs Crackenthorpe utterly disowns her being privy to any transactions of her man Francis since his elopement, about her picture, or otherwise. But the person taxed with laziness does sincerely promise Francis that whenever he comes and pays off the old arrears, in the first intimation, he shall have his picture drawn exactly to the life, at full length, and painted in its proper colours.

6 issued with a warrant for imprisonment

7 i.e. give the bride away

WEDNESDAY AUGUST 24 TO FRIDAY AUGUST 26 — *Number 22*

rs Crackenthorpe, seeing herself affronted by spurious paper, published in her name declares that she never had a hair-lip, wry-neck, cataract on her eyes, or cancered breast, as people will generally believe, seeing her exhibited like a patient on a mountebank's bill, and takes it very ill that they would not represent her at least as well as the Ballad does the *Fair Maid of Bristol.*[8]

*

There is now preparing for the press, and will be speedily published, *The History of Taralinda*, embellished with many uncommon and very modern intrigues. In which are interspersed some pleasant and elegant discourses between Taralinda and her mother. Translated from the Italian of Francisco del Pistorio, an author very much celebrated for his great strokes and bold touches in all the various parts and designs of masculine love.

Sold by W. Double-dealer, at the sign of the Snake in the Grass, near Gossips Hall, London.

FRIDAY AUGUST 26 TO MONDAY AUGUST 29 — *Number 23*

rs Crackenthorpe hearing no more of her man, Francis, would willingly entertain some young girl that does but understand the Town a little, and can write and read, who may do her business as well.

*

Mrs Crackenthorpe takes this opportunity of returning thanks to the gentleman and ladies who have all along encouraged her paper, and

[8] This note refers to a portrait of Mrs Crackenthorpe printed at the top of the Baldwin *Female Tatlers*. It was a simple engraving, in the style of most drawings on broadsheets.

doubts not of the continuance of their favour. But being now informed of a certain that the spurious paper foisted into the world under her name is contrived and carried on by the villainy of her man Francis, she thinks herself obliged to let the public know she disowns being anyways concerned with the publishing thereof, and to give a caution to all gentleman and ladies that they be not exposed on by that scandalous and trifling pamphlet. How ridiculous it is to suppose that she should give her consent to that paltry representation the wretches pretend to delineate her by in the front – more fit for a Ballad or a Quack's Bill than anything that looks like a diverting or instructive. And then the performance! How vain, shallow, and malicious, and scandalous to the lowest degree! I need not say, the public being sufficiently convinced of that already. And indeed, who can expect otherwise, when the poor devil is forced to pump for bread?

But lest any should be imposed on by entertaining him in their service when his poor scribbling is at an end, Mrs Crackenthorpe thinks fit to let them know something of his morals, as he approved himself since he left her service, and which she did but before suspect. He's one that has made it his business to set families together by the ears that he might reap some advantage by the quarrel; continually sowing dissentions between husbands and wives, parents and children, masters and servants, several instances whereof can be produced. But now he's discarded most good families, and seeks by flattery to reinstate himself. He's as vain as villainous, impudent and impertinent to the last degree, and to describe him throughout requires a volume, but this may serve to warn people lest they are abused by him. And for the rest of his character shall refer to the *History of Taralinda*, now in the press, or some other convenient opportunity.

*

Mrs Crackenthorpe desires all her friends to continue their correspondence, and direct for her as usual at Mr Bragge's in Pater-Noster Row, where this original and genuine paper is published, and where complete sets may be had from the beginning.

MONDAY AUGUST 29 TO WEDNESDAY AUGUST 31 *Number 24*

his Lady happening to be in the company with my Lady Sweetair and some more very agreeable ladies, my Lady Sweetair began to give some account of a very entertaining and remarkable passage that happened not long since at the Bath. But scarce had she spoken five words, when my Lady Speakall abruptly interrupted her, saying, 'Dear Lady Sweetair, it is very unaccountable that so intelligent a person as you are, should have your stories so stale! We had it three days ago at my Lady Farfetch's. I utterly abominate anything in conversation that is above the date of a dish of tea. How palled and insipid is a story of a week's standing!' Thus she began and without doubt would have continued on, to the great mortification of all the company, had not my Lady Senseless' footman, come with a message to her, which wrought their happy deliverance.

WEDNESDAY AUGUST 31 TO FRIDAY SEPTEMBER 2 *Number 25*

here malice prevails like an ill concoction that turns the most fabulous food into unwholesome and nauseous phlegm and crudities, it puts a base and sinister interpretation upon the most inoffensive words and actions, nay, often proceeds so far, as to give a scandalous turn to that which really merits commendation. This is the character of my Lady Strifemaker. Wherever she comes all faults are represented by her with magnifying optics, and many innocent things received as criminal from her ill nature. This makes her company universally avoided, and equally as welcome as a Tertian Ague. Her most nearest relatives cannot escape her, but she is intolerable to her servants, and seldom keeps any long enough to call them by their names.

Neither her husband nor her children can do anything but what she calls abominably disobliging in them to her. Silence is sullenness and a dogged morose temper, and a modest and moderate agreeable conversation, noise, clamour, or, at best, but impertinent prittle-prattle. A genteel and graceful air and deportment with her is rank pride and affectation, the least familiarity she terms sauciness, though it proceed from her betters. But it is egregious rude, and never to be forgiven if inferiors offer to open their lips in her presence, unless she first bids them.

FRIDAY SEPTEMBER 2 TO MONDAY SEPTEMBER 5 *Number 26*

he Public having had their appetites regaled and their taste wonderfully improved by the accounts already given of the pretty fellows, the very pretty fellows, the smart fellows and the etceteras, I have been much importuned to undertake the character of the unaccountable fellows, for I hate the filthy things, and would banish them my Drawing-Room, but only as I have engaged myself to receive all sorts of impertinents to make diversion for the ingenious and polite, as monkeys are sometimes made the entertainment of men of sense. Not to tire you at the door then, I'll admit you into my Drawing-Room, where Lady Clackit is over head and ears engaged in a robbery that had like to have been committed last night.

'Dear Mrs Crackenthorpe,' she cries, with much vehemence and emotion of spirit, fanning herself as if her heart would pop out of her mouth at every breath she expires, 'the fright is not over yet. Last night Sir Harry lay out of town . . . pough . . . pough . . . pough, just at the stroke of two, a violent clap happened – Bless me, Mrs Crackenthorpe, I am ready to sink at the remembrance of it . . . pough . . . pough – Have I not got a monstrous colour? – as if the beaufett[9] was broke open and all the plate was thrown upon the floor. It is incredible how I lay bathed in sweat, till my courage got the better of my fear, and I squalled out like a woman in a rape, "Jean, Tamas, Jeames, Herry, Rabert, Will, Gearge!" But finding my voice too feeble to reach any of the sleepy rascals, I waked my woman, and bid her rise and call the butler to see if the plate in use about the house was secure, for the gold plate was locked up in my own closet. When the butler was raised he durst not stir without disturbing the whole family, so the coachmen, the footmen, the grooms and the postillion were all up in arms. When I came down in my wrapping gown and, desiring to search the beaufett, found nothing amiss, but that a rat was got there, which had given this alarm to the whole family. I have really been disordered ever since, and have now a violent palpitation of

9 sideboard

my heart, which I believe the company may perceive by the shortness of breath. Pough . . . pough, I am in a fainting condition now, can scarce recover my spirits.'

This narrative lasting so long I was afraid the whole room would have been disgusted, there being no liberty given to any clack but my Lady's which is an infringement upon the freedom of society, and a plain violation of the Magna Carta of good breeding. Therefore to prevent any further disorder, by my Lady's reassuming her story, I interrupted her with a dram of right Union Brandy, upon which a surprising ejaculation she cries out, 'Heavens be praised for such a blessing! I have not tasted such a cordial before, for God's sake Mrs Crackenthorpe inform me where I may get a bottle of it.'

Resolving to break her measures of going on with her discourse if possible, I told her truly, tho' I had but one bottle of it left, her Ladyship should have it with her and desired she would call up her footman to receive it. 'Dear Mrs Crackenthorpe,' says she, without further thought, but in haste, lest she should lose the bottle, 'pray, let your servant go home with me, for Sir Harry is abroad and has taken the footman, so that I have nobody in town but Miss and myself.' Upon which the company burst out into a violent laughter, which threw my Lady into such an insupportable fit of the vapours Dr Megrim's *Sal Volatile* was not half so much use to her on that occasion as a urinal. Lady Clackit was ready to die with grief and anger, which nothing could relieve but absence, for now brandy could not help her.[10]

MONDAY SEPTEMBER 5 TO WEDNESDAY SEPTEMBER 7 *Number 27*

Mrs Crackenthorpe thinking herself highly affronted by that scandalous representation of her in the front of a spurious paper published in her name, and to comply with the importunity of her best friends, gives this public notice, that against the next month she designs to gratify her encouragers with her true effigies, at length, in a large copper plate, done by the best masters, to be given *gratis* to those who buy sets of her papers to be a frontispiece to each volume.

[10] This story was reprinted with judicious editing as *Female Tatler Number 61*, 23–25 November 1709, Emilia's Day. Such wholesale plagiarism indicates that Emilia was either involved in the fake *Tatler*, or a shameless hussy!

WEDNESDAY SEPTEMBER 7 TO FRIDAY SEPTEMBER 9 *Number 28*

They then began to propose expedients to prevent such calamities for the future. Nothing less would serve my Lady Briskbody, than having every mother's child of 'em shipped off for Ireland, and there forced to marry the wild bog-trotting Croggies, and their places supplied by a colony of Covent-Garden Sparks. After her my Lady Downright begins, . . . for my own part when I was at Mrs Formal, now Mrs Hopwell's Boarding School, I thought the Salisbury Beaus extraordinary well accomplished in most particulars. They dressed, ogled and made love with an admirable grace, that one might almost have ventured to compare their Close[11] to our park; and therefore I am bold to say, they certainly appear very bright and charming to these ladies who generally have had no better conversation than such sorry, unpolished, wretched tools.

FRIDAY SEPTEMBER 16 TO MONDAY SEPTEMBER 19 *Number 32*

Taking water at the Temple yesterday, I was ply'd by a jolly Waterman, who would needs carry me whether I would or no, under pretence he knew me and would not trust me to anybody else. 'Well Madam,' said he, 'I was very ambitious to carry you, because you are a Lady that knows everything, pray will you be so free then as to resolve an honest fellow a plain question? Which do you think the best road for a man to travel in to get preferment?' I was puzzled at once, and said, 'Indeed friend I am not able to answer your question.' Upon which with a fleering grin he cried out, 'Fie, fie, Mrs Crackenthorpe, you are not so half witty as I took you for, don't you know that the nearest road to preferment is by the way of Marlborough.'[12] 'And what do you think Waterman,' said I, 'of the nearest way to Honour? Must not you go the same road to come at that too?'

11 cathedral precinct

12 John Churchill, Duke of Marlborough, who was running the war

'Ay, Ay, Madam, that's true, but many a brave fellows knocked on the head before he can reach to his journeys end that way, and everybody's mothers don't take care to wrap up their children in their smocks to keep them shot-free. There's the brave Eugene[13] cannot fight in a whole skin, but he's always getting a broken head, and that is because his mother never minded to dip him well, as I have heard one of the seven champions was, I think they called him Achillus.' 'You mean well, Waterman, you are pretty near the mark, his name was Achilles, he was chief of the Grecian Heroes at the siege of Troy, and his mother dipped him in a river to make him invulnerable.' 'Well Mrs Crackenthorpe, don't you think our noble hero was dipped when a youngster in some lucky place or another.' I durst not enquire further into his meaning, for fear of a waggish answer, knowing those fellows very roguish, therefore bid him land me presently at Whitehall.

*

Just published: The dumps[14] of the vices of three figures, to which is added, *Hungerton's Antiquity of Gingerbread*.

FRIDAY OCTOBER 14 TO MONDAY OCTOBER 17 *Number* 44

Last night Madam Jollup out of the City made me a visit, who, at first sight, I took to be the Queen designed for my Lord Mayor's Pageant, and after a great many excuses, whereby she endeavoured to beg my pardon for her presumption. Mincing up her mouth like My Lady ——'s lap-dog, for a lick or a buss, she informed me it was ever her ambition to keep her better's company, and, knowing my conversation was with the most accomplished ladies at Court, she desired a familiarity with me, for the city Dames were too fantastical, that she did not know at which end to take 'em. And, besides, they were always a quarrelling about precedency, whereby she was obliged to give place to every dirty trollop, tho' her husband stood as fair to be a Church-warden as the haughty Deputy's half a score years ago.

13 Prince Eugene of Savoy the leading Imperial general

14 melancholy strains

But, as she was going to proceed, in slips Mrs Glisterpipe in as great heat as if the fermentation of the furmity-kettle[15] had been just over. 'Alackaday,' saith she, 'dear Madam Crackenthorpe, I beg your pardon for this rudeness, but the insolence of my neighbour, Jollup, an impertinent scoundrel, scolding, what shall I call her . . .?' 'Hold Madam,' saith the other, 'do you mean me? I profess, I came purposely to this good Lady, to complain of your sauciness.' Upon which, I had like to have had my china broke at loggerheads, had I not stepped in between them, in order to moderate their passions and make up the breach. But I had no sooner placed 'em on each side of me, than in comes Madam Quick-silver, puffing and blowing like a pair of second-hand bellows. 'Hussies, have I catched you in the nick of time? Madam Crackenthorpe,' saith she, 'I took you for another guise sort of a woman. Those impudent queans[16] had their education at Billingsgate, for never did poor woman live near such a couple of common scolds.' At which, they both flew at her with more fury than dogs do at a bear in the bear-garden. So down comes my tea-table, and they all three a top of it, with their head-gears well ruffled.

Upon which I was forced to call up my man Hugo to part them, which he had no sooner done, but each of 'em began to cast up their pedigree. Quick-silver affirmed, that her husband, Cocky Cockney, was admired by all the Ladies in the City for the handsomest black[17] man in the world. 'That's a lie, with your leave,' says Mrs Glisterpipe, 'for if the Witch of Endor did not sit on one side of him, and a monkey on the other, the oyster-wenches would let him be as weary of his amber necklaces as he is of you.' 'That's false, good Mrs Piss-pot,' says she, 'my husband is a Grace to the Yellow Regiment in the Militia, and walks like a Caesar at the head of his company.' 'Well, I hope,' saith Jollup, 'you will yet give place to Captain Longshanks after all, who cured him of a broken leg by the help of a Julep,[18] when he was taken in the siege of Sodom.' However, finding in short, they were like to go to Scratch Cat again; I desired my new acquaintances to withdraw, assuring them I would take their cases under consideration between this and Horn-Fair.[19] But it being post-night, business prevented me at the present, from gratifying their termagant liberties . . .

Mrs Crackenthorpe.
You are a dirty, confounded, impudent B——ch of a Harridan, if you proceed to expose me, I will cut your throat, by all that's good.

[15] brewing pan [16] shrews
[17] dark, swarthy [18] sweet drink
[19] annual fair held at Charlton, in south-east London.

Is it not enough for a man to be a Cuckold, but such antiquated bawds as you must expose one to the world? If you value your life, let me hear no more of this, you Jilt, you.
Andrew Doolittle
October 15 1709 Lawrence Lane

Good Mr Doolittle, why so hot? I sent you no summons as I know of; neither to my knowledge did I ever see you in my life. But if you will be a cuckold, whether your wife will or not, who can help it? Tho' from your modern language one may perceive how well you are qualified to govern a family, for when men fly out into these feuds without any prevarication, what rare examples do they give to their children and servants. I know of none that taught her the way but yourself. I am sure she was piously brought up and a constant hearer of that which is good, 'till you, by swearing, drunkenness, and ill-usage, made her run astray and the sinner overcame the saint. Therefore, mend you one first, lest your evil examples corrupt your whole family. Cat will after kind. As the master, so is his whole household, or the Mistress at least. You can no more suspect her to be virtuous when you are so profane, than she can believe you are honest when you are always in debauched company, or go a-courting Doll Common.

*

Mrs Crackenthorpe thinks fit to advertise the world, that a tailor in Budge-Row, having sent a letter by the half-penny packet to her man Francis, by inadvertency was delivered to herself. But to prevent such mistakes for the future, she declares that all such paltry stuff is fitter for him to be concerned in than myself, and that she will never have anything to do with those that carve their memorandums on cucumbers, for want of ability to buy pocket-books.

PART FOUR

Advertisements from The Female Tatlers

Purging sugar plums for children, and others of nice palates, nothing differing in taste, colour, etc. from sugar plums at the confectioner's, having been experienced by thousands to sweeten and purify the blood to admiration, kill worms, cure green sickness in maids, pale looks in children, rickets, stomach aches, King's evil,[1] *scurvies, rheumatisms dropsia, scabs, itch, tetters,*[2] *etc. Good in cases where purging is necessary, doing all that is possible to be done by purging medicine being the cheapest, fastest, pleasantest medicine in the world. Fit for person of all ranks, ages, and sexes; Price is the box, to be had only at Mr Spooner's at the Golden Half Moon in Lemon Street, Goodman's fields, near Whitechapel, with directions.*

*

The Most Famous Chemical Quintessence of Bohee

Tea and Cocoa nuts together, wherein the volatile salt, oil and spirit of them both are chemically extracted and united, and in which all the virtues of tea and nut are essentially inherent, and is really a pleasant, refreshing preparation, found upon experience to be the highest restorative that either food or physic affords; for be it all consumptive habits, decays of nature, inward wastings, weakly thin, or emaciated constitutions, coughs, asthmas, physics, loss of appetite, etc. are to a miracle retrieved and the body, blood, and spirit powerfully corroborated and restored. A few drops of it in a dish of Bohee tea, or chocolate is the most desirable breakfast or supper, and outvies for virtue and

[1] scrofula [2] skin eruptions

nourishment twenty dishes of either without it, nothing being more nutritive and supporting. Likewise to strengthen the back, prevent miscarriages, cause procreation and conception, it is beyond all medicines, as those that will take it will find, and scarce ever live without it. It is also the only sure cure for vapours and melancholy, for those diseases being occasioned by the poorness of the blood and spirits, this quintessence cures by its enriching and enlivening properties. It is only sold at Mr Laurence's Toy Shop, at the sign of the Griffin, the corner of Bucklersbury in the Poultry, at 5s. per bottle, with printed directions.

*

Lately published

Europe a slave England now break her chains discovering the grand designs of the French Popish part in England for several years last past. Sold by D. Leach in Elliotts Court, in the Little Old Bailey. Price 6d.

*

THE TOMB OF VENUS, or plain and faithful directions how everyone may infallibly be rescued both from the obvious and hidden relics of that dangerous disgraceful distemper which so many of both sexes are infected with, such as weepings after supposed cures, pains, swellings, breakings out, and also from the noxious remainders of ill-prepared medicines. Likewise a demonstrable method on which the most doubtful may depend, of certainly knowing whether they have the distemper or not. By a foreign physician. Sold by Bernard Lintott, Bookseller, at the Cross Keys, between the two Temple Gates, in Fleet Street, Price 1s.

*

O*f a certain safe and easy cure for the secret disease in either sex, by three doses (oftentimes by one dose) of a wonderful chemical bolus, which takes away all symptoms at once and cures even to astonishment; seven doses of it cures it, though of long standing and attended with the worst of symptoms, as those that once experienced it will allow, and readily own that it is a medicine of no equal, it producing more manifest effects of its wonderful efficiency by one dose than probably many other good medicines may by ten and is in truth what may be depended on for the most expeditious and effectual cure yet* *known, even when all other medicines have failed, and as it exceeds in goodness all other remedies whatsoever, especially in the cure of this disease, so does it for pleasantness, its taste not offending the most tender or nice constitution that is. To be had only of the author, Dr Wright at the Golden Head, in Bell Savage Yard, upon Ludgate Hill, where he or his wife are to be spoken with at any time of the day.*

*

MARTEN'S 6TH EDITION with great Additions of the secret disease, to plainly describing each degree and symptom, that anyone may know whether infected or not, its nature consequence and true way of cure, without hazard of reputation and life in the hands of quacks and pretenders. Illustrated with a variety of observations, histories and letters of remarkable cases, and cures in both sexes. By John Marten, surgeon, Price 4s. Sold by N. Crouch in the Poultry J. Knapton, in St Pauls Churchyard, P. Varenne in the Strand, and at the authors house in Hatton Garden.

*

THE CHARITABLE SURGEON, *Or the best remedies for the worst maladies revealed, altogether without mercury and wholly new in method and practice, wherein both sexes may, with privacy and small charge, without any other medicine or being exposed to quacks, cure themselves of that distemper which, if neglected, are dangerous as well as ignominious. By T. C. Surgeon, sold by E. Curl, bookseller, removed to the Dial and Bible against St Dunstans Church in Fleet Street, Price, 1s.*

*

DR JACKSON'S WORM POWDER, which has neither taste nor smell, cures pains, gnawings, sickness to the stomach, striving to vomit in the morning, faintness, sinking of the spirits, palpitation of the heart, twisting of the guts, intermitting fevers, hot and cold fits, consumptions, violent cholics, convulsions, rickets, wasting and weakness in children, and the green sickness; it opens obstructions and creates a good appetite, prevents fearful dreams and adds a lively colour to the face; the former and most other diseases incident to man, woman or child proceed from worms, and are cured by this excellent worm powder, which bring away worms of all sorts of lengths and shapes, and leaves the body in perfect health. Sold at my house, in 3 King Court, in the Great Minories, 3 papers sufficient quantity to cure a child, 6 pence a large quantity, for elder persons at a proportional rate.

*

Whereas I, Rachel Morbury, now living with Madam Huffy, in Church Lane in Great Chelsea, have been violent ill of the headache, for above this two years last past, but for the last half year in a more violent manner; so that I thought I must have left my place, and after I had made use of several medicines, without the least success, I at last received an effectual cure, by Mr. J. Moore, Apothecary, at the Pestle and Mortar in Abchurch Lane, London. I desire this certificate may be published for the good of mankind, under the same affliction witness my hand, Sept. 7, 1709.

*

A FAMED ELIXIR, for the wind which expels it to admiration, whether in the stomach, or bowels, all sewer or windy belch or hiccups, from indigestion, etc. It removes it upon the spot, and cures pains in the stomach, griping in the guts, stitches in the sides, the wind cholic to miracle; being no pretended, but a real and effectual medicine, fit for the use of old and young. To be had only at Mr Spooner's new living, at the Golden Half Moon in Lemon Street, Goodmans Fields near Whitechapel, at 2s.6d. a bottle, with directions.

*

Dr Clark, physician, and first sworn occulist in salary to King Charles and King James II, having within these months brought to sight Lady Yallop, Mrs Smith's child, born blind, Mr Lock, and more than 70 besides in and about Norwich. His ophthalmic secret being experienced by more than 1000 people cured of the Gutta Serena; *that is, when the eyes seem fair as those who see, yet are blind. It infallibly dissolves suffusion, the seed of cataracts and takes away dimness, mists, flies, gnats, sparks, cobwebs, and other false appearances, symptoms of approaching blindness if not timely prevented. This excellent means may be had by a messenger, or writing a true state of the case and conveyed into any remote part (with other proper remedies for all diseases incident to the eyes). From his house in Old Southampton Buildings, Holborn; a Golden Head over the door.*

*

Sir William Read, Her Majesty's Occulist, being very sensible that many of her majesty's soldiers must have received damage in their eyes or visive faculty, in the late, bloody and unparalleled battle, thinks fit to give public notice for the benefit of all such persons that he will constantly attend at his house in Durham Yard in the Strand, where all such persons, bringing certificates from their respective officers, shall be kindly received, and all due care taken in order to their speedy cure, gratis, as it has been his constant practice, ever since the beginning of the war. Note, Sir William Read couches cataracts gratis to all such poor people as shall be recommended to him as fit objects of charity, such as the poor Palatines. He hath several to couch this month and the next, at his house abovesaid, where he has successfully performed above one hundred such operations since Lady Day last. And any gentleman or lady shall be welcome to see that curious operation performed at his house aforesaid.

*

The famed chymical gargle for the mouth, teeth and gums, so delightful to taste that 'tis acceptable to the nicest person, and indeed for the pleasantness, safety and effects, the like was never known or made use of. It makes the teeth as white as ivory, fastens them when loose, kills the worms at their roots, and preserves them good and firm, even to old age. It perfectly cures the scurvy, erosion and bleeding of the gums, causing the flesh to grow (to admiration) where 'tis eaten away, and secures them from that pain. By washing the mouth with it every morning, it makes the most offensive breath so sweet as that it's admired by all, and speedily cures all distempers in the mouth, in old or young, whether soreness, heat, blistering, rawness, ulcers, thrush, cankers etc., (which last it's wonderfully famed for), the falling down of the palate, almonds of the ears, and all sorts of sore throats, whether swellings, inflammations, quinseys etc., either from cold, sharp humours or both. To be had only at Jacobs Coffee house, against the Angel and Crown, in Threadneedle Street near the Royal Exchange, at 2s.6d. the bottle, sealed up with discretion.

*

At Mrs Garraway's shop, the south entrance of the Royal Exchange, Cornhill, Mrs Markham, at the Seven Stars, a toyshop, under St Dunstan's Church in Fleet Street, Mr Helms at the King's Head in Westminster Hall, bookseller, are to be sold the royal unparalleled wash-ball, which is largely experienced to be the safest (being faithfully prepared without the least grain of mercury etc.) and of the most powerful force, by its admirable virtue for cleansing the skin from all discolour, as sunburn, freckles, swarthy, yellow, or tawny colour &c. It's approved by those ladies and gentlemen who use them, to be the greatest beautifier in nature. It gives liberty to show its redness on the cheeks and the blue veins on the hands neck and temples. It's the most esteemed amongst gentlemen, above anything extant. By washing therewith it fortifies the head from cold, comforts the head, brain and nerves, also strengthens the memory, by supporting those tender parts by its noble scent and virtues. Each ball sealed with this seal: a serpent, dove, wheatsheaf, lion, with this motto round it, *I de salus populi.*[3] With them printed directions, and the virtues more at large.

*

The true cephalic or head snuff, which in twice or thrice using, does infinitely more good than fifty times using any other sort, for by its peculiar operation and effects it cures the most stubborn and dangerous distempers of the head, such as apoplexies, epilepsies, lethargies, vishegoes,[4] *megrims,*[5] *pains in the head, humours in the eyes, imposthumes,*[6] *vapours, loss of memory, deafness &c. two papers at most times making a perfect cure, it being what is daily prescribed and approved by the most eminent physicians. 'Tis to be had only at Mr Varen's, a bookseller at Seneca's Head, near Somerset House in the Strand, price 1s.6d. the paper, with directions.*

3 'No. 1 for the health of the people' 4 faintness
5 migraines 6 abcesses, swellings